Drag Queens and Beauty Queens

Drag Queens and Beauty Queens

Contesting Femininity in the World's Playground

LAURIE A. GREENE

RUTGERS UNIVERSITY PRESS

NEW BRUNSWICK, CAMDEN, AND NEWARK,
NEW JERSEY, AND LONDON

Library of Congress Cataloging-in-Publication Data
Names: Greene, Laurie A., 1961– author.
Title: Drag queens and beauty queens: contesting femininity in the
    world's playground / Laurie Greene.
Description: New Brunswick: Rutgers University Press, [2021] |
    Includes bibliographical references and index.
Identifiers: LCCN 2020012070 | ISBN 9781978813861 (paperback) |
    ISBN 9781978813878 (cloth) | ISBN 9781978813885 (epub) |
    ISBN 9781978813892 (mobi) | ISBN 9781978813908 (pdf)
Subjects: LCSH: Miss America Pageant. | Miss'd America Pageant. |
    Beauty contests—New Jersey—Atlantic City. | Gay community—
    New Jersey—Atlantic City.
Classification: LCC HQ1220.U5 G73 2021 | DDC 306.76/60974985—dc23
LC record available at https://lccn.loc.gov/2020012070

A British Cataloging-in-Publication record for this book is available from the British
Library.

♾ The paper used in this publication meets the requirements of the American National Standard for Information Sciences—Permanence of Paper for Printed Library Materials, ANSI Z39.48-1992.

www.rutgersuniversitypress.org

Manufactured in the United States of America

For Naomi, Nathan, and Noah

Everything is held together with stories. That is all that is holding us together, stories and compassion.

—*Barry Lopez*

Contents

List of Illustrations

Preface and Acknowledgments

In many ways this book is for me a labor of love. As research progressed, I found myself more and more enamored with this much maligned tourist destination, Atlantic City, and in awe of its little-known, rich histories. Recounting of the history of marginalized communities is always important, even more so when the population in question is absent so many of its storytellers. Gay Atlantic City, having lost most of a generation to the plague of HIV/AIDS, is such a community. This book presents part of the history of gay Atlantic City, in lieu of intergenerational oral traditions usually tasked with passing down this lore.

So many people assisted in the research process. I would like to thank every individual member of the *"New York Avenue in the 1970s"* Facebook page, in particular those who shared their memories and photographs: David Lavoie, Jeanne Chiaradio, James Farber, Donna L. Visco, Ann Fox, and Robert Muir. To friends and neighbors who made community introductions, and corrections to my retelling of their lives; a special mention to Jean Antolini, always the essential critic, and a sometimes photographer. Thanks to my dear friend and talented artist and producer, Melanie Rice, who gave me initial access to the world of professional drag and drag pageantry. Much gratitude to director Mark Dahl for allowing access to contestants during the chaos of rehearsals and pre-performance dressing rooms. To every member of the ACGLBT Alliance, who volunteer tirelessly to make the Miss'd America Pageant a success. A special thanks to Sharon Garland, who, as always, took things "off my plate" at the last moment. To Georgette Watson, COO of the South Jersey AIDS Alliance (SJAA), who gave essential feedback about HIV/AIDS in Atlantic City. To Patti Smith, who opened the crated archives of New York Avenue nightlife, which somehow survived superstorm Sandy. To John Schultz and Gary Hill for sharing newsreels, videos, clippings, and memorabilia of gay Atlantic City and who took time to sit down for interviews. And finally, to the Stockton University student researchers who helped with interviewing and transcription: Kate O'Malley, Katherine River Sage, Genesis Sandoval, Heather Gordon, Shoanne Seijas, and Aleyah Hassan.

The photographic images for this book are mostly the work of the talented photographer Paul Dempsey, who also re-photographed and sharpened old images and those taken from my smartphone. His contributions serve to enliven the text, and provide important visual examples of drag pageantry, the Miss'd America Pageant, and the gay community in Atlantic City.

I am indebted to all the former contestants of the Miss'd America Pageant who shared their dreams, aspirations, and assessments, and to the iconic Sherry Vine, Jackie Beat, Manilla Luzon, and other drag queens not part of the Miss'd America Pageant, who generously offered insights into this project. There are not enough words to express my gratitude to two very talented performing artists, editors, fact checkers, and honorary mayors of Atlantic City, HRH Mortimer (Mortimer Spreng) and Sandy Beach (Robert Hitchen). Their contributions to both Miss'd America and this book are invaluable, and integral to any telling of a more complete history of Atlantic City. This story is yours, and I hope I do it justice.

Finally, I would be remiss not to mention the important editing suggestions, friendship, and moral support offered by the following people, without whom this book would not have been possible: Kimberly Guinta, my patient and insightful editor at Rutgers University Press; Joe Rubenstein, who continues to be my "editor in chief"; and Edward Clark, dearest friend, confidant, and cheerleader. I am grateful for the often-critical theoretical feedback of my grown children, Naomi, Nathan, and Noah; know that I did listen! And finally, to Arlin Padilla and Valdenir Oliveira, who kept me sane by teaching me to salsa dance (and danced with me), and the Chain Gang and many others, who have given me support and friendship.

In researching this book over the past decade, I have come to better understand the ongoing challenges facing the LGBTQ+ community. LGBTQ+ youth continue to suffer disproportionately from homelessness, drug addiction, mental illness, and victimization through exploitation and violence. For transgender youth, the incidence of suffering is staggering. Drag in many cases affords a respite from these sufferings, the drag community providing a supportive "family" structure to counter the deficits that lead to these social ills. Drag is also fertile ground for activism, as drag queens have always been vocal advocates for those facing discrimination and serve as the face of LGBTQ+ culture to the larger community. In particular, drag is a safe space for all who challenge the conventional understanding of gender, sex, and sexuality, either intentionally or because of their own nonconforming identities. Many of the drag queens I now know dedicate themselves to giving back, using their platforms as entertainers to serve these youth and to raise the next generation of strong, proud, queer adults. Thank you; may drag continue to serve these ends as it evolves to reflect the next generation of innovators and explorers at the front lines of gender.

Laurie A. Greene

Drag Queens and
Beauty Queens

GAY ATLANTIC CITY 1970s AND 1980s

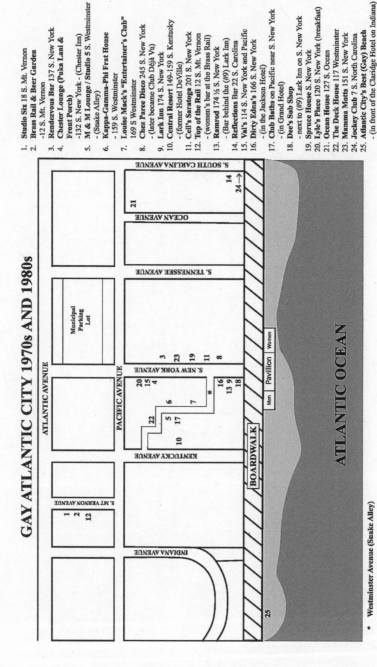

* Westminster Avenue (Snake Alley)

Credit: Sharon Garland

1. **Studio Six** 18 S. Mt. Vernon
2. **Brass Rail & Beer Garden**
   - 12 S. Mt. Vernon
3. **Rendezvous Bar** 137 S. New York
4. **Chester Lounge (Puka Lani & Front Porch)**
   - 132 S. New York - (Chester Inn)
5. **M & M Lounge / Studio 5** S. Westminster
   - (Snake Alley)
6. **Kappa-Gamma-Phi Frat House**
   - 159 S. Westminster
7. **Louise Mack's "Entertainer's Club"**
   169 S Westminster
8. **Chez Paree Disco** 245 S. New York
   - (later became Club Déjà Vu)
9. **Lark Inn** 174 S. New York
10. **Central Resort** 149-159 S. Kentucky
    - (former Hotel DeVille)
11. **Cell's Saratoga** 201 S. New York
12. **Top of the Rail** 12 S. Mt. Vernon
    - (women's bar at the Brass Rail)
13. **Ramrod** 174 ½ S. New York
    - (Bar behind the (#9) Lark Inn)
14. **Reflections Bar** 22 S. Carolina
15. **Val's** 114 S. New York and Pacific
16. **Dirty Edna's** 166 S. New York
    - (in the Jackson Hotel)
17. **Club Baths on Pacific near S. New York**
    - (in Grand Hotel)
18. **Dee's Sub Shop**
    - next to (#9) Lark Inn on S. New York
19. **Spruce House** S. New York
20. **Lyle's Place** 120 S. New York (breakfast)
21. **Ocean House** 127 S. Ocean
22. **The Deck House** 117 Westminster
23. **Mamma Motts** 151 S. New York
24. **Jockey Club** 7 S. North Carolina
25. **Atlantic City's Best (Gay) Beach**
    - (in front of the Claridge Hotel on Indiana)

Introduction

DOING AC

At Boardwalk Hall the digital marquee announces upcoming shows: a hip-hop concert, a comedy carnival, and tours of the largest pipe organ in the world.[1] To the right is Kennedy Plaza, and on the far right stands a life-sized bronze statue of Miss America. She holds a crown in her outstretched arms. Beneath that crown, a woman poses as her companions take pictures. They rotate until each has a chance. On the wall behind them are murals of prominent Miss America winners, including Suzette Charles, Miss New Jersey, 1983, who served as Miss America in 1984 when Vanessa Williams lost the title in a scandal over nude photographs. Two little girls in flowery dresses fidget while they wait their turn to pose. A man feeds the seagulls from a dirty paper bag and is scolded by two policemen. In the distance, the Ferris wheel on Steel Pier changes colors, and past Casino Row, the small run-down stores line the Boardwalk: Peanut World, Irene's, Big G's Tattoos, Sally's Psychic Shop, Massage Paradise, James Salt Water Taffy. Two tabby cats walk across the boards. There's a beach colony of cats here; there always has been on the corner of New York Avenue and the Boardwalk.

To the right is the beach; to the left, framed by the Ocean Club and *Ripley's Believe It or Not!*, the wooden ramp descends to what used to be arguably the most famous, infamous, street in Atlantic City. Now, it is mostly empty, overgrown lots strewn with debris. Parking lots fill the rest of the spaces between random buildings. Philip and Joe, once denizens here, look around and then at each other. They both smile as they point to where favorite spots once stood. They tell stories, of sexual encounters, memorable performances, people who are no longer here to tell stories of their own. Some of these, I imagine, they may not really want me to hear; or maybe they do.[2]

Atlantic City: A City "Down the Shore"

Atlantic City is a place that defies simple description or explanation. It is in constant motion, like the ocean that creates its beaches and bays, a place always reinventing itself, the comeback kid, the underdog of cities. It lacks an industrial base; the economy is and has always been based on tourism. Atlantic City, "the World's Playground," has entertained millions in its more than 150 years. The Boardwalk has been its Main Street, its attractions always changing: bootleg alcohol, jazz, gay nightlife, and now casinos, . . . but always against a constant backdrop—the beach. As with many tourist destinations, people move in and out, and like the tides, some wash ashore and stay for a while, and some recede back out to sea. And so too, the economic and social history of the city itself is a series of ups and downs, of economic booms and busts. The booster phrase "the World's Playground" has given way to "Atlantic City: Always Turned On," and now, in an effort to attract a younger, hipper crowd, a trendy "Do AC."

Atlantic City's volatility is bolstered by its renegade reputation. It has always been a place where cultural and social norms were challenged or ignored. The tourist-based economy of the resort town encouraged business owners to provide whatever was needed to make the visitors happy. During Prohibition, for example, this meant contraband alcohol. Atlantic City flouted the country's restrictive laws, acting as a mainstay for illegal production and sales of alcohol. Residents and tourists alike made their way to secret clubs or speakeasies or made bathtub gin at home. Organized crime syndicates emerged in the area to supply locally produced alcohol to the many customers demanding it across the country. Prohibition was essentially unenforced by the local authorities, and the city's beachfront location and docks allowed rum runners to bring their goods onto shore by boat. Add to this a powerful city crime boss, Nucky Johnson (made famous once again in the television series *Boardwalk Empire*),[3] who allegedly controlled everything from the smuggling operation to the law enforcement to the restaurants where alcohol was served, and Atlantic City was essentially a wide-open town, flagrantly violating the federal law. As Johnson famously stated unapologetically: "We have whisky, wine, women, song and slot machines. I won't deny it and I won't apologize for it. If the majority of the people didn't want them, they wouldn't be profitable, and they would not exist."[4]

Aided by its proximity to major population centers like Philadelphia, New York City, and Washington, D.C., and its reputation for unfettered fun, Atlantic City rapidly expanded. Between 1880 and 1940, it was known to be a premier world vacation resort. From the 1920s to the 1960s, Kentucky Avenue on the north side of town enjoyed a thriving jazz scene and vibrant African American culture. Numerous bars and clubs, like *Club Harlem* on Kentucky, and *Chicken Bone Beach*, a few blocks away on Missouri Avenue, presented the best talent and biggest stars from the world of jazz. Until the 1970s, Kentucky Avenue and its black community was the pulse of the city and a mainstay of its tourist economy.[5] On adjacent New York Avenue, the gay population of Atlantic City exploded in the 1970s. This book is an effort to describe a portion of the history of New York Avenue in Atlantic City: the gay community and drag culture that thrived there from the 1960s through the 1980s, and the decline of gay nightlife in the 1990s. In doing so, I hope to add to the scant recording and analysis of communities of marginalized people, who rely principally on oral traditions to record their history. This is particularly important, since the AIDS epidemic in Atlantic City nearly wiped out an entire cohort who might have passed down this lore to the next generation.

Where the "Gurls" Are: When AC Was GayC

Bryant Simon, in his book *Boardwalk of Dreams*, describes the rise and fall of Atlantic City as a tourist destination. In his words, Atlantic City "manufactured and sold an easily consumed and widely shared fantasy," built upon a "grand deception."[6] It was a place where white working-class and middle-class tourists, many the children of immigrants, could celebrate their inclusion in American society through their consumption in the posh vacation resort. But the exclusive nature of resort vacationing was made possible by the exclusion of people of color and other marginalized groups. Simon's account is a stark reminder of the contradictions inherent and often invisible in all tourist economies, and *Boardwalk of Dreams* describes some of the ugly realities of racism and homophobia that created communities of poor, disenfranchised laborers who served as underpaid workers in the resorts. Two cities emerged—a "perfect White City—the Boardwalk, hotels, and theaters—and a funky 'Midway' of nightclubs, street corners and backrooms."[7]

This book in many ways takes off where Simon's book ends; it aims to describe the vibrant culture and lives of one of these communities living off of the Boardwalk.[8] The community that emerged on New York Avenue and the adjacent winding Snake Alley was a place where gay men and women lived, worked, and celebrated gay life. The decade of the 1970s was the apex of gay life in Atlantic City; the thriving and boisterous gayborhood, a four-block area backing the beach, boasted over a dozen bars and nightclubs and a myriad of rooming houses catering to gay clients and residents. This picture of gay life is not simply nostalgic, nor is it meant to deny many of the ugly realities of the lives of people in a racist and homophobic society who eventually endure the devastation wrought by the

AIDS epidemic. Instead, it is an important illustration of the fact that despite these circumstances, and the poverty and struggles that prejudice creates, the gay community in Atlantic City flourished. New York Avenue was not just a midway for tourists to gawk at a spectacle. It was a place the gay community called home.

Adjacent to the gayborhood, on Kentucky Avenue, the Northside was the center of African American jazz culture in Atlantic City.[9] Like the Kentucky Avenue jazz scene, which was an expression of African American culture, the drag scene on New York Avenue was intrinsic to its culture of origin (gay culture) but desired by outsiders. In the 1960s and 1970s, when liberation movements (women's liberation, black power, gay rights, and so on) steered the direction of social and cultural reforms, the gay culture in Atlantic City produced, among other things, a vibrant drag performance scene.

Many of those who frequented the gay clubs after hours were visitors from the entertainment industry. Popular entertainers and their crews—hairdressers, stylists, and choreographers, many of who were gay—found comfort and a welcoming environment in the clubs and bars on New York Avenue. Likewise, the Miss America Pageant has been held in Atlantic City almost uninterruptedly since 1921. For the production staff of the Miss America Pageant, each September, New York Avenue was a home away from home; for while the pageant contestants changed each year, the crew remained largely the same. Production crews were sometimes joined by the family and friends of pageant contestants at the clubs, although the contestants themselves were forbidden to attend.[10] The friendships formed between individuals in the local gay community and the Miss America Pageant crew in the clubs on New York Avenue only partially explain the strong connections, both felt and functional, between Miss America, the gay community, and what would, in 1993, be birthed as the *Miss'd America Pageant*. This book is an effort to explore the important ways in which a portion of the gay community in Atlantic City has and continues to form its identity through its relationship to the Miss America Pageant, and how this same community has significantly impacted the evolution of the Miss America Pageant in return.

Drag has been a fixture in the gay community in Atlantic City since the 1950s, enjoying its heyday in the 1970s. A quick tour of the Facebook page *"New York Avenue in the 1970s"* attests to the vibrancy of the community and the ubiquitous drag scene there. Drag queens from Atlantic City speak about the 1970s with nostalgia and refer to the queens who performed in the clubs and bars—Dee Dee Lewis, Tinsel Garland, Chunkie Marinara—as legends, from whom they learned the craft of drag and developed a sense of belonging. The drag scene persevered in the 1980s despite the changing economy of Atlantic City and the devastating impact of HIV and the AIDS epidemic. Atlantic City was once a place to party for gay and straight alike, but the threat of AIDS resulted in the loss of many community members, and in the stigmatization of New York Avenue and the "gay lifestyle."[11] The Miss'd America Pageant was created as a way to revitalize the gay community in Atlantic City in the wake of the damage wrought by AIDS and this stigmatization.[12] It was an attempt to cope with the physical, social, and emotional impact of AIDS and the threat that it and other forces posed to the survival of the gay community in Atlantic City. When creating a ritual to counter these threats, the gay community looked to the traditional functions of drag performance through the language of camp and to their local experience of pageantry, Miss America. Miss'd America utilized a traditional drag performance format when it first began, featuring comedic skits and talent presentations. The songs were all prerecorded and then lip-synced at the time of the performance. No winner was chosen in the first pageant in 1992. Over the next few years, Miss'd America began to take on more of the Miss America Pageant format. A runway was built, a winner crowned, and eventually all four categories of competition were contested (swimsuit, evening gown, talent, and interview). This book describes the origins of the Miss'd America Pageant and how the structure, function, and meaning of this pageant have evolved alongside the Miss America Pageant since 1993.

Drag has become a much bigger part of popular culture since the birth of Miss'd America in 1993, in large part due to the popularity of the reality show *RuPaul's Drag Race*.[13] The impact of *Drag Race* on drag performance and pageantry over the past ten years is significant. In light of this popularization and the changing conversation about gender in American culture, the definitions of femininity, masculinity, and drag itself have changed. This book explores the challenges the Miss'd America Pageant faces in light of these cultural changes, similar to the continuous challenge for relevancy posed to the pageant that inspired it, now referred to as Miss America 2.0.[14]

How This "Bitch Is Turned Out"

Chapter 1 begins with a brief overview of pageantry and a more particular history of the Miss America Pageant.[15] Pageantry is a place where cultural values and identity are contested within the context of performed ideal femininity, and this is illustrated in the ways that the Miss America Pageant is structured and how it has changed in response to criticisms over the years, most prominently from feminists. The rise of drag pageantry is discussed as one means to present an alternative to hegemonic values and gender identities. Drag pageantry is at one level an homage to cis-female beauty pageants, and at another a critique of their narrow presentations of gender.[16] The importance of the popularization of drag, principally through the popularity of *RuPaul's Drag Race* and the impact it has had on drag pageantry, is then discussed and illustrated in the Miss'd America Pageant.

Chapter 2 starts with a definition of drag and a discussion of the culture of drag performers within the gay community in Atlantic City. Drag culture in Atlantic City was a "community of practice" through the 1980s, after which it went into decline. Several shared practices are briefly described, as well as the methods of developing these practices within the context of the local drag community. Important shared values and beliefs are described for the Miss'd America Pageant contestants illustrating the now larger, more dispersed community of practice, which exceeds local boundaries.

Chapter 3 describes in greater detail the character and history of the gayborhood in Atlantic City. The important meaning of place to the gay community is detailed in the remembrances of New York Avenue and the birth of the Miss'd America Pageant in response to the stressors that threatened the community. Traditions of volunteerism associated with the AIDS crisis were the prime motivators for the creation of the pageant as one tool for fund-raising along with other efforts made to combat the epidemic. Finally, the evolution of the pageant is documented, from its original local focus to its rise in national pageantry.

Chapter 4 begins with a discussion of the importance of "camp" sensibility in drag performance and in gay culture. Drag performance is further explored through the experiences of drag performers who have participated in the Miss'd America Pageant. These ethnographic accounts are presented in light of the meaning and centrality of camp. The importance of camp in the Miss'd America Pageant—in drag style, performance, and language—is discussed, along with the changes in camp expression in the modern version of the pageant. The chapter ends by looking at the *queering* of the Miss America Pageant, most visibly in the birth and development of the popular *Show Us Your Shoes Parade*—a parade introducing each of the Miss America contestants in a playful context, whose origins are undoubtedly found on New York Avenue.

Chapter 5 offers a comparison of the Miss'd America and Miss America pageants through an examination of the four elements of competition: swimsuit, evening gown, talent, and interview. Depictions of femininity are framed as both "object"—"displays of the body in different comportments—and "subject"—performance in talent and interview. The ethnographic evidence shows that drag pageants and beauty pageants share certain values, including the value of hard work, perseverance, and talent, but differ in the way that they interpret the elements of pageantry and the meaning of individual expression. Whereas beauty queens value the ability to express individuality within the boundaries of conformity so as to have a wide appeal and not offend, drag queens push against boundaries and see creativity and uniqueness as valued qualities. Offense comes with the territory, as Sandy Beach once said after telling a joke the day after a celebrity killed himself: "Too early? It's *never* too early."[17] Drag queens value instead the questioning of boundaries often resulting in offense but tempered with humor.

How I Got the "Tea" on Them

> Because you have seen something doesn't mean you can explain it. Differing interpretations will always abound, even when good minds come to bear. The kernel of indisputable information is a dot in space; interpretations grow out of the desire to make this point a line, to give it direction. The directions in which it can be sent, the uses to which it can be put by a culturally, professionally, and geographically diverse society are almost without limit. The possibilities make good scientists chary.
>
> —Barry Lopez
> *Arctic Dreams*

My research in Atlantic City was carried out over a four-year period from 2016–2019.[18] I have tried to describe both of the iconic pageants of the resort town and the development of its vibrant gay community, so intimately related to pageantry. For much of the material I am indebted to current and former gay residents of Atlantic City, including drag queens and others who worked or partied on New York Avenue during its heyday. Intensive ethnographic fieldwork extended over three consecutive Miss'd America Pageants and to a lesser extent the Miss America Pageant, including interviews with organizers, contestants, and audience members. Every effort was made to hear the accounts of those who were present in the beginning, who created and participated in the evolution of Miss'd America. The ethnographic descriptions and quotations from informants were taken from recorded interviews and participant observation. Appendix B lists the dates of these recorded interviews and observations. The text references these and formal observations as field notes. I am grateful to every contestant of the Miss'd America Pageant who gave me their time, knowledge, and often very personal stories—in particular, to the early local queens Morgan Wells, (Lemon Fresh) Joy Marnier, Alexia Love, Brittany Lynn, and first and foremost HRH Mortimer and Sandy Beach, whose personal narratives encapsulated gay Atlantic City and who were always available for assistance, information, and clarification. Finally, a surprising amount of information was gathered from Facebook postings (the *New York Avenue in the 1970s* group and the *Official Miss'd America Pageant* page) and published op-eds, commentary, and current events in the Atlantic City and Philadelphia local press, as well as from video recordings of past Miss'd America events. I am also indebted to John Schultz and Gary Hill, who graciously opened their Miss'd America Pageant archives.

I have made every effort to write an academically accurate and informative analysis in plain, jargon-free language. My hope is that this book will be accessible and useful to the community in Atlantic City, and that this might serve to inspire others to tell their stories. On occasion, technical terms or theoretical concepts were unavoidable. For easier reading, as much as possible, explanatory comments and references to useful academic resources are included in the endnotes of each chapter rather than in the text. As with any works, even book-length ones, so many stories— important stories—have been inescapably omitted. In writing, every attempt was made to include all of those who were kind enough to generously share their lives with me. Though every attempt was made to accurately take account of this important ethnohistoric moment, people's memories are imperfect, and sometimes accounts of dates and times and people were out of sync. Though I have tried to be as accurate as possible, checking printed materials and asking for clarification, know that the

essence of each account is most important, as memories sometimes differ. The most poignant example of this came three years after I interviewed
all of the "originals" from Miss'd America (as the drag queens from the
first ten years were called). They had all insisted there was no swimsuit
competition until the 2011 pageant. I later viewed a 2002 video of an early
Miss'd America Pageant, with drag queens parading in swimsuits. In fact,
the eighth annual Miss'd America Pageant 2000 (held in September 1999)
was entitled "TarzAnne: In the Swimsuit Adventure."[19]

This book is very personal to me, and in many ways I am an insider in
this culture. Ruth Behar, in her explorations into the anthropology of
experience, notes poignantly that when observers allow themselves to be
vulnerable, their fieldwork can "break their heart." Certainly, I am and
continue to be deeply impacted by this fieldwork and the people who are
its subject. I have lived near or in Atlantic City for over thirty years and
have watched many of the events that I describe unfold. I am queer and a
participant in the ongoing activism in my community, and many of those
interviewed I count as acquaintances, if not friends. As a result of this
research and my community engagement, I was asked to sit on the board
of the ACGLBT (the Alliance),[20] the nonprofit organization that at the time
ran the Miss'd America Pageant as a fund-raiser every year, although my
role was in youth education. Despite these "insider" and intimate connections, I do not think I could have chosen a more "male" venue for fieldwork (local lesbians called the drag scene "the dick farm"). Drag is a part
of the gay community in Atlantic City and elsewhere, but its activities have
a decidedly male focus, its culture dominated by men. Drag performers
have volunteered and continue to lend their time and energy to various
gay causes, predominantly those of interest to gay men (those related to
AIDS, as a prime example), as is true of the Miss'd America Pageant and
other efforts in the Atlantic City drag community (gay bingo, fashion
shows, cabaret benefits, etc.). As Fiona Moore asserts, drag is "associated
with masculinity through its symbolic and social links to gay culture . . .
its activities have a male focus."[21]

I stand as an anomaly as well, in otherwise conservative and provincial southern New Jersey, where I am a "liberal outlier." I am also a *shoobee* (local term for tourist/nonnative). Some of the tensions in the local gay community arise from these oppositions, but delving further into that topic is outside of the scope of this analysis. It does serve to illustrate, however, that the gay community in Atlantic City in general, and the drag community there in particular, is anything but homogeneous. I hope, therefore, that this research adds to the published work of others across disciplines[22] by challenging conventional accounts that too often treat gay identity as "unproblematically monolithic,"[23] and hope that my analysis is read as an ethnographic description of a particular community of people, experiencing a unique set of historical circumstances in a dynamic and ever-evolving place.

The names of most informants and drag queens have been maintained, in part because they are local or national celebrities and wanted their names indicated (as drag names), although pseudonyms may be used for their birth names, along with those of local residents.[24] I have chosen to refer to those interviewed as drag queens with the pronouns *she/her/hers*, even when they might not use these feminine pronouns exclusively. On occasion, I use the male pronouns *he/him/his* for the same informants when they speak from the perspective of their male (boy) persona. This choice was made for clarity rather than as a statement about pronoun choice or identity.

As with any local history, emotions associated with relationships and events run high, and the recounting of events is in some cases contradictory. This is certainly the case for views on how and why New York Avenue and the once vibrant gay community there went into decline. It is also true for the way in which the Miss'd America Pageant itself has evolved. I have chosen to present many of these controversies and varied remembrances in the book without resolving them. I am sensitive to the conflicted experiences of so many people who love Atlantic City and feel ownership of their beloved pageants. I have no intention of causing any rifts or

suffering to a community already under stress from so many sources—
historical, social, political, economic, and epidemiological. In fact, I hope
this research is testimony instead to the resiliency of a local gay community and its integral contributions, not only to this struggling and oldest
of American tourist destinations and to the creation of a now nationally
renowned gay circuit pageant, but also to the Miss America Pageant, a
national, iconic institution, which has laid claim to the (feminine) ideal
in American culture.

CHAPTER 1

Pageants and Pageantry

Boardwalk Hall is buzzing with women and girls of all ages wearing evening gowns with sashes, some sporting tiaras on their carefully coifed heads and made-up faces. This is no ordinary Sunday night. This is the finals of the Miss America Pageant, arguably the most famous modern beauty pageant in the world. Two young girls, maybe six years old, walk by hand in hand, their parents or chaperones trailing behind. They are in floor-length gowns, one blue and one yellow. They carry their bejeweled crowns in plexiglass boxes in their free hands. Both have their hair in an updo and their faces made up like any beauty queen. They smile their perfect red-lipsticked smiles as they pass, each wearing a sash proclaiming their status of "Little Miss *so and so.*" A parent calls after them, and hurries ahead to fix the train of one girl's dress, which is dragging in a less than perfect fashion across the floor of the old convention center. An older woman passes with a sash that reads "Miss Senior Utah." She is statuesque and wears her crown with a familiar confidence.

Most of the pageant viewers are packed into the floor seating or the sections closer to the stage and runway. A staff member comes by and asks if we would like to be on television. Those who reply yes are brought down closer to the stage, where they huddle behind those being interviewed on camera, and cheer, waving their arms, giving the appearance of a large crowd to television viewers. Two television screens frame the stage for the full effect. The screens go blank and the crowds quiet down each time there is a pause for a commercial break. In the stands, beauty queens walk around to get just the right position along the railings as they pose for photographs like professional models, the stage behind them. They seem at ease in this setting. Chaperones and parents talk about the preliminaries, who they think will win, the politics of pageantry, and their own competitors' recent wins or losses.

The celebrity judges will be tasked with scoring the accomplished young women competing in the Miss America Pageant in four areas: fitness (formerly swimsuit), then talent, evening gown, and finally interview. After the opening musical number and introductions, the fifty-two contestants, representing the fifty states, the District of Columbia, and Puerto Rico, are winnowed down to the top ten contestants. As each of the ten is announced, their supporters, seated together, respond with cheers and hold up homemade signs or lighted letters designating their states: New Jersey, Texas, North Carolina! The screens go blank for a commercial break, and the contestants leave the stage. A voice comes over the loudspeaker: "When we count down from ten, cheer as loudly as you can for the television audience. Let's give it a try!" The instructions are acknowledged as people continue to talk among themselves and pose for pictures. When the countdown starts, people return to their seats and begin to cheer as the first competition begins. Toddlers in tiaras munch on potato chips; teenagers giggle for a moment and then return to their pageant faces. One by one each contestant, wearing a two-piece swimsuit and heels, walks out as one of the presenters describes their hobbies, accomplishments, and social platforms. The contestants smile as they walk to the front of the stage, pose, turn, and return to their positions. The crowd cheers. The screens go blank, and the pageant takes another commercial break.[1]

The World Is the Stage

Miss America still flows like the Mississippi, drifts like amber waves of grain, sounds like the crack of a bat on a baseball, tastes like mom's apple pie and smells like dollar bills. . . . . . . She really is the body of state, and the country is in her eyes

—Frank Deford, *There She Is*

This book describes a process of evolving community identity in Atlantic City, New Jersey, by examining the dynamic relationship between a pair of spectacles, the iconic Miss America Pageant, and its drag counterpart, the Miss'd America Pageant, both important to gay life in the once vibrant and now abandoned New York Avenue gayborhood. The Miss America Pageant has been described locally as the "gay holy grail" despite its reputation as antiquated and irrelevant in most urban environments. The Miss America Pageant's connections to Atlantic City and the gay community there run deep along both economic and social lines. The Miss America Pageant is admired by the gay community in Atlantic City, and the gay male and drag community in particular, because of its long-standing social and economic impact on the area, and because the pageant is understood by gays as essentially a camp performance. Alongside the mainstream Miss America Pageant, the drag alternative Miss'd America Pageant has had immense influence on the construction of gay identity in Atlantic City and has in turn "queered" Miss America.[2]

Camp is a complex and much debated phenomenon that includes parody, irony, humor, contradiction, and theatricality.[3] In addition, camp is a decidedly gay sensibility, but more particularly, a gay male sensibility, with strong influences on gay male identity in Atlantic City. Although lesbians and others attend(ed) pageants and frequented the once overflowing clubs on New York Avenue, their connection to the two pageants, drag and straight, is of a far less intimate order. Finally, as Esther Newton declares in her essay "Role Models," "camp is in the eye of the homosexual beholder,"[4] a fact that is vividly illustrated in the interpretation of pageantry in general, and Miss America in particular, as "camp" by gays in Atlantic City, despite the fact that the female pageant contestants themselves might not share this interpretation.

BEAUTY PAGEANTS: POPULAR CULTURE AND CONTEMPORARY CONTESTATIONS

Beauty pageants are a fixture of popular entertainment in American culture. By definition, popular culture is associated with the everyday, the mainstream, and that which is commonly accessible: in short, culture produced for mass consumption and commercial gain. As a form of popular culture, pageantry is no exception. The performance of gender in traditional beauty pageants, detailed in this research, is deeply contextualized in cultural meaning about the body and how it is purposed. Beauty contests are, in other words, not simply about femininity or female beauty or even competition, but about the negotiation and enactment of cultural values.[5] Likewise, drag pageants, through the use of parody, bring into harsh focus the heteronormative values by which conventional notions of gender are upheld and alternatives to these conventions are expressed.

Exactly what can be learned from the popular phenomenon of pageantry? As past academic analysis has shown, and this book intends to illustrate, pageantry is deeply rooted in the social, political, and economic ideals contested within contemporary culture. As a public spectacle, pageantry allows for the expression of norms, as well as alternatives to these conventions, in a context that appears inconsequential. As one can see elsewhere in culture, the ritual character of beauty pageants allows for this questioning of the conventional beliefs and behaviors in an accessible and nonthreatening context. It is through the evolution of these rituals of pageantry and the acceptable enactment of alternative roles and identities that we can witness culture change and observe mechanisms of power, and strive to create and maintain values, beliefs, and practices.[6]

The History of Pageants

The roots of pageantry are ancient; choosing a woman representative to stand as a figurehead for a group in Western culture can be traced to ancient Greece.[7] Both physical beauty and aesthetics were important in Greek culture, and beauty contests were held for both men and women: *euandria* (literally, "beautiful manliness")[8] and *kallisteia* ("female beauty").[9] Contestants were judged on their appearance and other aspects of gender perfection such as "strength and physical fitness" (male)[10] and "singing and dancing" (female).[11]

Modern American pageantry is said to have been started by P. T. Barnum, who in 1854 promoted many different contests as part of his popular entertainment empire—judging dogs, flowers, babies, and then, of course, women. Barnum's original live female beauty contest was met with controversy; it was considered obscene according to the values of Victorian puritanical high society. After widespread protests ended live pageants, Barnum began running contests in newspapers, featuring photographs of women in bathing suits; winners were selected by local newspaper readers.[12] In 1864, Barnum, fueled by popular Western beliefs about the savage East, began to display "Circassian Beauties" as a live "exotic" freak presentation. Circassian Beauties were fabled female slaves from the Caucasus region, said to be the most beautiful women in the world, and also the most sought after as sex slaves for harems.[13] Perhaps the first female bodies to be displayed as specimens of beauty in sideshows, these most perfect specimens of "white women" possessed inferred (yet not overtly displayed) sexuality. As Robert Bogden and Linda Frost both note, these beautiful women represented "unsullied purity," and in part, interest in these Caucasian specimens was fueled by Northern anxieties about racial mixing,[14] particularly in the wake of emancipation in the United States. According to Frost, "In her role as a symbol of endangered-yet-rescued whiteness, the Circassian slave mirrored Northern whites' representations of white American woman herself, potentially endangered by 'dark' and savage forces suddenly 'unleashed' in the South."[15]

The Circassian Beauty was a representation of the Victorian cult of "true womanhood."[16] Characteristics of these presentations included, as in all sideshows, techniques to control the audience's viewing, like those found in chapbooks describing the biographies of each Circassian Beauty—her capabilities, temperament, place of origin, and the manner of her rescue and procurement.[17] These biographical facts were read aloud by showmen as the women sat silently posed or engaged in demure activities. Biographies emphasized the chaste and delicate nature of these most perfect examples of whiteness[18] and also models of modesty, propriety, and the womanly arts, literature, painting, and the like,[19] who at the same time embodied sexual pleasure. As Frost goes on to note: "Barnum's writer describes [Circassian Beauty] Zoe Meleke as the very model of Victorian womanhood—modest, intelligent, and pure, racially as well as sexually—visually, the beauty is something quite different, a sexualized figure, intended to entice ... the Circassian Beauty embodies sensual pleasure and, more importantly, a tremendous sexual power that is resolutely female."[20]

The display of women and their overt, enticing sexuality, as well as the narrated presentations of them as chaste, intelligent, and demure, is a model of Western female display that I argue later becomes a blueprint for presenting women's "chaste sexuality" in beauty pageants like Miss America. As will be noted in more detail, in the swimsuit section of the Miss America competition, contestants do not speak, but are instead accompanied by a narrated biography as they walk across the stage or down the runway, as a way to mediate the overtly sexual display of the chaste contestants' bodies.

ATLANTIC CITY, POPULAR ENTERTAINMENT, AND THE RISE OF PAGEANTRY

At the turn of the nineteenth century, Atlantic City was already positioned at the center of the development of the new "popular amusement" industry, providing spectacles such as sideshows, dime museums, and other displays deemed tenuously acceptable for upstanding Christian citizens. "Freak shows" were billed as both entertaining and educational, lauding the newest discoveries in science and exploration. Experts—scientists, doctors, notable celebrities—attended these spectacles, conferring on them a degree of legitimacy and authenticity, despite any gaffing (deliberate deception) that might underlie freak presentations.[21] The World's Fair was the iconic event celebrating human advancement in exploration and in the sciences, but the midway (the area at the borders of the official fairgrounds) attracted more audience attention, where popular fears and curiosities were satisfied in sideshows and carnival amusements; the stretch of beach towns from Atlantic City to Coney Island became the epicenter of this pseudoscience. The Atlantic City boardwalk itself was a place where one could enjoy such formal voyeuristic pleasures. At Arkansas and the Boardwalk, across from the Million Dollar amusement pier, was "Dr. Couney's Infant Incubator" display, where passersby could view newborns in their new "mechanical wombs." Hundreds gathered every day to gawk at the premature infants and marvel at the technology that acted as their life support. Small, wrinkled, and tightly swaddled preemies were hardly the cute babies Americans loved to view in boardwalk stroller parades, but the drama of their fight for survival was hard to beat. Customers peering through the glass got to watch a life-and-death struggle that had a mostly satisfying ending.[22] Ripley's Believe It or Not opened a museum of curiosities on the Steel Pier in Atlantic City from 1955 to 1958 and later a museum on the corner of the Boardwalk and New York Avenue in 1996.[23] Informal freak displays were also common; dwarfs set up mini-villages just off the Boardwalk, and buskers performed on the Boardwalk and the beach nearby for loose change.[24]

It was in the 1880s that the first Bathing Beauty Pageant took place as part of a summer festival to promote business in Rehoboth Beach, Delaware, with minimal success. In 1920, the same year that women were granted the right to vote, the Miss America Pageant began as the Fall Frolic, promoted by Atlantic City businesses in order to attract and keep tourists in the resort city beyond Labor Day, the traditional end of summer. In 1921, Atlantic City's Inter-City Beauty Contest debuted. The winner was determined by a set of judges along with the crowd in attendance, whose applause counted for 50 percent of the vote. The following day featured a bathing suit competition called the Bather's Revue, consisting of about 200 bathing beauties from other pageants, vying for a trophy called the Golden Mermaid. As part of the festivities, an annual parade was held, with floats from businesses, civic organizations, and the pageant contestants. In 1922, the first Miss America was crowned as Miss Washington D.C., but because a new Miss D.C. had already been appointed by the time the next Atlantic City contest rolled around, the winner was given the title *Miss America* in 1923.[25] "She represents the type of womanhood America needs," opined labor leader Samuel Gompers, "strong, red-blooded, able to shoulder the responsibilities of homemaking and motherhood. It is in her type that the hope of the country rests."[26]

Miss America: Femininity, Feminism, and the Beauty Queen

The Miss America pageant has been the subject of many books, dissertations, and articles detailing both its history and significance.[27] Since the pageant's inception, Miss America has provided a barometer for women's place in American life, and likewise, the Miss America Pageant itself has evolved over time in response to changes occurring in American culture. What began as a swimsuit competition on the Atlantic City boardwalk in 1921 eventually developed into the more familiar four-category format, where contestants are judged in swimsuit, evening gown, talent, and interview competitions. In 1938, the talent competition was introduced so that the young women could be judged on more than just their appearance,[28] although that same year, the pageant chose to limit eligibility to single, never-married women between the ages of eighteen and twenty-eight. There was the infamous Rule 7, abandoned in 1940, that required

Miss America contestants to be "of good health and of the white race,"[29] and all contestants were required to list just how far back they could trace their ancestry on their formal biographical data sheet. As a PBS commentator put it, "The Miss America Pageant's continual crusade for respectability, ancestral connections to the Revolutionary War, or perhaps the Mayflower would have been seen as a plus."[30] This genealogy requirement was consistent with the popularity of the eugenics movement at the time, and the abandonment of Rule 7 in 1940 only coincided with the opposition of Hitler and his eugenic utopian philosophies.

In 1945, scholarships were first awarded to pageant winners, in addition to a screen test opportunity and a fur coat,[31] mostly due to the reported advocacy of Jean Bartel, Miss America 1943. Bartel is credited with raising $2.5 million in war bonds and giving the Miss America Pageant legitimacy by convincing the CEO, Lenora Slaughter, to award pageant winners scholarships, now the centerpiece of the pageant's claims to be a scholarship (not beauty) competition.[32]

In 1968, scores of feminist activists arrived in Atlantic City to declare "No More Miss America!" Despite popular lore, no bras were burned in the "freedom trash can," but protesters did attempt to incinerate many other "tired gender stereotypes," including "the Degrading Mindless-Boob-Girlie Symbol" and "the Woman as Pop Culture Obsolescent Theme."[33] The protests of 1968 are said to have helped usher in the modern feminist movement in the United States and stand as a watershed event in American cultural history. They also stand as a defining moment in the history of the Miss America Pageant. Since that moment and to this day the pageant strives to define itself in light of the evolution of feminism and changing notions of femininity. If pageants were seen as "obscene" in the Roaring Twenties, and as an indication of the debasement of American values, they were recast as misogynistic by the feminist movement, a label the Miss America Pageant has yet to shed.[34]

In the 1980s, in response to continued feminist critique and the impact of women's liberation and other social movements, the Miss America

Figure 1.1. Freedom trash can, New York Radical Women, Miss America Pageant protest, Atlantic City Boardwalk, 1968. Photo credit: William Sauro, *New York Times*.

Organization made efforts to downplay the beauty aspect of the pageant, adding the Social Campaign Clause, through which "contestants could campaign for a better society."[35] Through the addition of the social platform, pageant organizers imbued the competition with social values, and gave a voice to contestants.[36] By adding a social campaign element to the awarding of scholarships, allowing women to continue their education, and by the creation of the Hostess Committee, comprising respectable women recruited from Atlantic City "high society," the competition took on an air of respectability, despite the paradox posed by the contestants parading around in their swimsuits.

In 2018, the Miss America Organization, hounded by accusations of misogyny and sexual harassment, fired its CEO and hired former Miss America and Fox News anchor Gretchen Carlson to be the new head of the pageant. Fighting continued accusations of misogyny and irrelevance, Carlson aimed to bring the pageant into the twenty-first century and announced major changes, resulting in the new and improved Miss America 2.0. As part of the changes, the pageant eliminated the swimsuit competition, the focus of claims for women's objectification; took away the iconic runway and theme song made popular by Bert Parks; expanded options in the evening gown competition, allowing girls to wear "what they feel most comfortable in"; and maybe most significantly, reframed the nature of the pageant, calling it a "scholarship contest" rather than a competition. The reaction to these changes from pageant participants and supporters was swift and, by and large, negative. State pageant organizations that failed to follow the new guidelines or protested them were reprimanded, and in some cases lost their licenses. Calls for the firing and replacement of Carlson and the resignation of a number of board members, including former Miss America Kate Shindle, soon followed. Protests from fans in and around Atlantic City peaked as the pageant neared, fueled by allegations from the reigning Miss America, Cara Mund, that she had been silenced, bullied, and abused by the Miss America Organization. Illegal banners lambasting Carlson and calling for the re-examination

Figure 1.2. Miss America 2.0 protests Gretchen Carlson, Dover and Atlantic Avenues, Atlantic City, 2018. Photo credit: Laurie Greene.

of these reforms appeared all over Atlantic City just days before the pageant was set to begin preliminary competition. At the writing of this book, the Miss America Pageant is facing the loss of another television contract, and most probably the support of Atlantic City business interests. The pageant, in attempting to redefine itself outside of pageantry, had apparently lost its support. What becomes of the Miss America Pageant has yet to be seen, but its survival is tenuous and its critics vocal.[37]

THE PAGEANT AS CULTURAL BATTLEGROUND

Previous academic analyses of pageantry speak to its complexity. Most notably, despite popular perception, beauty pageants have been revealed to be deeply and inherently political.[38] As Cohen, Wilk, and Stoeltje assert in their cross-cultural analysis, beauty pageants worldwide "evoke passionate interest and engagement with *political issues* central to the lives of contestants, sponsors, organizers, and [the] audience."[39]

The Miss America Pageant is an important cultural phenomenon that underlies and has inspired the creation of other beauty pageants, including the drag pageant named after it, the Miss'd America Pageant. The Miss America Pageant is a model for pageantry not only in the United States, but worldwide, as well as a template for the function of pageantry in modern popular culture. Despite criticisms of the Miss America Pageant as anachronistic, its engagement with and contestation of timely political and cultural concerns is marked. In 1976, in the face of the ongoing military conflict in Vietnam, for instance, the Miss America Pageant agreed to allow talk of the war in the interview competition. In general, contestants are often asked to answer politically charged questions in their interviews. During the 2018 Miss America Pageant, the political nature of interview questions could not go unnoticed:

> First up, Miss Missouri was asked if she thought that President Donald Trump had colluded with Russia during the presidential campaign. She said that she would have to say that he was innocent of collusion, as there is not currently enough evidence that he is guilty. She also believed that the investigation into the collusion should continue. . . . Miss Texas was asked about Charlottesville protests, and if she agreed with Trump that there [were] "very fine people" on both sides of the protests. She said that she thought Trump should have made a statement earlier than he did, and that it's important to make people feel safe in the United States. . . . The eventual winner, Miss North Dakota, was asked about

her thoughts on the U.S. withdrawal from the Paris Accords. She said that she did not think the United States should have withdrawn and that she disagrees with the decision. After the show, she later clarified that while she disagrees with the Trump administration on this issue, she does still support the president. . . . Miss New Jersey was asked about her thoughts on removing Confederate statues. She said that they belonged in museums, but not discarded altogether. . . . Miss District of Columbia . . . was asked if she'd support legislation banning full-contact football in elementary and high schools due to the risk of concussions. She said that she would, as she's worried the sport could have a detrimental effect on young brains.[40]

Not only are Miss America contestants asked to comment on hot button political debates; they are also asked to do so without aligning themselves with any particular faction in the culture wars. A quick search of the Internet reveals dozens of websites and books coaching contestants on their performance in interviews. All these sources strongly assert that good pageant interview questions are tricky, since "no contestant wants to alienate any viewers; . . . the answers must satisfy everyone."[41] As Mike Perko, executive director of the Montana Miss America Organization Pageant, noted, having accepted the resignation of a titleholder after she stated her anti–Vietnam War views, "Girls [sic] are not discouraged from having political opinions but are asked not to express them openly."[42] Coaching sites and pageant commentators bemoan what they see as the slow creep of politics into an event that is pretty expressly nonpolitical. In a critical op-ed on September 11, 2017, Christine Rousselle stated, "People don't want to be inundated with politics all the time, yet there seems to be no sign of anyone wanting to stop."[43] The deft way that pageant contestants answer questions to avoid alienating the American television viewing audience is obvious in the answers from the 2018 Miss America Pageant. Cara Mund, the winner, went so far as to clarify her answer after winning the crown to ensure the open nature of the debate and her support of America values, embodied in the office of the president, if not in President Trump himself. The notion that the pageant is important as entertainment and that politics and entertainment cannot coexist (in polite conversation, with good taste, in civil interaction) is a familiar American perspective. It is echoed not just in the many press articles critical of interview questions like the ones cited, but also, for example, in discussions of #metoo protests at awards shows, kneeling to protest racism at sporting events, or the politicizing of children's books. As another op-ed by June Rice about the 2018 Miss America Pageant asserts: "When I heard the questions, I thought they were out of bounds. The contest was for beauty, intelligence, and charm. I guess those questions did test whether the ladies could answer a controversial opinion and still be charming. I still do not think the questions were fair because the answers are so sharply controversial. I would have hated to answer those questions, not knowing the judges' opinions on them."[44] Public sentiment aside, pageantry and popular culture are inherently political; they are a barometer of the political climate of the moment.

The studied ability to appeal to everyone when engaging in a conversation about potentially offensive topics such as politics illustrates another important feature of pageantry as an arena for the assertion of culturally specific values. In her analysis of beauty pageants, Sarah Banet-Weiser notes that, as the name suggests, the Miss America Pageant intertwines the concept of gender with that of the state and offers a glimpse into the "constantly changing and always complicated stories about nation itself: who counts as part of the nation? What does it mean to be a specifically feminine representative of the nation? How are social concerns—such as racism, multiculturalism, and 'family values'—mediated in and through women's bodies on the public stage? And what are the social and cultural conditions through which particular kinds of representation can occur?"[45] Each of these questions has been the centerpiece of both spectacle and controversy at the Miss America Pageant at one time or another, and these critical political debates lie at the foundation of attempts to modernize the pageant, including the 2018 changes culminating in the pageant's rebranding as Miss America 2.0.

The beauty pageant is also important as both mediated spectacle as well as a performance of construct wome "palpable, on displ disciplinary practi been the focus of m Cohen, Wilk, and Stoeltje see page structures of power are engaged: the power to control and contain the meanings mapped on the bodies of competitors, the mechanisms of this power, and the spaces where this power is resisted.[48] The aforementioned controls are many; in beauty pageants they serve to regulate (or discipline, in Michel Foucault's terms) femininity and national identity through the presentation of women's bodies. This book explores, among other things, the way the power is exerted in traditional beauty pageants like Miss America, and in comparison, in drag pageantry like the Miss'd America Pageant.

Moral principles are also contested in pageantry; concepts of appropriate behavior for women are presented to define ideal womanhood. Rules determining eligibility, judging, and circumscribing appropriate conduct for contestants and crown holders become statements about what a woman should be, and part of the disciplinary structure defined by Foucault. It is typical that pageants have requirements: indigenous pageants require, for example, the knowledge of local language, residency on reservations, and tribal membership as prerequisites for participation.[49] To become a contestant for the Miss America Pageant in particular, one must be between the ages of seventeen and twenty-five; be a United States citizen; meet residency requirements for competing in a certain city or state; meet character criteria as set forth by the Miss America Organization; be in reasonably good health to meet the job requirements; and be able to meet the time commitment and job responsibilities as set forth by the local, state, and national competition(s) in which one competes.[50] Every contestant and titleholder in the Miss America Pageant must abide by the following personal characteristics:

> (Section 2.6.1)—You must be female; (Section 2.6.2)—You cannot be married, previously married, or divorced; (Section 2.6.3)—You must not have a child—be currently or previously pregnant, or be the adoptive parent of any child; . . . (Section 2.6.5)—You must not have been charged for any minor offenses in the last 24 months; you cannot compete if you have ever been convicted of a "criminal offense"; . . . (Section 2.7.5)—You cannot get engaged during your year of service without written permission from the Miss America Organization; [and among other legal obligations] . . . (Section 6.7)—If any statements you make in the contract are untrue, if something changes your eligibility, if you have inappropriate mannerisms, do not follow the rules, or suffer a disability that keeps you from fulfilling duties, the MAO can take your title from you.[51]

These rules and requirements make clear that pageants, like assessments of beauty, are more than skin deep; they are a regulation of femininity from within the culture and polity of a nation. These regulations are expressions of power that consider gender identity, marital status, sexual and social behavior, and even the form and comportment of contestants' bodies—their mannerisms, and potentially disqualifying disabilities.

In addition to the regulations for eligibility, while in Atlantic City, pageant contestants are disciplined in their behaviors under the watchful eye of chaperones (called State Travelling Companions, or STCs) and a local hostess assigned to guide and advise them during their stay. The hostess ensures that the contestant stays clear of controversy by enforcing draconian rules, some of which in 1970 included the following:

- She may not answer a telephone—the hostess answers that, and if the party on the other end is a newspaper or television reporter, she hangs up.
- No man—and this includes her father, who presumably knows her quite well and has no ulterior motives—may enter the [bed]room.
- She may speak to no man without a hostess present, and this includes all male relatives.
- She may not walk on the beach or boardwalk with any man or go shopping or sightseeing with one or relax with one poolside.
- She must occupy a private room with no connecting door, since such things are conducive to sin.
- She may not leave her room, even to mail a letter, unless the hostess is with her.
- All places serving liquor are off limits, and she is in deep trouble if she sneaks a snort in the privacy of her own room.
- Smoking is forbidden.
- She may accept no gifts of any sort.
- She may kiss no man.
- All interviews with reporters and photographs must be authorized by the pageant.[52]

After casinos opened, these restrictions were expanded to include exclusion from casino gambling locales. Miss America Organization CEO Albert Marks described the industry as "a zoo" and said that Miss America should not "associate with any less than perfect operation."[53] Kate Shindle, in her memoir *Being Miss America*, speaks of growing up in Brigantine, New Jersey, and her mother's role as head of the Hostess Committee: "STC[s] are in charge of everything the contestants do at the hotel—using the gym, getting up on time, not being late for pick up. If you are a contestant, you and your STC have adjoining rooms and your door to the hallway is locked at all times. You do not answer the door. Your name is not on the reservation; everything goes through the STC . . . the hostesses take over once the girls are downstairs."[54]

Contestants are disciplined in a way that ensures that ideal femininity will be preserved and protected from the various corrupting forces that threaten it. This discipline extends to every aspect of contestants' lives, both public and private, and encompasses the shape (good health/fitness), comportment (behaviors and mannerisms), and sexual behavior (never pregnant, single) of women's bodies. Evidence of violations of these ideal womanly virtues even outside the confines of pageantry are enough to disqualify contestants. Most notably, Vanessa Williams (Miss America 1984), the first black Miss America, lost her crown after old nude photographs of her posed in sexual acts with another woman were published in *Penthouse* magazine.[55] It was not until thirty-two years later, in 2015 (crowning Miss America 2016) that the pageant formally apologized to Williams for her ouster. As CEO Sam Haskell told Williams on stage: "Though none of us currently in the organization were involved then, on behalf of today's organization, I want to apologize to you and to your mother, Miss Helen Williams. I want to apologize for anything that was said or done that made you feel any less than the Miss America you are and the Miss America you always will be."[56] Despite this apology, the rules have changed little since the inception of the pageant, and even then, change comes not without great struggle. It is one reason the pageant is often viewed as a relic—outdated and out of touch.

POPULAR CULTURE AND COMMODITY CULTURE: THE PAGEANT

Popular culture can be "simultaneously conventional and unpredictable, liberating and reactionary, personal yet anonymous, and grounded in materiality while also being a realm where fantasy is played out."[57] Beauty pageants ultimately provide an idealistic resolution to the tensions surrounding issues of gender, race, sexuality, and inequality within culture. Are women sexual objects subject to male gaze and desire, or repositories of respectability and morality? Are women intelligent subjects with social agency, or commodities valued for their bodies and reproductive capabilities? Are women of color as beautiful as white women, and is race even significant? What values underlie the America Dream, and are these attainable by all Americans? These questions are broached and contested through the "vehicle of the 'female' body, which comes to represent nationalism in terms of a particular image of femininity" in the Miss America Pageant.[58]

At various times during its contestation, the Miss America Pageant has highlighted one or more of these tensions, most notably with its selection of winners, who appear to reflect the debates and events unfolding at that cultural moment. The first Jewish American to compete and win was Bess Myerson, whose reign coincided with the unfolding of the atrocities of the Holocaust in 1945. The first black winner, Vanessa Williams, in 1984, was, along with her unlikely successor, Suzette Charles, at the center of a more complex debate about both whiteness (skin tone) and morality (based on the publication of nude photos of Williams in *Penthouse*). The first deaf Miss America, Heather Whitestone, in 1995, attested to the hard work and discipline at the heart of the democratization of success and personified debate in the increasingly politicized deaf culture. The first openly gay contestant, Erin O'Flaherty, competed in 2016 amid continuing debates about marriage equality and gender nonconformity. In each case, these contemporary challenges to the feminine ideal as stated by the Miss America Pageant are ameliorated through a popular trope, "We are just like everyone else";[59] the "pageant is pro-woman and a reflection of the ever-evolving modern women."[60] In an interview in 2002, Heather Whitestone commented: "The best thing was that being Miss America gave me the opportunity to bring a positive awareness to other people about the deaf community. We all have a heart and a mind, and we're more than just hearing or deaf people! Being Miss America gave me an opportunity to teach the world about deaf people and that deaf people can speak too!"[61]

The saliency of the value of democracy and the democratization of difference is not only held in the Miss America Pageant but is part of the American ideology. When speaking of the first openly gay Miss America contestant, Erin O'Flaherty (Miss Missouri), Rita, a former Miss America contestant, was perplexed by the fact that the local lesbians in Atlantic City were so disappointed by O'Flaherty's uneventful march down the Boardwalk in the Show Us Your Shoes Miss America Parade, having expected her to be "gayer" in her presentation: "She's a pageant girl . . . other than the fact that she is gay . . . they don't get pageant culture! I know they were disappointed she didn't look *different*, but whaaa? . . . . They don't get [to] buy in to the regulation . . . your body completely regulated. . . . We had to sign a contract that said we had never been pregnant, never been married, never been divorced, never had children . . . had a tattoo . . . they were so super strict about how you were supposed to look and how you were supposed to dress . . . let alone talk. She can't lead with that [lesbian]!"[62]

The annual spectacle ushers in the Miss America competition and features the fifty-one Miss America candidates celebrating the "spirit of their home state through costume and one-of-a-kind wearable handmade art-shoe creations, floats, marching bands, dancers, twirling groups, and a variety of other amazing parade groups."[63] Rita's assertion the "she can't lead with that" is a clear expression of support for the American ideal of democratization. As O'Flaherty herself asserted in her many interviews, "It's a little hard because I think some people think I'm one-dimensional [just a lesbian] and I'm not."[64] The fact that Miss Missouri was already marked as gay may have subjected her to deeper scrutiny focusing on her comportment as an embodied lesbian and Miss America contestant. This may explain why during the Show Us Your Shoes Parade she was rather demure when passing the screaming, bawdy gay crowds on New York Avenue and the Boardwalk—compared to other contestants who responded with high fives and shrieks, one even grabbing a rainbow flag and waving it in the air.

Adding to the analysis of popular culture as a complex phenomenon is the knowledge that it is firmly situated in commodity culture.[65] Products of popular culture are used to spur economic activity while they sell cultural ideology. Some of this commodification is obvious—beauty products and fashion, for instance, are sold with the selling of ideal feminine beauty. The connection between the Miss America Pageant and commodity culture is firmly rooted in its inception. The pageant was begun as a marketing scheme, after all, held in Atlantic City just after Labor Day in 1921 as a way for newspapers to increase their circulation and for the resort's businesses to extend their profitable summer season. Newspapers across the country held contests judging photographs of young women, and the winners came to Atlantic City for a competition where they were evaluated on "personality and social graces."[66]

HERE SHE COMES: THE MEANING OF MISS AMERICA

Femininity, national identity, and morality are presented in pageantry; nonetheless, opposing interpretations of pageants exist within society and culture. As Frank Deford, sportswriter and former Miss America judge, poignantly stated, "Miss America is maligned by one segment of America, adored by another, [and] misunderstood by about all of it."[67] Feminist detractors for example, passionately object to beauty pageants as arenas for the objectification of women's bodies and the control of their sexuality.[68] Supporters, however, believe in the strong sense of empowerment for young women found through improved self-confidence and the development of professional skills gained from pageant participation.[69] Contestants themselves express the choice they have in their participation—their agency rather than any exploitation: "We're up there because we want to be up there . . . we're up there and it builds confidence, it's not degrading. Other women may think it is, well, okay, don't curl your hair."[70]

In her memoir, former Miss America Kate Shindle suggests that despite decades of "stereotypes, expectations, scandal, myths, media scrutiny, public skepticism, and questionable leadership choices," Miss America continues to attract intelligent, passionate women who share strong "camaraderies" wrought through the rigors of competition, and who themselves have pushed "the pageant to be more progressive" and substantive than its caretakers aspired for it to be.[71] Shindle views contestants with great admiration. They stand out in her mind as exceptional women, despite the inherent contradictions and problems with pageantry. Rita shares a similar high regard for her pageant experiences, even the pageant's most maligned enactment, the swimsuit competition: "To wear a bikini up there in front of so many people, that takes confidence . . . the thought of wearing a bikini in front of all those people was mortifying. I wore a classy one-piece . . . I did build a lot of confidence and interviewing skills, and I am great with people, talking in front of people. . . . That's what pageants teach you, how to be confident and strong."[72]

Most contestants, like Rita and Kate Shindle, claim elements of liberal feminist discourse as part of their self-presentation, with statements about self-confidence, assertiveness, the importance of careers, and perhaps most importantly, the agency contestants possess—agency to both participate in and craft their individual presentations as beauty queens. Beauty queens in this model are transformed from exploited pariahs to feminist superheroes; they are real women who embody the values of American culture: individuality, hard work, and perseverance. They embody the American Dream, for through the enactment of these values, any woman can become Miss America.

Miss America Meets Stonewall:
The Rise of Drag Pageantry

Drag pageantry is a highly developed form of pageantry for female impersonators (and in some cases transgender women[73] and cisgender women), styled after traditional beauty pageants, most notably the Miss America Pageant. Drag pageants first appeared in the gay community during the 1970s post-Stonewall era and were held in gay bars and discotheques. The importance of gay bars as the center of gay social and political life in that period cannot be overstated. The Stonewall riots attest to the saliency of gay bars as important sites for identity creation and contestation, a phenomenon that was also the case in Atlantic City. Though drag pageants evolved largely within the context of gay nightlife, all were influenced by and many mirrored the format of the influential Miss America Pageant.[74] Small local pageants abounded in gay bars throughout the United States. The first national gay pageant, Miss Gay America, was held in 1971, and since then, dozens of local, state, and national pageants have been created and continue to be held.[75]

In 2009, the first season of *RuPaul's Drag Race* brought drag out of gay bars and into popular culture; since then, drag pageants and drag nightlife have been forever changed. The popularization of drag as a result of the commercial and media success of *Drag Race* has been much debated in the drag community. Some see the "homogenizing" effects of the powerful media success of *Drag Race* as a detriment to the individuality and creativity of local drag performances. Popularization, some critics believe, has also detracted from the potent political force that drag once commanded. As drag queen Mimi Imfurst described it, ever since RuPaul went "mainstream," drag has fought to maintain its "subversiveness."[76] Drag queen Evelyn Syde spoke to the difficulty of doing "funny" (campier) drag anymore, in light of the influence of *Drag Race*: "[In Austin, Texas] people only want to tip RuPaul queens (if you are on TV); no one wants to tip local queens anymore, except straight people and bachelorette parties. . . . It's harder to do funnier numbers, I mean things that aren't top 40 . . . that's what they expect. One of my favorite things to do was rap about donuts and eat them on stage. *That* was my kind of drag! The campy, funny . . . this is who we are. It's hard to do that now."[77] Former *Drag Race* contestant Thorgy Thor has been very vocal about how *RuPaul's*

Drag Race has damaged drag and drag pageantry; "*RuPaul's Drag Race* has sort of killed drag for queens who are not on the show." Thor suggests that producers of *Drag Race* purposely demonize pageant queens through what has become known as "the bitch edit."[78] This is when a queen is "edited" by producers of the show to look deplorable. As in other reality TV shows, on *Drag Race*, participants are portrayed in ways that turn them into basic archetypes, that is, "the underdog," "the funny one," and, of course, "the bitch."[79] Targeting traditional pageant queens as villains is an attempt to ensure that *Drag Race* serves as the only way for drag queens to get national recognition even though drag pageants have been around for much longer.

Drag Race has also been the subject of even more glaring controversy within the gay community. In its first season, *Drag Race* was accused of "transphobia" as a result of remarks made by RuPaul.[80] *Drag Race* did not feature its first transgender competitor until 2016, and Miss Gay America and the Miss'd America Pageant still require contestants to be unaltered surgically "below the waist" (although Miss'd America does allow presurgical transgender contestants to be on hormones).[81] The reasons for these eligibility restrictions lie at the heart of competing definitions of drag itself within the drag (and gay) community. Many of the Miss'd America contestants spoke of the value of "traditional drag," which requires anatomical men to create the illusion of femininity without the unfair advantage of performance-enhancing drugs and body-altering surgeries.[82] Regardless of where one stands on specific requirements, suffice to say that transgender queens have played an important role in drag history, and have always faced discrimination from some within the LGBTQ community, including the drag community and the highly visible and influential *Drag Race*.

Fans of *Drag Race*, on the other hand, point to the ways that popularization has resulted in increased visibility of drag queens and indirectly of gay culture, providing a positive image of the LGBTQ community and reducing the stigmatization of drag performance. For example, Arnold

Myint (a.k.a. Suzy Wong) recounted an interaction he had with an older woman sitting next to him on a flight while he was on his way to compete in Miss Gay America. After the woman asked if he was a singer, Myint told her, "Oh no, honey, I'm a drag queen. She said, 'Oh, that's cool,' and that was that. She didn't even blink."[83] Drag queen Alexia Love compares the danger that crossdressing posed in public in the 1990s to her life as a drag performer now: "Nowadays, you have a drag queen at a party, and it brightens up the whole thing . . . I do bridal events, like at the Borgata . . . the girls love it. They love it so much they want you to hang out with them for the rest of the night. You walk through the casino in full drag, and you know, *you are queen of the casino*! [*Laughs.*] Now . . . everyone wants to have a drag queen around . . . have one as a friend . . . it used to be a gay guy, now it's a drag queen [laughs].")."[84]

Fifi Dubois (Miss'd America 2015) expresses the acceptance of drag that has come with its familiarity to the general public through pop culture, echoing the sentiments of many drag queens who were interviewed: "I do think it's cool that there are 13 year old kids that want to go and see a drag show, and there is a way for them to watch it on their TVs at home, and that I don't have to walk around explaining what a drag queen is to random strangers—'oh, why are you dressed like that, what is this?' I don't have to explain it now because it is so mainstream. You can 'Wikipedia' it. You can see it on your television. You can ask your Alexa and she will explain it to you quite well. When I got my Amazon Echo, I asked her what was the definition of a drag queen [laughs] and she gave me a really great definition."[85] Suffice to say, *RuPaul's Drag Race* and the subsequent mainstreaming of drag as popular entertainment has had a great impact on drag performance, drag pageantry, gay nightlife, and changing perceptions of the LGBTQ community.

As will be described in chapter 2 in detail, the Miss'd America Pageant was created in 1992 as a spoof of the Miss America Pageant, held on the day after the iconic pageant at the gay bar *Studio Six*, off of New York Avenue in Atlantic City. Since then, the pageant has evolved, transforming from its decidedly local referential roots to become a national pageant, subject to and reflecting the national and even international standards and meaning now associated with drag performance. It is interesting that the gay community and the drag subculture in particular should glorify beauty pageants and reproduce them, even in a satirical guise, considering their rejection of the male heterosexual power structure. Gay and pageant subcultures adore pageants in similar and disparate ways. This book explores the similarities and differences between the Miss America Pageant and its unofficial drag "counterpart" the Miss'd America Pageant in Atlantic City in order to better understand the importance of popular entertainment within the context of culture.

CHAPTER 2

Atlantic City, Drag Culture, and a Community of Practice

The backstage dressing areas at the Borgata Hotel and Casino are crammed with racks of gowns, glittered stilettos, and enormous wigs on Styrofoam stands. Long tables spill over with a chaotic array of makeup boxes, jewelry and accessories, glue guns, and duct tape. Breastplates and hip-pieces are draped off hangers next to sequined swimsuits, rhinestoned gowns, and tulle underpieces. A large octopus boa, nearly eight feet long, wraps itself along the clothing rack, a suitcase, and eventually the floor. Cleo Phatra tends to the elaborate costumes on her side of the room. Though not competing this year, she comes as the costumer and head of the entourage for drag queen Mimi Imfurst. Noah, her assistant, fixes some stones on a dress as he arranges shoes and carefully places the contents of a makeup box on a section of the shared tables. A wig almost two feet high is being teased and hair-sprayed just to his left.

Shi-Queeta-Lee has already begun painting her face. White makeup covering her dark brown skin, she creates contours to her already pronounced cheekbones and recounts the time she impersonated Michelle Obama at the White House. One of the dancers, stretching in a straddle on the floor beside her, breathes out deeply, listening in awe. Shi-Queeta-Lee laughs as she begins to apply the next layer of eyelashes with the confidence and calm of a seasoned performer. Across the room, the slim and fit Stasha Storm is sitting still while her wig is fitted. She teases her dressers in Spanish as they discuss the excitement of the impending competition. Her dancers beside her on the floor stretch as they hum parts of the music and mark the choreography with their arms and fluid upper bodies. Next to her, Farrah Mascara is pulling a third layer of panty hose over her foam hips. She looks in a long mirror as she adjusts her breasts, then looks over, grunts, and flashes her huge, dark eyelashes, lips slightly parted. Champagne Bubbles sits back as her makeup artist applies her face; she is glamorous, even half constructed with a stocking on her head. Glitter is applied to her eyelids and her platinum wig fitted. She looks up as she lifts her eyebrows for the next application of shadow.[1]

DRAG AND CULTURE

The performance of gender mimicking, blending, and ambiguity is found in many cultures and takes many forms. As one of these forms, drag can be simply defined as the performance of gender by an individual possessing a contrary anatomy.[2] Unlike cross-dressing or the gendered presentation of transgendered individuals, drag is a public performance that requires an audience aware of the fact that drag queens are not women, but men (or that drag kings are women).[3] No matter how real the presentation of femininity by drag queens, the contradiction, based primarily on anatomy or behavior, is apparent to the audience, and the tension created through this contradiction affords drag its potential expressive power. The "collusion between the audience and the performer" highlights the important role of the audience in maintaining the disruption between sex and gender in drag.[4]

This book is a study of drag queens who compete in a parodic form of drag pageantry, the Miss'd America Pageant. More specifically, it is an ethnographic description of the Miss'd America Pageant that considers not only the meaning of pageantry to a particular audience, but also the changes to that audience, that pageant, and the iconic pageant it parodies, the Miss America Pageant. Miss America and Miss'd America are not just pageants showcasing ideal femininity. They also play an important part in forming and expressing the identity of a larger community in Atlantic City, New Jersey: a segment of the gay community whose social lives are centered around New York Avenue.

ATLANTIC CITY DRAG: A COMMUNITY OF PRACTICE

The term *community of practice* was first used in 1991 by organizational theorists Jean Lave and Etienne Wenger to describe the kind of tacit learning that occurs between individuals who are members of and invested in organizations of common interest. Communities of practice are created through "the process of social learning that occurs when people who have a common interest in a subject or area collaborate over an extended period of time, where they share ideas and strategies, determine solutions, and build innovations."[5] According to Wenger, communities of practice are groups of people who share a passion for something and learn how to do it better as they interact regularly.[6] As Wenger notes, a community of practice is different from a geographical community, although they may overlap. Unlike geographical communities, "communities of practice develop around things that matter to people. As a result, their practices reflect the members' own understanding of what is important. Even when a community's actions conform to an external mandate, it is the community—not the mandate—that produces the practice. In this sense, communities of practice are self-organizing systems."[7]

Communities of practice exist on three axes of interaction: (1) *what they are about*: a joint enterprise as understood and continually renegotiated by its members; (2) *how they function*: the relationships of mutual engagement that bind members together; and (3) *their capability*: the shared repertoire of communal resources (routines, sensibilities, artifacts, vocabulary, styles, etc.) that members have developed over time.[8] Communities of practice typically evolve through various stages of development

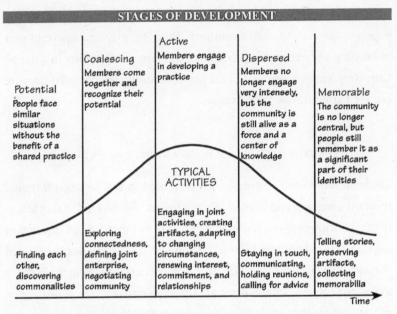

STAGES OF DEVELOPMENT

Potential
People face
similar
situations
without the
benefit of a
shared practice

Coalescing
Members come
together and
recognize their
potential

Active
Members engage
in developing a
practice

Dispersed
Members no
longer engage
very intensely,
but the
community is
still alive as a
force and a
center of
knowledge

Memorable
The community
is no longer
central, but
people still
remember it as
a significant
part of their
identities

TYPICAL
ACTIVITIES

Finding each
other,
discovering
commonalities

Exploring
connectedness,
defining joint
enterprise,
negotiating
community

Engaging in joint
activities, creating
artifacts, adapting
to changing
circumstances,
renewing interest,
commitment, and
relationships

Staying in touch,
communicating,
holding reunions,
calling for advice

Telling stories,
preserving
artifacts,
collecting
memorabilia

Time

Figure 2.1. Life cycle of a community of practice. Communities of practice move through various stages of development characterized by different levels of interaction among the members and different kinds of activities. Credit: Etienne Wenger, 2018.

characterized by different levels of interaction and different kinds of activities. Figure 2.1 describes the ways in which communities of practice develop. We can use this progression to understand the historical evolution, in part, of the gay community on New York Avenue in Atlantic City.

The drag community in Atlantic City is a clear community of practice, where individual relationships and community identity have been structured around the shared practice of drag and the shared passionate concerns of the gay community, first in confronting endemic homophobia, and then in combatting the epidemic of AIDS. The ethnographic data also show that the Miss'd America Pageant became one important organization through which identity was created, negotiated, and shared, and that this identity and its community evolved as both the pageant and the community dynamics changed. Drag queen Sandy Beach recounted the necessity to create the pageant when he described the beginnings of the Miss'd America Pageant as a joint enterprise:

> The AIDS crisis had raised its ugly head and no one was out there help-ing and raising money for that. And we figured, we have to help our friends that are dying . . . as more people got sick, we started to make sure people got their groceries and medications, and even getting buried. . . . We paid to cremate quite a few people the funeral homes wouldn't touch. We all came together. We knew we had a built-in audi-ence from Miss America the night before, and we would get that crowd to help us, the way we had always helped them [the pageant]. And we all donated everything, including our tips and all our time, and it was a labor of love, a bittersweet labor of love.[9]

As an illustration of the strong relationships developed through drag practice, drag queen Alexia Love also speaks about the early days of the Miss'd America Pageant and the feelings of community and common pur-pose that she remembers fondly:

> My best memories are being with all the girls, Joy, Mortimer, Brittany, and Morgan. . . . The best times we had with each other were when we were in the dressing room getting dressed, helping each other. We would cut up and laugh so hard. . . . catching up on past events and stuff, fig-uring out how to sew, doing makeup, doing wigs, we learned it all on the fly! . . . and that would be the best time. We'd call it our church time, well, not *church* time, we'd be in the back laughing and it would be like church hymns, like singing. That was the best time."[10]

The development of a shared repertoire of communal resources is evi-dent in the practices that evolved as part of in-group interactions. In the early days of Miss'd America, as we shall see, local queens, well known to everyone from the bar/nightlife scene, competed for the title, and camp humor that was based on the kind of *reading* that drag queens commonly engaged in with each other abounded—a sometimes scathing critique of one's appearance, lack of talent, intelligence, hygiene, and, most of all, sexual behavior. This verbal jousting was attributed to one's ability to size someone up instantly and find the clever one-liner. Drag Queen HRH Mortimer (Miss'd America 1995) described his inability to keep up with the best queens and their cutting *reads*, how they knew just where "they could not go" and instead went "right to the edge." He recalls how he stayed quiet to avoid being a victim of the teasing, but also the lasting intimacy of the bonds this shared practice of verbal jousting created: "When they started 'reading' each other . . . I always kept my mouth shut. It's an art form. . . . I didn't know how to 'read' people . . . to sum people up in a couple of phrases or ideas. Drag queens are vicious . . . just vicious . . . but there is a lot of love . . . the camaraderie . . . the core girls, Lemon Fresh Joy, Morgan Wells, me, Chunkie Marinara, A.J. (Alexia Love), Ms. Ten'e, Sandy Beach, Brittany Lynn, we have friendship bonds that no one will be able to get inside of . . . we bonded over the blood, sweat, and tears."[11]

As the historical trajectory of the Miss'd America Pageant and the gay community on New York Avenue are recounted, ethnographic testimony reveals the changes in this shared community to be an excellent model for understanding the process of identity creation in general, and the role of the Miss'd America Pageant in particular in the Atlantic City gay community. For it was not only the drag queens who became invested in this shared community of practice, and then resisted its dispersal, as the pageant grew to focus on national rather than local concerns. Everyone who became a member of this community of practice, the Miss'd America Pageant, shared its mission combatting the AIDS epidemic and homophobia, and valued their place in the shared enterprise of Atlantic City pageantry. The practices associated with the pageant, whether it be the production of the pageant itself, the act of drag performance, reading each other, or other products and practices, such as the Show Us Your Shoes Parade, retain strong emotional meaning for the members of this community even now.

As recently as September 2018, years after the physical demise of New York Avenue and its gay clubs, the community threw a party. The impending reopening of the former gay 1980s club, the Saratoga, as a Cajun restaurant called Bourré, initiated a triumphant reunion of the former queens and other denizens who once lived, worked, and partied on New York Avenue and the adjacent streets. The gay community reconvened to reminisce, tell stories, raise money for local gay causes, and remind old and new of the place and the activities that still form part of their collective identity as a community, although some are now deceased, or dispersed in Philadelphia, New York City, and sometimes further away. The Show Us Your Pride event was hosted by drag queen Sandy Beach, credited by all in the community as the Miss'd America Pageant's originator,[12] although, as we will see, the pageant's roots go further back historically. At the event, the mission of the community was reaffirmed: raise money for the SJAA (originally South Jersey Against AIDS, now the South Jersey AIDS Alliance—an organization dedicated to serving those stricken with HIV/AIDS) and MANNA (an organization that provides food for AIDS patients), and to erect a plaque commemorating the community that shared this space and the pageant that originated there as an expression of its identity. The proposed plaque reads:

New York Avenue: Where the Party Began

Since the 1920s, New York Avenue has served as a safe haven for the LGBT community. For decades, boisterous hotels and nightclubs made New York Avenue a gay tourist destination, a hangout for celebrities, and a place for everyone to let their hair down and party. In the 70s, the now infamous "Show us your shoes!" was chanted by drag queens who watched the Miss America Parade from the Boardwalk and their apartment balconies, helping to inspire the modern Show Us Your Shoes Parade. This plaque is dedicated to the memory of hundreds of thousands who lived here, worked here, visited here, and had the times of their lives on New York Avenue!

Though drag events have increased in the casino showrooms and brunch venues in Atlantic City, the community of drag has all but disappeared. Drag brunches, *RuPaul's Drag Race All Stars*, and other drag events hosted by casinos are evidence of the ascendency of drag as a popular culture phenomenon rather than a performance style expressive of local gay culture and its concerns. This is revealed in the way that the craft of drag was learned in the past versus today. While Miss'd America contestants today express gratitude for relationships within their "drag families," they talk as well about the importance of the Internet and YouTube and television as ways of learning their craft. Many queens also identify as "drag orphans," lacking real "drag family" ties. The original Miss'd America drag queens from Atlantic City describe the development of their craft in different terms; they learned from older queens how to "paint their faces" or "the importance of hips" or "how to find your talent." The remainder of their craft, whether it be how to speak, how to dress and make costumes, or even how to manage the business of performance, was learned from their peers, who navigated the club scene in Atlantic City with them. At dinner in 2019, HRH Mortimer, Morgan Wells, Alexia Love, Brittany Lynn, and Joy Marnier reminisced:

JOY: I know everyone speaks drag language. Those words were those words. . . .

MORGAN: I mean [they] are the words now, but I will say this, I moved here from Philadelphia in 2002, but the whole *brick*, only you girls would call someone a brick! When I go somewhere else and say *brick*, they look at me like [*makes a crazy face; laughing*]. That was an Atlantic City word! *Brick*!

JOY: Miss Morgan says that all the time and I say, "Are you sure?" I mean, you gotta know what a brick is!

[*All the girls talk over each other about why you call someone a brick.*]

MORGAN: *Brick* means too hard!

HRH: A monster.

JOY: BRICK means brick; a face like a brick wall; you got a haaard, squaaaare, manly face; you ugly! You just ugly [*laughing*].

BRITTANY: I can't get a word in with all these old pigeons yapping away.

HRH: So, like we said, Brittany's a monster . . . [*Laughing.*]

JOY: We were talking about bricks girls! *Bricks!*

BRITTANY: Like when we were talking about how all the words are the same if you watch that documentary The Queen, that black and white one with Sabrina from like 67 and the big New York drag queen-of-the-year pageant, if you watch that they use the same terminology . . .

LAURIE: Well, how did you learn it?

BRITTANY: I learned it from watching all of them, because they're just a bunch of old drug addicts [*gestures to the group*].

HRH: And I learned it from the generation that was before me, like Dee Dee Lewis, yeah, Tinsel, Tinsel Garland.

ALEXIA: You just picked it up.

HRH: Diane Jones . . . yeah, what's her name . . .

BRITTANY: Diane Jones . . .

ALEXIA: Oh my goodness, Diane!

MORGAN: Yup, that's how . . . ain't no other way.

JOY: Pillars, all pillars of the drag community here . . .

ALEXIA: Dee Dee taught me how to put my makeup on.

HRH: Yeah, that's the one thing we all learned together from them. We'd all sit in the dressing room with each other and then you would watch how each other does their makeup and then you learn how to do the tits . . . and you are like, "How'd you do that?"

The gay bar was described as a "refuge," a "home," their "church," and in these bars, skills and stories were shared, practices developed and learned, and identities formed. HRH describes his first time in a gay bar: "[The] first time I walked in to a gay bar, I saw two guys having sex on the dance

Figure 2.2. Practice for Miss'd America Pageant, the Originals, 2011.
Photo credit: Christopher Hartney.

floor and I was like . . . I didn't know that's how we did it. We were all kids.
Nobody cared how old you were. You were in a gay bar [*all laughing*]. I
ordered a Chablis! How gay is that? I'll have a Chablis! [*Laughing.*] You
can't carry an ID that says you're 'gay' as good at that [*laughing*]."[13]

The girls describe their memories of camaraderie with the old girls in
the bathrooms and dressing rooms of the clubs:

ALEXIA: You know what I miss most? The dressing room and the
bathroom. It was great when we had real bars, gay bars . . . we would

all catch up. That was so much fun. Talking . . . just talking about . . . ·
I don't know . . . everything.

HRH: Laughing in the dressing room for hours, literally three hours.

ALEXIA: And hours, that was our church. Me and Mortimer used to
sit in the bathroom, the big men's room, and people [would] come
and say, "Hi, how are you?"

HRH: And we'd just talk about everything . . . and people be like,
"Where the hell were you two? We thought you left three hours ago."

ALEXIA: We had the best time. We talked about everything, *anything*.

JOY: I remember people bringing you drinks!

HRH: They would get us drinks; remember . . . Miss Patty? "Miss
Patty, can someone go and get us a vodka and tonic?" [*All laughing.*]

MORGAN: And the dressing rooms! Anyone who comes back and
sees that says, "You bitches are turning this dressing room out!" and
I say, "Yes! We turning that dressing room out and we have cock-
tails, I don't care if it's nine o'clock in the morning!" They'd be there,
all the girls, some getting ready, some just there. Oh, it's always
kitchen table talk, honey.

JOY: We were the jug girls. We always have a jug and our wigs on a
little funny. But a beautiful gown! [*Laughing.*]

HRH: And [the talk] was ruthless and fun and hysterical.

ALEXIA: And very honest Miss Thang, Miss Southern Comfort 2006
(gestures to Morgan)!

HRH: We used to come out on the stage and say to the audience, "You
missed the real show!" It's the honest truth because the real show was
in the dressing room because we were . . . it's just hysterical back there
because we have known each other for so long, and like, the jokes just
come back and forth, and we laugh so hard about everything![14]

The pre-existence of vibrant and respected drag in the 1960s and 1970s as
part of the gay Atlantic City community was noted by all the queens at

the dinner as an important part of their success as drag queens coming
up in the 1980s. Values and practices were created, shared, and passed on
to them, the next generation, who admired the generation that came before
them:

HRH: The drag queens back then especially, they were ... everyone
    loved the drag queens. I mean, Dee Dee Lewis, my god! And Tinsel
    Garland, they were like goddesses to us, and all the gay men that
    were around town. And Molly Makeup!

ALL: Uhmmmm

HRH: When they walked in the bars, everyone knew who they were,
    and they were *fabulous*! Everyone payed attention to them ... and
    then we were the second generation coming up after them and we
    got the same thing after a while.

MORGAN: It was a special group.

[*Pause*]

HRH: And now everyone's a fucking drag queen.

BRITTANY: That larger than life comedy, that like came like real
    natural, and they were just like all like, well especially Tinsel ... you
    can't top Tinsel. She was just it!

ALL: Yeah ... uhmmm, that was then.

HRH: Tinsel was one of my mentors ... she gave me my first couple of
    outfits. She said, "You need to use this and just get on stage."

JOY: Mable Redchop was probably the first drag queen I *really* saw on
    stage where I was like ... *wow*. And her banter was like, *amazing*.

ALEXIA: And Chunkie (Marinara)!

JOY: And then she left, and then Tinsel came in, and that was like a
    whole 'nother ball park of banter that came in, and I'm like ... Oh
    my god! I've got to learn this. This is fabulous, and funny. I've got to
    get in.

LAURIE: What kind of banter do you mean?

HRH: Oh, yeah ... Tinsel is sharp as a tack, oh my god he's so funny.

Joy: Just being on stage and just being quick-witted and not only having a routine, but being able to come back at the audience and like . . . if they said something that was a little off color, or something that was razzing her one day she always had a comeback. A *good* drag queen knows how to banter, knows how to handle the audience, no issues about people or about things.

HRH: There was that one time that Tinsel threw that guy down the steps for heckling her . . . [*laughs*] that was great! "Don't forget, I'm a man in a dress!" And threw him down the steps. [*All laughing.*][15]

Particular skills and knowledge found in drag culture that are needed to create the illusion of femininity are important components of drag performance. These skills were learned through mentorship, creativity, and necessity. Tucking, the process of hiding one's genitals, is of particular importance, as is how to create breasts and hips. As the originals reminisce:

ALEXIA: Eliminate the "problem"—tuck it!

HRH: Oh yeah.

MORGAN: And it's a different process for everyone. Some people don't have that much to put away, and some people have the full monty!

HRH: Sometimes you can just do a little pushback, and sometimes you got to do the whole strap!

ALEXIA: You watch older girls do it and you are like . . . whaaa?

MORGAN: Sometimes you got to push your balls up into their sockets.

JOY: Yeees!

HRH: Vicki Dominatrix used to make hips out of stuffed animals she found upstairs at the [club] Rendezvous. She would forget her hips and she'd find a teddy bear and she'd rip that teddy bear apart. She would find old records and stuff and make dresses out of them. That's how it was.

JOY: At least for the ones with talent! The ones that learned by watching and listening when they shoulda been.[16]

The prevalence of a camp sensibility was highly valued in performance. The "old style" queens were "over the top," unpredictable and funny. They improvised and didn't aspire to the kind of "polished" looks that have evolved in modern drag.

> HRH: I think modern drag lost its camp sense along the way, but it's coming back!
>
> ALL: It's coming back yes!
>
> HRH: I went to perform out in Vegas, and I brought all my outfits and my big hair and they thought I was from another planet, and then the pretty girls went out there and they loved them. They cheered! It was crazy. And then one of the drag queens came back and said, "I wish I could do what you do, because you are fabulous!" She's like, "These people don't understand what you are doing." Because they lost it. The audience lost the want of the camp . . . they wanted the pretty girls all of a sudden. But they aren't the same audience we had. They aren't gay men. They are mostly straight people with no idea about what we do and why, I guess.
>
> JOY: Camp was no longer . . . it got lost.
>
> HRH: It [drag] lost its wildness, like, you don't know what this bitch is going to come out and do next time. But they are running out of ideas so . . . just being a girl gets boring I guess.
>
> JOY: Look at the lashes now! As many lashes as you can on the top!
>
> MORGAN: They wearing top lashes on the bottom and the tops are . . . I don't know! Diana Ross used to do it in the seventies, but nobody else; nobody. Now you have to.[17]

The Atlantic City queens valued, and still value, the camp style and presentation. This is evident whenever they get the chance over the years to perform in Atlantic City. The odd drag bingo event at the Borgata Casino, and drag brunches, now held at Bourré on New York Avenue (the former Saratoga Club), feature the original queens lip-syncing, telling bawdy jokes, teasing audience members, or singing scatological parodies of pop tunes. A recent drag brunch featured Morgan Wells, Sandy Beach, and Brittany Lynn presenting these "old school" performances. Brittany, acting as MC with local comic Michelle Tomko, took shots at local "celebrities" in the audience, and courted cute young straight men. She sang a parody of a tune from the Broadway show *Chicago* entitled "Chipotle Gives Me Gas," featuring farting sounds while lifting her skirt. Sandy Beach sang the iconic song "I Am What I Am," ending with the classic drag queen "reveal" where she took off her wig in dramatic fashion. Morgan Wells sported spectacular costumes in each number, some electronically lit, all meant to transform as she performed a striptease while weaving through the audience lip-syncing. This sensibility can be seen in the descriptions of the early Miss'd America Pageant, as the originals describe:

> HRH: It was very local, but it was *always* very *funny* and it was, it was, well, it was really stupid because we would record all the vocals two weeks before and never rehearse it again until we got on that stage, and we wouldn't remember our words.
>
> JOY: Oh, yeah, it was a mess, all the lip-syncing, but it was *our* Mess [*laughs*]. It looked like a Chinese kung fu movie.
>
> HRH: Yeah with the bad lip-syncing, the Japanese chop suey movies!
>
> ALEXIA: It was Baaaaad.
>
> JOY: Yeah, bad, it was bad! And we loved it. Everyone loved it.
>
> MORGAN: It was never good; I never liked it [*laughs*]. So bad, maybe it was good!
>
> HRH: But that's what it was, it was just so dreadful, it was *amazing*!
>
> JOY: It was campy.
>
> ALEXIA: Yeah. That's what's good about it. It was just plain bad!
>
> HRH: It was the height of camp. We would just be as bad as possible. But it was good because it brought us all together.
>
> JOY: I mean, you would sit there and you would listen to this stuff, this *crap* that Sandy would write, and you would think, "This is just awful, these old jokes," but then when you really got into it, it was

Figure 2.3. The Originals in drag, Miss'd America Pageant, 2012.
Photo credit: Patti Smith.

like, "Oh, well, this is *funny*! It's really actually *funny*!" [*Laughs.*] It
was a hoot. Not to mention, sometimes the bad delivery that added
on to it.

HRH: The *layers* of jokes about the whole thing were always so funny.
Only we knew all of that. What was behind it, the humor and the
story.[18]

The sense of loss of this vibrant culture was palpable in these gatherings,
along with the nostalgia expressed in the retelling of stories of a time
remembered fondly. The feeling of being left behind or forgotten by the
modern version of the Miss'd America Pageant is also marked. It is here
where emotions ran high and ambivalence about the modern pageant
can best be heard. In describing the process of the evolution of the
Miss'd America Pageant and their connection to the pageant over the
years, the original queens explain why they continued to play a role in

the professional version of the show, despite their feelings of loss and disenfranchisement:

> MORGAN: We all went through this process because we were the original girls. We went through the process of the change when we moved on to Boardwalk Hall; but Sandy was still doing her thing for the show [Miss'd America] and then somebody decided that *that* was not professional enough and we need to get rid of Sandy . . . so they did that.
>
> HRH: That [the decision to drop Sandy from the show] was a big problem for all of us because we didn't know if we wanted to . . .
>
> MORGAN: . . . to go along with that.
>
> HRH: . . . or to support Sandy, and like, no, we don't want to go along with the show, because we liked Sandy's vision, or . . .
>
> MORGAN: We didn't want our part to be erased, because like . . . they wanted to erase us, because they didn't want that [first] six years to be part of this [the modern Miss'd America Pageant] anymore . . .
>
> JOY: And we stood right there with our dresses on and said, "Look here, we right here, bitch, and we are better and we are stronger than all this."
>
> MORGAN: And that's exactly what we did. Whatever they weren't gonna let us do, well, we were doing it.
>
> HRH: That's exactly what we did, because when we heard that they wanted to just basically wipe us all off the map we were like, "Oh fuck no." We don't know *who*, but we felt that that's what they wanted. We were like "NO, this is our legacy and you are not wiping away our legacy. You know, so we were a part of it on the ground . . . so you aren't going to reap the benefits of it here, when we are the ones who helped you get here."
>
> MORGAN: And it was twenty years of here and five years right here!
>
> JOY: And to be clear, those twenty years were *excellent* money-making years, so it wasn't like it was something that changed . . . it was

more . . . because of that dark undertone, the seediness, the struggle. We made so much more money, because it drew more people in . . .

HRH: And so we shoved ourselves right in their faces, we were like, "*Hello*, we are in it [the new pageant]! We are doing this [the new pageant]!"

ALEXIA: Yeah, because the Studio Six Pageant was seedy.

MORGAN: I mean people from the [Miss America] Pageant wouldn't even come to [the Miss'd America Pageant at Studio Six].

JOY: But now it's like mainstream; I think the [original] whole undertone [of seediness] brought more people in than it actually does now.

HRH: That hardcore group of people that really loved Miss'd America, I mean they *loved* the original concept of it . . . I mean a lot of them are still going, but my mom doesn't go, 'cause, it's not about local folks anymore, or benefiting our people, people we know directly. She liked the whole Sandy Beach years, with the skits in the beginning, the whole camp part with how we did all the stuff to get into Miss America and then we missed it! And that's why it's called *Missed* America.

MORGAN: Those story lines were very local, and you had to be from here to get the jokes, and it was ours, like, it made us something at that time, when it was hard to watch people. People [were] getting sick.

HRH: It was local. We had jitney jokes and you know there was always something about the jitney.

MORGAN: And we always had the jitney. They would drag the jitney on the stage every year—I think they still do that????

JOY: No more jitney. You had to know the people; there's nothing local now.

ALEXIA: Nothing.

HRH: Actually, yeah, we are even all sucked out of it now. The formers; we're not doing anything anymore, which is kinda sad I think.

MORGAN: Yeah, we used to at least be in the opening number, up
until two, three years ago. We used to do a walk, we'd do some stuff,
some dancing . . .

JOY: That's all cut now. We getting dressed up and there's no party.
For nothing.

MORGAN: Because now that it's in a casino, they are . . . they want to
keep the pageant down to two hours. They want people to come in,
watch and then go out and gamble . . . so they cut us out of the opening number. We are now a filler in between the contestants.

JOY: Which is actually not so bad, I mean we go out; we look fabulous;
we get our two minutes and we leave [*chuckling*].[19]

The disenfranchisement felt by the originals, Sandy Beach included, is
well known to the ACGLBT Alliance who runs the pageant, and former
Studio Six owners John Schultz and Gary Hill, who own the trademark.
Attempts have been made by the Miss'd America Pageant organizers to
address these bad feelings. HRH Mortimer and Morgan Wells serve on
the board of the Alliance, and Sandy Beach was officially honored for his
early contributions to the founding of the pageant after a period of tension and bad feelings. Suffice to say that there is a strong sense of nostalgia for the days when the Miss'd America Pageant was "theirs" and their
community was strong. The sense of the loss of the gay community in
Atlantic City in general and the loss of the pageant in particular continues to fuel these conflicting feelings.

MASCULINITY AND CONTEXTUALIZED POWER

Drag queens are often thought of as effeminate men, or even men who
want to become women (transgender women or transfemmes).[20] Though
drag queens may exhibit effeminacy in their gender expression as "females"
or even as men out of drag, this impression does not fully encompass the

complexity of their female impersonation. Drag queens use their feminine persona as a means for enacting masculinity, where femininity becomes "merely the real estate upon which" drag queens might obtain and exert status and power.[21] Drag can be, therefore, a way of successfully expressing masculinity, one available to homosexual men, who otherwise may lack access to heterosexual male power. Evidence for drag as an alternate expressive route to masculinity comes from many sources. In his study of gay beauty pageants among the transvestite Bantut in the southern Philippines, Mark Johnson acknowledges the heteronormative gender dynamics that are maintained between drag queens (cis-males) and the drag kings (cis-females) who act in their service during pageant competitions.[22] In his analysis of drag in popular culture, Steven Hopkins points to the "significant benefits . . . to becoming a drag queen, especially to those who are contextually successful." He observes that "one such motivation is the individual's increased involvement in the gay community by making a further identification with the group beyond that of just homosexual. This represents the opportunity to experience a second 'coming out.' Others claim that drag offers a chance to be involved in entertaining and to receive attention for performing. . . . [There are] gendered rewards that many queens claim to receive from female impersonation."[23] The idea that drag queens are powerful and enjoy agency is a common reason for doing drag. Adriana Trenta describes her drag persona as her male persona (Kevin), without all the fears and inhibitions, and speaks of her own second coming out as a drag queen:

> When I was closeted, I was very much a tormented soul. I really wanted to express myself with as many colors as possible, and I really felt myself sticking with the grays and neutrals of the universe. And I came out, but it wasn't enough, 'cause, well, Kevin can be a little awkward. . . . I fell in love with it [drag], so I came out again as a drag queen . . . like pop stars and the modern-day divas and the *energy* that they evoke on stage and that they are not afraid to be beautiful, dangerous, sexy, like

> they are in *total* control of themselves and I admired that, so . . . I choose
> to emulate them, and that's why I do drag.[24]

Adriana and others recognize that coming out as gay is often not enough to make one successful in the gay community. In a subculture that affords power to those who exhibit traits such as physical perfection, exemplified by leathermen and the hypermasculine physique,[25] many gay men who are shy, or fat, or too thin, or in some other way conventionally unattractive lack the currency to access power and status. Drag becomes a vehicle whereby gay men might achieve this masculine power in an alternative form apart from ideal gay masculinity.

The notion that pageantry is a venue for accessing power is supported by Beverly Stoeltje, who argues that beauty pageants are ritual responses to changing gender relations and as such carry great potential for "signification in culture."[26] She adds that "while some contests add remunerations or scholarships, the more substantial reward in the majority of queen contests is 'symbolic capital'"[27] It is through this signification and the competitive process that queens vie for power and status (symbolic capital) within their local (and sometimes national) contexts. The acquisition of this symbolic capital within locally contextualized events and communities is an important aspect of drag pageantry, where queens are able to acquire great status and prestige through the meaning expressed in ritual performance and competition as champions of homosexuality. Rather than losing power, as one might presume, by identifying as female, drag queens gain power through successful performance, and in this sense construct their symbolic masculinity. The potential for achieving status within their communities is the reason given by many for becoming drag queens. Farrah Mascara, for instance, spoke about why she likes doing drag:

> I just play around with maybe the insecurities I might have had before
> or like the fact that I've always been just a really feminine man, and I
> get to embrace that, whereas, you know, growing up you're not taught
> to embrace your femininity and I think being feminine can also be

powerful and it's not always looked at that way. So being a boy growing up, being very feminine. . . . It's a bad thing, being bullied . . . [stiffens and looks down] and now it's a good thing [looks up and smiles] when you like take control of it. When I'm Farrah, my insecurities fade away.[28]

Farrah sees power in her femininity in local gay contexts, femininity that affords her a loss of power in heteronormative American society, where it is symbolically indicative of weakness, especially when expressed by men. Femininity as a marker of weakness is so pronounced when enacted by men in these contexts that it justifies bullying (an expression of power over another). Drag queens, on the other hand, are likely to torment (bully) heterosexual men who come to their shows in a reversal of the heteronormative power dynamic (see Newton, *Mother Camp* [1979], and Rupp and Taylor, *Drag Queens* [1993], for examples). The taunting of and flirtation with heterosexual men by queens is part and parcel of drag performance in local clubs, even though pageantry rarely provides this opportunity. Although not a part of the modern Miss'd America Pageant, the early performances did feature this traditional taunting, as Alexia Love recalls: "I would go out into the audience. I would bring people [men] on the stage. I would put them between my breasts and shake my breasts on them. I would dance with them, make them uncomfortable, reach out and TOUCH them! When Alexia came out, she was over the top, but when AJ was there, I was very low key . . . Alexia Love was outrageous. Alexia Love is one of a kind."[29]

Absent these formal affronts in the Miss'd America Pageant today, heterosexual male audience members do, however, as often noted in post-pageant interviews, acknowledge their discomfort, while at the same time admitting they were "a little turned on by one of the queens."[30] Other comments included "[I] can't believe those aren't real!"; "I don't really see them as male or female, but something else altogether"; or "[I was] a bit uncomfortable; I'm glad I'm here with her (points to female partner)," signifying a recognition of the power that drag queens possess, a power that may be intimidating.[31]

Figure 2.4. Shelby Late, "beating" his face for Miss'd America, 2018.
Photo credit: Laurie Greene.

Other researchers have noted the power of the drag persona as a way
to overcome perceived deficiencies in the performer's masculine persona.[32]
Drag queen Shelby Late also described the way that doing drag allows her
power she cannot command outside of drag:

> Most of Shelby comes from my insecurities as Ian. I'd say that Shelby is
> not afraid to ask for you to explain something, whereas Ian is a little bit
> guarded in admitting that he doesn't know everything or. . . . She gives
> me courage. She is not inhibited by what other people think of her intel-
> ligence, although she might seem to be an airhead. Ian is . . . very
> much . . . I'm an overthinker . . . yeah . . . so . . . to have Shelby be some-
> one who is a little less . . . [pause] well, she'll ask it! And then she sur-
> prises you and does know it! So, she's smarter, more in control of things
> than you think! [*Ironic smile.*] [33]

Evelyn Syde describes her own motivations in a similar fashion: "Drag for
me is a mask. I don't walk around every day loving myself and thinking
that I am good at anything . . . and drag is one of those moments when I

put it on that I can be the best form of myself—outgoing, interested to meet people. I have a severe anxiety disorder and drag is a way for me to get over that . . . and that's what I like about Evelyn."[34] The power found in this personal transformation is also, according to Evelyn Syde, a characteristic of the great Texas drag legends that she admires and aspires toward in her own performances. She notes that their power arises from their actions within the local context of their communities, and that with this power, drag carries an added responsibility:

> Drag queens have always been the icons, the role models. You know, I always say, a crown is a microphone and people listen to us. Even when we are *not* wearing a crown people listen to us. I haven't come up with why, why they listen. I think it's because they put us up on stage with a microphone. In Texas, I tell a lot of the baby queens, you've got to be really careful, really careful, because people listen to us and they look up to us because, well, we've always been there though. . . . From the time the trans women threw a brick, and every time I'm there at Stonewall, it's just mind blowing, and [*tears up*] I think about that legacy, the queens at the front of the parades, and the queens that have to step in . . . I think we are easy to be found, it's a visibility politic, and that's why we have to be careful with it. There is a great responsibility that comes with drag, and you can't take it lightly.[35]

The notion that drag queens have a great responsibility that extends outside of the context of performance is an indication of the power that they enjoy within the gay male community. Enacting femininity allows drag queens to access power not readily available to cis-women or homosexual men in American culture. What they are asserting instead is an alternative masculinity, one without the restrictions usually associated with expressions of (heteronormative) masculinity—restrictions that are more about what thou shalt not do (femininity) than about what thou shalt do.

Drag queens are not only *queens*, they are also *divas*. Possessing these attributions is another indication of drag queens' symbolically powerful masculinity. "Queen" is in and of itself a status distinct from other females. Queens are, after all, royalty and enjoy absolute power within the context of a monarchy, a status and influence usually reserved for men. The iden-tification as diva further signifies this power. "Diva" is often code for a demanding, bitchy, or difficult female, one who can assert her authority to get what she wants, no matter how excessive. The characterization of drag performers as queens and divas points to their ability to express male power and privilege even when presenting as female. As one exasperated female stagehand said of some of the more difficult 2016 Miss'd America contestants and what she saw as their "unreasonable demands and disre-spectful treatment" of the production staff, "They might be dressing as women, but they are still behaving like fucking men!"[36]

Female contestants in traditional beauty pageants may also attempt to exert power, but their expressions tend to be covert,[37] instead signifying valued, conventional female qualities like cooperation, humility, and grace. As one former Miss America contestant noted, "We form lifelong friend-ships, all the girls. We help each other with everything; we root for each other. People think we are just competitive, which we are, but more than that we support one another."[38] Drag queens, on the other hand, may openly and unapologetically assert their power over each other and the audience in their role as divas, revealing the maintenance of their under-lying masculinity.

Sex, Gender, Sexuality, and the Body in Drag

Though straight men, transgender women, and even cis-females perform as drag queens, the vast majority of drag queens today, and all but two queens interviewed here, self-identify and live their lives as gay men. Leila Rupp and Verta Taylor note in their ethnography of the 801 Cabaret in Key West, Florida, that drag queens possess a range of gendered identities from masculine, to transgendered, to something in between.[39] In the research undertaken for this ethnographic study, the drag queens interviewed (with two exceptions) made a point of emphasizing their masculine identity and their lack of desire to actually become a woman. Many felt that this was a common misunderstanding about drag queens, while at the same time acknowledging the validity of transgendered drag performers. As drag queen Stasha Storm remarked, "Don't judge the makeup and the dress as the person that's wearing it!"[40] The Miss'd America Pageant queens felt instead that notions of sex, gender, and sexuality were complex and distinct. As drag queen Savannah Savonier explains: "Here's something I use to remember: Sex is in your pants, Gender is in your mind, and Orientation is in your heart. Sex is what your genitals tell you, and gender is what you personally feel like you are. Personally, my gender matches my sex, but for many, they don't match."[41]

Michel Foucault notes that "the body is the primary site for inscription of cultural truths, . . . and an important site for self-transformation."[42] In *Discipline and Punish*, Foucault theorizes the docile body as a malleable object on which disciplinary force is acted. The body is an object that we can read—its movements, its postures, its "positionality"—to reveal the forces that have shaped it. Bodies become texts on which to inscribe dominant ways of doing things. In order for the body to be disciplined in this way, it must be receptive and accept powers that work on it.[43] In this view, the body is the battleground for contesting the categories of gender, sex, and sexuality. It is expected that one accurately displays this essential information clearly in one's dress, hygiene, speech, and comportment. Failing to do so is considered criminal in a culture that is highly disciplined. Violence against gay men and the murder of trans women are stark reminders of this in the Atlantic City gay community. Jeanie told frightening stories of gay boys being beaten up in parking lots on New York Ave., and Johnny, a resident who frequented New York Ave., recalled a local character who turned tricks as a woman:

I met Angel a few years back . . . To listen to her stories, you wondered how she survived. She was a transsexual, back in the day when trans-

sexual was something you just saw on Phil Donahue. She performed in
the clubs on NY Ave. She prostituted herself; she developed a heroin
problem. She didn't like to tell her clients she was trans, so sometimes
they would reach between her legs, and feel something they didn't want
to feel . . . well one person got very mad at her and stabbed her 41 times
and then threw her out of the car and left her for dead . . . but you can't
kill an old queen.[44]

Significant violations of body presentation are subject to social stigmatization, but violations of gender, sex, or sexuality are grounds for physical
violence and retribution when enacted outside of the context of performance. In the ritual context of a drag show, the quotidian meaning
associated with presenting a gender that is false is suspended. A man pre-
tending to be a woman is given dispensation where there exists a safety
zone between audience and performer, and where the audience is com-
plicit in the ruse. Removing this liminal space calls the meaning of the
false presentation into question; it is no longer primarily a performance
but a transgression against social mores. Drag queens, therefore, are as
likely to be revered on stage as they are to be beaten up in an alley, further
emphasizing the contextual nature of their status and power.

Categories of sex, gender, and sexuality are often conflated by outsiders, while contested by drag queens themselves. What you see represented
in one's body may or may not be a representation of their sex, gender, or
sexuality. Some drag queens do not identify as gay. Drag queen Sapphira
Cristal explains her pansexual identity and her relationship to her understanding of gender and identity, born out of her drag experience:

I'm not gay. It confuses people. I'm a strange guy. I'm pansexual; I have
my preferences, but I don't really care what's here [points to crotch] or
here [points to chest], I just like people. I'm a really beautiful woman,
and it made me think . . . anyone can be a beautiful woman, put on
makeup, change their hair or outward appearance, to be what someone else wants to see. So maybe that's not important. Maybe we should

think about something else when we talk about the quality of a person. And I don't mean your skin. I mean what's in here [points to head] and here [points to heart]. Who *is* this person?[45]

The drag queen contestants of the Miss'd America Pageant that I interviewed all expressed a fluid sense of gender identity and emphasized the uniqueness of people as individuals and the failure of labels to capture the essence of a person. That being said, most contended that even though they were dressed as women, they are *men*; they had no desire to actually be women. Drag queen Roxi Starr, for example, explains: "I have no desire to be a female in any sense. Roxi is a character that comes out and expresses a whole other side of me that *is* me, that helped to break some barriers in the world and learn *who I was*. I think Roxi has always been in there. It is a really liberating experience."[46]

Some drag queens prefer to be referred to by the feminine pronoun, especially when they are dressed in drag. This identification under the "she" pronoun does not extend into their personal lives as Robert, or John, or Mark, but is preferential in performance contexts as Jessica, or Penelope, or Farrah. During an interview, the following resulted between two legendary drag queens when I addressed them as women:

> SHERRY VINE: We are *men*, call us *he*, like men. Address us as men, I'm a he, not a *she* . . . I just play a girl on TV [*high-pitched voice*]. All the best roles are the girl's roles. Men are not as captivating as women on stage.
>
> JACKIE BEAT: What do you mean? [*In a baritone voice*] Call me a *she*. [*Laughter.*] I want to be Blanche, not Stanley.[47]

Other drag queens identify as female. Gender-fluid drag queen Jenna Tall, the only drag queen who still performs in Atlantic City each week, starring in the Saturday midnight drag show at the lone remaining gay bar, the *Rainbow Room*, likes to present as female outside of drag, and preferred the feminine pronoun when being addressed, and Virginia Slimp (pseudonym), transitioning to female, had this to say about what she saw as the "coded discrimination" in drag culture: "Drag has different historical and cultural contexts. The most simplistic definition of drag is that it is a man dressed as a woman. But if drag is about being a glamorous woman, and in my opinion, in order to be that, you have to be trans, they exclude trans women, because they think they have an unfair advantage, but why exclude someone's 'art form' just because the transformation is more or less permanent?"[48] At the very least, drag culture alerts us to the diversity of the expression of sex, gender, and sexuality and illustrates the complexity and fluidity of these categories. It also illustrates how bodies and their presentation are an important—if not the most important—markers of these distinctions. Bodies are used by society and culture as Foucault suggests, as "texts on which to inscribe dominant ways of doing things," and this inscription is certainly manipulated and contested by drag queens as they portray feminine characters on stage.

In her groundbreaking theoretical analysis *Gender Trouble*, Judith Butler describes all gender as subjective performance, identity that is reproduced through the act of *performativity*. Gender, she claims, is not essential to an individual, but culturally constructed through the acts of gendered behavior, a set of practices that are historically specific and conditioned by race and class. Gender, therefore, is not outside the way a woman (or a man) dresses, acts, and speaks, but is instead constituted by these and other practices[49] "because there is neither an 'essence' that gender expresses or externalizes nor an objective ideal to which gender aspires, and because gender is not a fact, the various acts of gender create the ideal of gender, and without these acts, there would be no gender at all."[50] Many drag queens interviewed for this research question this strict reading of performativity. While recognizing that gender is performed, they also claim that essentialism is at the heart of their performance. According to drag queen Farrah Mascara: "The way that I act on stage or present myself on stage, when I get dressed, put on things, it just takes over instinctively. The costume draws something out of me, which is already there. It is natural.

My male persona is more of a performance ... I have had to practice being a man, lower my voice on the phone, for example, shake the hand a little firmer, masculine up. Probably my day to day life is more than a performance ... Farrah is easy."[51]

People who think that drag queens mock women baffle drag queen Cha Cha. She questions ". . . how could you do that when you are not a woman? But you do not need to have a vagina to feel like a woman, or a penis, you don't, to feel or behave like a man; it's all in you and how you feel."[52] Drag queen Cleo Phatra explains this differently: "Drag elevates itself beyond the specific gender binary and it allows itself to become a starting point for discussing gender, and we see gender and speak about gender, and it's a good diffuser for being able to discuss trans issues. A lot of trans females use drag as a vehicle to explore their gender."[53] Gender performance in drag, then, may function as a way to express the essential character of a person, according to drag queens, to discover an authentic aspect of self (Butler's absent "subject")[54] that is lost in the mundane performance of gender off the stage and out of the ritual context. To limit gender to performance, however, simplifies what is a complex and fluid act of identity expression where male and drag personas overlap and some aspects of performance are experienced as more natural than others.

The common assertion of masculine gender identity may have been marked in the interviews conducted for the Miss'd America Pageant contestants partly because the pageant requires contestants to be anatomically male and disqualifies contestants who have made any permanent changes below the neck. This requirement results in the virtual lack of transgender contestants in the modern pageant, although the original pageant, lacking such restrictions, did have transgender contestants, with Ms. Ten'e taking the crown in 1999. The majority of drag queens in Atlantic City, however, perform what they would call traditional drag, requiring the creation of the illusion through creative problem solving and theatrical performance. It is with much pride that drag queens boast about their ability to make "something from nothing," lacking resources for the expenses of pageantry, and to make "nothing from something" when referring to the problems associated with camouflaging their genitalia (tucking), especially in the swimsuit competition. The association of drag with masculinity is also based largely on the fact that modern drag performance originated in and continues to evolve in gay male bars, and as such remains a central part of gay male culture and nightlife. This is still the case even with the mainstreaming of drag to a wide audience due to the popularity of *RuPaul's Drag Race* and other pop cultural expressions of drag.

SOMETHING FROM NOTHING AND NOTHING FROM SOMETHING: DRAG AS CREATIVITY

Drag is, according to the Miss'd America contestants, a form of creativity. It is a kind of imaginative expression of gender that guides drag performance rather than a realistic expression of femininity. Through these theatrical performances, many of the contestants spoke of a powerful sense of freedom that cannot be achieved in their lives as gay men. For some, drag was an extension of their careers in acting and the theater: a role that they might play either because they enjoy it, or because they do not have access to other roles as professionals. As Cleo Phatra stated:

I started doing drag because I'm a singer and a musical theater actor and I have been told since high school that I am too heavy to ever be taken seriously in theater until my forties and . . . well . . . it was devastating, 'cause to be so in love with something and so good at something and to be told you really just have to wait twenty years. Like, what the fuck?! I'm not waiting twenty years to do nothing! I've always felt very insecure as an actor because I've always been told I wasn't what an actor's supposed to look like. Through drag I was able to accept the fact that I'm okay as I am. My talent can stand on its own.[55]

And Cha Cha recalls her foray from theater into drag in New York City:

> And then I moved to New York for a little bit because I wanted to pur-
> sue acting on Broadway, and . . . it didn't happen [*laughs*]. It didn't hap-
> pen, and I was so depressed and so down that I didn't know what to do
> and I needed money, so one day I was looking through the magazines,
> and I saw a karaoke contest, and I said, "Well, you know, I sing, but I'm
> never gonna win a karaoke contest," and a little voice inside said, "Why
> don't you do it in drag?" And I thought, "Yeah, that's a good idea," you
> know as a gay karaoke, and I need the cash prize so yeah, I dressed in
> drag with whatever I had, and I went . . . and I kept winning.[56]

She goes on to speak about the freedom found in the "mask" of drag,
behind which one is able to find a sense of courage and freedom of
expression:

> When I'm in drag it's like wearing a mask, nobody knows what I look
> like. I don't look like this [gestures]; nobody knows me. It's like I'm
> guarded behind the makeup. I can feel everything. I can feel, I can taste,
> I can smell, I can do everything—anything! But I know it's not me. It's
> someone that takes the wheel for a couple of hours and lets me just sit
> on the passenger wheel and enjoy the ride and feel everything, and then
> I get home and I take the wig off and I'm back to normal. That's the guy
> that struggles with depression.[57]

Cha Cha is one of many drag queens who use their drag as a tool for dealing with difficulties in their lives as performing artists. The importance
of creativity and expression, and the strength gained through performance, is one feature that this research will show distinguishes drag pageantry from female pageantry in general and the Miss America Pageant
in particular. This creativity is valued at all levels of performance and has
much to do with the "something from nothing" / "nothing from something" value in performance.

The Intersectionality of Drag: Race and Class as Axes of Gender

In both Western and non-Western cultures there is a long history of men performing as women on stage. Whether in Elizabethan times or in African rituals, women have historically been banned from certain spaces, including acting in the theater, and going to war, so men have played those female roles. Laurel Halladay describes how the banning of women in combat areas necessitated all-male theatrical companies where male actors portrayed females when entertaining the troops in both World War I and II.[58] As women became more acceptable figures in public spaces, and female impersonation in the West became increasingly associated with homosexuality, these "drag troops" were disbanded.[59]

But drag should not be viewed as something left to gay men. Nor is it just subverting the female identity, as Butler would have it. It is more complex; Ragan Rhyne writes of drag and camp that it is a "political mode of critical performance" through which the categories of class and race intersect with gender. And bell hooks, for example, broadens Butler's analysis of the famous New York ballroom documentary *Paris Is Burning* (1990) by requiring us to take race and class (and sexuality, culture, and place) into account if we are to understand the gendered expression within these performances. Ragan Rhyne writes that white drag in film must be understood as the "performance of gender, race, and class as a process of negotiating the boundaries of each" and that scholars must pay attention to the way in which femininity is enacted along these intersectional matrices.[60] Jeffrey McCune points to the importance of musical genres, in particular gospel music and the centrality of the black church, in black drag performance in light of the complexity of the relationship between the black church and the black gay community.[61] Jennifer Spruill[62] and Amanda Lock Swarr[63] explore the ways in which drag responds to notions of racial representation in light of political change in post-apartheid South Africa.

Figure 2.5. Shee-Queeta-Lee, in Talent, Miss'd America Pageant, 2013.
Photo credit: Paul Dempsey.

Drag is not simply a reflection of gender roles in society; it expresses aspects of race, class, and sexuality that are intrinsically linked to expressions of gender. Drag, therefore, must be understood as a performance of race, class, and sexuality as well as gender: codes of gender performance being constructed through these other axes.[64]

In this book, place assumes an important dimension in the intersectional matrix. Early Miss'd America drag identities were very much expressions of the struggles of the local Atlantic City gay community and its unique relationship to the Miss America Pageant. As a former host of the Miss'd America Pageant, Jeff Wilson reminisces:

> We knew all these "girls" from the neighborhood, and then there they were up there, talking about us, at a time when no one else would, or maybe at a time when we needed to talk about who we were, to come together because so many [of us] were dying or sick. They didn't have to say as much; sometimes it was just a look or a wink in a direction . . . at someone's house . . . or about something that happened the night before, in jokes . . . stuff shoobees[65] couldn't possibly know. It's what we needed to do to know we were still here.[66]

The modern Miss'd America Pageant lacks this strong expression of local values and common experience, in that contestants now come from around the country and even the world rather than the local community to compete.

Expressions of local identity are still apparent in some drag performances, although the audience may lack the ability to read these expressions. Drag queen Evelyn Syde, for example, spoke at length about her Midwestern sensibilities when constructing her drag persona: "She's a real polite, soft spoken gal. It's all in the nuance; sometimes that doesn't go over in Austin" (where she now resides, performs, and is finishing her PhD in literature).[67]

Drag queen Cha Cha spoke passionately about her experience as a Chicana in Los Angeles, and the way that women like her sisters and mother are treated in the small Oaxacan town where she grew up: "It's what I'm portraying in my talent performance (a rendition of 'Jailhouse Tango' from the show *Cabaret*), I hope the audience can see what I'm doing. The way machismo works in Mexico is oppressive to women."[68] Drag queen Pattaya Hart speaks about the "girlie boys" in Thailand, where she lived until recently, working as a financial adviser: "It's a tradition where I grew up, and I try to show that in my drag persona, in Pattaya. That's the city where all the famous girlie boys have shows. People might not know that about my country. If you are Thai, you know a lot about me by that name."[69]

The role of the audience and their level of "collusion" is more complete in local settings where codes of local identity are clearly communicated. In the modern Miss'd America Pageant, as we shall see, local identities are less likely to be expressed, as drag queens instead emphasize national rather than local identity and concerns within the gay community—ones that they believe the audience can read.

QUEERING POP CULTURE AND THE POLITICS OF DRAG

The history of modern drag in the United States is best known through the struggle for gay rights. Since the 1970s and the Stonewall Riots, drag has become a way that gay men construct feminine bodies as a confrontation of the oppression of heterosexual male privilege. In writing about drag culture in the 1970s in the third edition of her urban ethnography *Mother Camp*, Esther Newton explains her title: "'Mother Camp'" as an honorific implies something about the relationship of the female impersonator to his gay audience . . . 'camp,' the latter word then referring to the whole system of humor. This reflects my belief that camp humor ultimately grows out of the incongruities and absurdities of the patriarchal nuclear family; for example, the incongruity between the sacred, idealized Mother, and the profane, obscene Woman. If camp humor takes such problems as its special subject, then the drag queen is its natural exponent."[70] Drag then, within the gay community, is inherently political. It is a critique of masculinity and the nuclear family structure based on this masculine privilege, using the contested female body as the battleground. The female body is defined by its presentation, whether real or satirical, rather than any actuality of the body. In fact, it is performed in direct opposition to the real, lived body.[71]

CHAPTER 3

New York Avenue

WHERE THE PARTY BEGAN

Mortimer breathes in deeply and gestures broadly with his arms at the now vacant lots and run-down buildings on the west side of New York Avenue. The Saratoga was there (he points behind us) and the Chez (Chez Paree disco). He turns and walks toward the world-famous Boardwalk and makes a right on Westminster (commonly known as Snake Alley), a winding back street that connected New York, Kentucky, and Mt. Vernon Avenues in the old gayborhood. The parking lot to the right used to be the Entertainers Club, the oldest bar on the East Coast. Louise Mack, who loved gay people, owned the building, and the bottom floor was her little speakeasy nightclub, which always catered to gay men. It was one of those places where you had to knock on the door and have the code word to get in. Mortimer continues to walk, looking around and gesturing toward two large parking lots on the opposite side of the street, where the Grand Central Hotel and Studio Five once stood before they burned down. He laughs as he kicks an abandoned beer bottle toward the curb.

Gay rooming houses and hotels once choked the streets here, and it was "all gay everywhere." He turns and frowns as he rounds another corner, the ghosts of properties where it was easy to pick up young men for sex, the "rent boys"—especially in the 1980s. We turn onto Kentucky Avenue, where Snake Alley ends, now a deserted parking lot, as he describes the hotels and gay businesses that used to line the west side of the street. On the corner of Pacific and Kentucky Avenues on the right-hand side was the Coffee Mill, and on the left-hand side the Atlantic City Electric Company. Across the street was Kelsey's Restaurant and what used to be a pool hall and pizza parlor, rooming houses, and a little grocery store. He pauses and points across the street to a small house, which still has a plant in the window. This is where drag queen Sandy Beach lived. Mortimer points out a little window where he remembers losing his virginity. He shakes his head, surveying the empty space.

Turning right on Pacific Avenue, we walk past an empty lot that was once Lyle's, a gay breakfast place where everybody ended up after staying out all night partying. Two prostitutes walk by, followed by their pimp, arguing about cigarettes. Turning right, back down New York Avenue, he summons the ghosts of gay clubs once again: the Saratoga, the Chez, the Rendezvous, where he used to perform in drag, and where he saw his first gay sex inside the club, right on the dance floor. On the right side stood the Chester Inn, its restaurant called the Front Porch, and there was an underground club called the Pukalani with a pool. Across the street was an Italian restaurant, Mama Motts, where he had his first gay date. It's all gone now.[1]

THE NEW YORK AVENUE GAYBORHOOD:
SPACE, PLACE, AND CULTURE

This book recounts the experience of a community—a community defined in part by a place and the unique characteristics of that place. All of us have a sense of place about locations that are important to us, and strong meanings and emotions linked to these intimate spaces. Hometowns, idyllic vacations spots, grandparents' houses with their sights and smells; these places are linked to familiar landscapes that comfort us even when they are not particularly beautiful or comfortable. Writers like Barry Lopez and Wallace Stegner speak about the importance of place in shaping human experience. As Stegner notes in his essay "A Sense of Place," a place becomes significant not only because of its physical existence and the events that happen there, but because it is remembered and recounted in the memories of a community:

> [A] place is not a place until people have been born in it, have grown up in it, lived in it, known it, died in it—have both experienced and shaped it, as individuals, families, neighborhoods, and communities, over more than one generation. Some are born in their place, some find it, some realize after long searching that the place they left is the one they have been searching for. But whatever their relation to it, it is made a place only by slow accrual, like a coral reef. . . . No place is a place until things that have happened in it are remembered in history, ballads, yarns, legends, or monuments. Fictions serve as well as facts. [2]

These remembered stories are histories, and the most salient role of the anthropologist, one might argue, is to help tell the stories of situated others. As Lopez states: "Everything is held together with stories. That is all that is holding us together, stories and compassion," (Barry Lopez, Facebook post, October 30, 2011.)

Literary critics and social scientists have applied the concept of linguistic performativity to understand phenomena outside of the realm of speech acts.[3] Judith Butler, for example, describes performativity as "that reiterative power of discourse to produce the phenomena that it regulates and constrains." [4] In applying the notion of performativity to the analysis of place, the essayist Michel de Certeau asserts that storytelling and memory, as forms of speech, are culturally creative acts and that the continued existence of culturally definitive spaces, such as hometowns, requires their repetition in telling. In this sense, *storytelling becomes in his view a performative action*: "The story plays a decisive role. It 'describes,' to be sure. But every description is more than a fixation . . . [it is] a culturally creative act. . . . It even has distributive power and performative force (it does what it says) when an ensemble of circumstances is brought together. Then it founds spaces. Reciprocally, where stories are disappearing (or else are being reduced to museographical objects), there is a loss of space: deprived of narrations."[5]

In Atlantic City, New York Avenue is such a space, providing a focal point for gay culture and a place where memories were created and identity was celebrated, and where yearning for the vibrancy of this time now gone is still intensely felt. The stories told by my informants about the creation of the Miss'd America Pageant exist within the intimacy of this space and the people and places that enlivened it. These stories speak of a halcyon period of gay life in Atlantic City, between the sexual revolution and the beginning of the AIDS epidemic, and then to the eventual demise of the street and the community that acted as its lifeblood.

As Rupp and Taylor and Patrick Sisson note, bars are central social institutions and act as building blocks in the gay community.[6] This was certainly the case for Atlantic City's gay community, where the gay bars on and around New York Avenue became the incubator for drag/camp performance at the center of community identity, activism, and advocacy: "Drag shows have a long history as central institutions in gay communities and as places where, at least in tourist towns, straight people come in contact with gay life. From the drag balls in cities such as New York and Chicago in the 1920s to the famous Finocchio's in San Francisco in the 1940s and the popularity of RuPaul and Lady Chablis in the 1990s, men dressed in women's clothing have served as a visible segment of the gay community and have also enthralled straight audiences."[7]

New York Avenue, and the gay scene in Atlantic City, existed well before the historical period relevant to this study. In the first half of the twentieth century, as Atlantic City sought to market itself as a premiere resort destination, gay life occurred by and large in the shadows, and gays experienced harassment, incarceration, and violence. Gay bars and clubs were raided; liquor licenses were revoked by the ABC (the New Jersey liquor control board); and club owners were fined or occasionally jailed.[8] In 1967, Val's, a gay bar on New York Avenue, challenged the liquor board's power to close down bars for "no other reason than the presumed

Figure 3.1. Mortimer's Café flyer with HRH Mortimer in drag, Studio Six, circa 1994. Photo credit: Patti Smith.

presence of gay men and women on licensed premises."[9] With the help of the Philadelphia-based Homosexual Law Reform Society (HLRS), an important early gay rights organization, Val's won their suit in the New Jersey Supreme Court, and shortly after that, "New York Avenue turned gay, it exploded."[10] The events that occurred on New York Avenue during this period are significant. They speak to the vibrancy of the underground gay scene, and foreshadow the more significant riots against the New York liquor control board at Stonewall in 1969 that ushered in the modern gay rights movement.

In the 1970s, New York Avenue was becoming the epicenter of a vibrant gay scene. In its heyday, it boasted eleven packed clubs on one block and a cabaret presenting drag shows and other entertainment. New York Avenue was the place to be seen, the promised land for many gay people, and the adjacent Snake Alley (nicknamed such because of its narrow twists and turns) and Mt. Vernon Avenue housed the overflow of bars and clubs that defined gay nightlife in Atlantic City. Today, the "New York Avenue 1970s"

Figure 3.2. Friday night out at the Rendezvous Bar, circa 1980.
Photo credit: James Farber.

Facebook page shares memories, memorabilia, and pictures from the time.
Photos point to the freedom the gay community experienced during this
period. Celebrities commonly patronized the New York Avenue strip; a
visit to the Facebook page shows pictures of locals with Joan Rivers, her
husband Edgar, and her dog; Tommy Tune; and Aretha Franklin. Casino
headliners patronized the clubs after they performed their shows, among
them Cher, Connie Francis, Neil Sedaka, Matt Damon, Bruce Willis,
Donna Summers, and Vanessa Williams.[11] There was a gay beach at Park
Place and the Boardwalk, in front of the Claridge Hotel, "because [the
hotel] looked like a penis," according to HRH Mortimer, who still bartends at the rooftop hotel bar in his non-drag persona. The beach was
packed with boys and girls in skimpy bikinis or "nothing at all."[12] Jeanie
tells about her experience as a young lesbian, first visiting New York Avenue in 1975: "You'd go out on a weekend night in the 70s, early 80s and it
was four deep at the bars, all the bars. . . . Marion White had a rooming

house next to the bar, and all the Philly girls would come down and stay here. It was a crazy . . . everyone just danced from one bar to another. Women's volleyball in the parking lot, Philly girls against shore girls. It was great . . . so many celebrities came to everything."[13] "Atlantic City was one of the only places where you had dozens of gay bars and hotels all in one place, in a four-block radius where everyone lived," recalls Robert, an Atlantic City resident.[14]

In 1971, John Schultz purchased the Brass Rail, a bar on Mt. Vernon Avenue, and later added the Studio Six nightclub to the complex. During the energy crisis of the early 1970s, President Nixon asked businesses to close early to conserve fuel, but because the front door of the all-night club lacked a key, when all the other clubs closed the Brass Rail stayed open. Taxicabs lined up at the front door late at night, bringing customers who still wanted to party. "Once I got the reputation [for staying open], the money started coming in," Schultz said.[15]

Two buildings framing the Boardwalk and New York Avenue, the McCorry and the Fralinger, contained apartments occupied mostly by gay men and drag queens, who told stories of wild parties that went on day and night. Many bars touted drag shows where transvestites and trans-sexuals comingled with gay men with money and local drag celebrities like Tinsel Garland. The resorts and boarding houses on Snake Alley were always jam-packed as well, as were the adjacent streets. "New York Avenue had no off switch," said Frank, an Atlantic City resident.[16] John Schultz recalls of the heyday of gay New York Avenue:

Atlantic City was a place to have sex all the time. I bought my first bar in 1970. I mean, I was king of the [scene]. . . . I had the Grand Central Resort; it was 135 rooms. I had Studio Four, Five, and Six, the Show Biz Cabaret. . . . They called my franchised resorts the Sexual Disney World of the gay life. I had nine bars running at one time. It was a *gay nucleus* here. They all came; they all fell in love with it; they all had sex; they all went on the beach; they all went after the beach to the bars.[17]

Sex tourism has been part of Atlantic City tourism since the prewar years, and homosexual sex tourism is well documented. The display of bodies on the beach and boardwalk, vibrant jazz clubs, and bawdy entertainment often resulted in the relaxing of conservative sensibilities.[18] Customers looking to purchase sex knew they could come to the area to look for tricks. According to historical accounts, clothing became a marker of gay sexuality, a way of indexing or communicating homosexuality. As early as 1896, journalists reported seeing men wearing "brightly colored silk garters with their black bathing suits"; in 1925, "cunning looking men wearing trick pants, pale purple hose, tan shoes with two-inch soles and lavender neckties" were seen the Boardwalk, as well as "men wearing high heels."[19]

In the 1970s, New York Avenue "shook, boogied, and rocked"[20] while the rest of the city rotted away from neglect. On New York Avenue, business was booming, and clubs were packed with music and dancing until daylight, when revelers left for breakfast at local cafés or work, or less frequently, to sleep. Bryant Simon's analysis provides an important historical perspective, highlighting the neglect of traditional urban historical analyses, which fail to account for disenfranchised populations[21] and the important complicated nature of postwar cities, where the history of gay men—and to a lesser extent lesbian women—and urban spaces are intertwined. He notes: "Urban historians generally begin their accounts in the final days before the fall of downtown and front porch-centered city neighborhoods. From there, they show how the pernicious forces of disinvestment, deindustrialization, and finally white flight have destroyed the nation's urban spaces. Often the narratives end with a final sad picture of a now empty, but once great, city. The story of the rise and fall of New York Avenue, however, highlights an overlooked counter-narrative of place making, and not just decline, in postwar urban history."[22] New York Avenue may have flourished in the 1970s because, as one longtime gay resident remarked, "no one else wanted to be here!" So, as the city around them faltered, the population decreased steadily, and tourism fell off, gays moved into the city, "set up shop, and lived [their] fabulous lives" unnoticed.[23]

Figure 3.3. Membership cards, Gay Atlantic City, 1970s–1980s.
Photo credit: Jean Antolini (card owner James Farber).

Then, by the mid-1980s, New York Avenue ceased to exist as the center of nightlife and cultural liberation, and with its disappearance the gay community all but left for Rehoboth Beach Delaware, and towns in Maryland and Asbury Park, New Jersey. The reasons for the demise of New York Avenue as a destination location are complex, but "expanding on the already vibrant gay tourism was not part of the plan."[24] The first casinos in Atlantic City opened in 1978,[25] and New York Avenue was tagged as a casino development zone. Business owners on New York Avenue cashed in on development schemes, but developers and investors failed to follow through with plans, leaving "torn-down buildings and empty, trash-filled lots" in the place of popular clubs and boarding houses.[26] After tearing down all the properties on New York and St. James Avenues, the Mint Group reneged on the development deal, and to this day the lots remain vacant. Finally, in 1981, an entire swath of the street burned down in a mysterious fire originating at the Grand Central Resort, making national news.[27]

In addition to the changes they made to the physical and economic landscape, once established the casinos hired many of the local drag entertainers away from the remaining clubs to work front- and backstage jobs for higher, union wages. Sandy Beach, the originator of the Miss'd America Pageant, recalls the impact of casino development:

In the early 80s the casinos came and scooped us up to work for them. They picked the best looking, the smartest, and the most personable. I got hired right away by the Golden Nugget. New York Avenue was already dying . . . the Chester, the Lark Inn, and Dirty Edna's, the Saratoga, Rendezvous, and the Chez Paris and a bunch of the hotels had been ripped down. Those big empty parking lots were all hotels [*he points*]. We became the "Golden Boys"' . . . we did drag and the male leads. We did both, you started out as a guy, went into drag, and then back again . . . it was show biz.[28]

Technology certainly had an impact on gay meeting places in the 1990s, as it continues to have today. Apps like Tinder, Jack'd, Scruff, Hornet, and Grindr have transformed the ways that gays (men in particular) socially connect. The impact of hookup and dating apps on gay communities cannot yet be determined, but most informants interviewed felt that gay bars everywhere struggled because people could now access virtual places to meet. John Schultz, who divested all his stakes in gay bars in Atlantic City with the sale of Studio Six in 2005, sees the impact of technology much the same way. The invention of the telephone answering machine and want ads in the *Philly Gay News*, and the aging of the baby boomer population, changed the way gays socially interacted in the 1970s much as apps for cell phones do today. As Schultz observed:

In the 70s, from 1968 to '78, 50 percent of the population of the US was under twenty-five years old! And gay people didn't think about owning a car or getting married. They spent their money partying and vacationing . . . and all of a sudden, a lightbulb goes off in their head because that twenty-five-year-old group, well, they realize ... they change to thirty-five ... I want to buy a house or a nice apartment ... and that took a toll on gay nightlife, and social media wiped it out. And *now*, you don't have to go to a bar, just go online. ... *Philly* can't even keep bars open![29]

Eventually, the remaining clubs on New York Avenue and Snake Alley moved out, and many in the gay community left town. New York Avenue ceased to exist as a gay meeting place, even though it had once rivaled any in the country. Today, Atlantic City still lacks a gayborhood, its only gay bar, the Rainbow Room on Florida Avenue, having closed its doors in 2019. A stroll down New York Avenue today reveals empty, overgrown lots, abandoned buildings, prostitutes, and drug dealers. Though gentrification in Atlantic City has begun,[30] it is not a revitalization of the gayborhood, but of the hipster variety—a local coffee shop, 100-tap beer hall, yoga studio, and chocolate bar stand shoulder to shoulder on adjacent Tennessee Avenue, and the Saratoga Club, once a well-known gay nightclub, is now a Cajun restaurant and bar. All that remains in evidence of the area's storied past are the bronze markers embedded in the sidewalks where the clubs once stood, a reminder of the days when New York Avenue was "the place where the party began."

The loss of gay places had repercussions in the drag community. In the absence of venues to perform and people to view performances, drag lost its popularity in Atlantic City, and along with it, the passing on of drag traditions. As the original Miss'd America queens discuss today, the strong drag community no longer exists, and drag queens look for other work either in drag or as men. HRH Mortimer now bartends for a number of establishments, and Morgan Wells makes costumes for drag queens as the owner of Morgan Wells' Drag Closet:

MORGAN: There is no drag culture here at all.

HRH: 'Cause there is nowhere to go.

JOY: There is nowhere to perform. Right.

MORGAN: There is no young girls . . . that are wanting to follow us.

HRH: We had the Studio, we had the Rendezvous, we had the Saratoga, and a bunch of bars to perform at, and now we have nowhere
to go.

ALEXIA: The Rainbow Room, I [am] scared to walk in there to get
mugged, take all your jewelry off!

JOY: It's not even that. Some of the thing is that you don't have . . .
money is an issue . . . they don't want to pay you. You can't be paid
five dollars still, which is like 70s money, 80s money, to be able to
still do what we do. The second part of it is you don't have the clien-
tele and . . .

MORGAN: The old girls, where the young girls come and see that
show and then emulate it! You know . . . they are the next group. We
don't have any of that anymore. That's lost.

HRH: There is no next generation after us. . . . There is nothing.

JOY: There is nobody to teach.

MORGAN: We would be the group of girls that the young girls would
be coming to see, but we're not performing nowhere.

HRH: Yeah . . .

MORGAN: [points to A.J.] . . . except bridesmaids' parties; she pops
out at bridesmaids' shows, that's it! That's no life! [Laughing.]

HRH: And you guys (Morgan and Joy) are on cruise ships!

JOY: OMG!

HRH: We did have some young girls for a while. We had Claudia and
Lady Labelle . . .

ALEXIA: Lady Labelle was our age.

HRH: But she [had] just started; she wasn't doing drag. That's what I
mean, but that was like during the last years at the Studio. Once the
Studio ended, that was pretty much it.[31]

The closing of Studio Six is seen as the end of drag performance and the
vibrant gay community in Atlantic City. In fact, Studio Six did not close,

Figure 3.4. Gay Beach, Indiana Avenue in front of the Claridge Hotel, 1981. Photo credit: Robert Muir.

but became a straight bar and was eventually sold by Schultz. Having eliminated most of the nightlife competition and opened clubs to capture every segment of the gay and straight population through his self-described business model, when Schultz sold his establishments, most gays in Atlantic City believe that the gay scene in turn ended.

New York Avenue, AIDS, and AIDS Volunteerism

Over the years, one comes to measure a place, too, not just for the beauty it may give, the balminess of its breezes, the insouciance and relaxation it encourages, the sublime pleasures it offers, but for what it teaches. The way in which it alters our perception of the human. It is not so much that you want to return to indifferent or difficult places, but that you want to not forget.
—Barry Lopez

By the late 1980s the instability of the casino economy, rampant political corruption, and the influence of organized crime all posed challenges to the survival of the gay community in Atlantic City. Further, throughout the 1980s the AIDS pandemic began to devastate gay communities around the world, including in Atlantic City. The year 1989 marked a loss of what is estimated to be about one-third of the gay community in less than a year's time.[32] Sandy Beach remembers how the Saratoga Club show was decimated by AIDS: "The whole show died, all the entertainers."[33] And HRH Mortimer recalls:

> Now we started hearing about so-and-so being sick. Oh, I heard so-and-so was at the AIDS doctor, Miss Thing saw him there. Oh, did you see so-and-so? He don't look good. . . . Once we hit the 90s, the crisis was on our doorstep like a hurricane. How can I convey to you the horror of that era? Well, you know . . . it's really hard to give you an idea of what was lost during those days. Imagine, if you will, that a third of your Facebook friends were to die within a year. I lost that and more. At one point, I started going to funerals more than I was going to the club; one of my closest friends committed suicide when he found out he was HIV positive . . . and then the backlash started . . . now we were pariahs, and not just to the straight community, who blamed us for the disease we had no idea we were spreading, but among our own people.[34]

The AIDS epidemic and the crisis it created played a pivotal role in reshaping the gay community and gay identity in Atlantic City, as it did elsewhere. In Atlantic City, drag queens were on the front lines of volunteer and activist efforts, raising money for treatment and care for the sick, promoting awareness about the suffering in their community, and proclaiming their existence in the face of increasing stigmatization. The Miss'd America Pageant was just one response to the AIDS crisis that was created by the local gay community. Drag queen Alexia Love remembers the first Miss'd America Pageant as a community response to the AIDS epidemic:

> Everything was for the South Jersey AIDS Alliance. Every time we performed, all the money would go to the SJAA. It was shocking because

Figure 3.5. Atlantic City AIDS Quilt, Atlantic City Boardwalk, AIDS Walk. Photo credit: Georgette Watson.

you would come out and you would hear that someone else passed away, or someone else was sick, or someone couldn't work, or lost their job . . . or was in the hospital. It was a very depressing time because you lost a lot of friends, a lot a people. You weren't even aware they were sick at the time. There was only one medication and it was really expensive, and it didn't always work . . . they were dying quicker. . . . AIDS brought people together, but people were afraid; people were very afraid. It was a scary time. Very depressing. People came out more then. There were so many places to go, if it weren't for AIDS . . . now it's nothing . . . [there's] nothing there [*she points*], which is very depressing."[35]

As it evolved, the Miss'd America Pageant grew to replace New York Avenue as a focal point for gay pride and identity in Atlantic City, and an outlet for the strong emotions experienced in the wake of so many deaths. A performance in 2003 illustrates this focus:

Brittany Lynn moves onto the stage, a six foot six Joan Crawford in a brown and gold caftan. In her hand a wire coat hanger; she grabs a large plastic doll as she lip-syncs, alternating from the sound track from *Mommy Dearest* to the song "Little Girls." She dances around the stage with the hanger and the doll, and at the end of the song screams, "What are you doing in this closet? Don't you know I've told you, no wire hangers! Ever!" . . . and then lip-syncs the rest of the "wire hanger" scene, Later in the show, during the interview, she proclaims her platform to be "Lesbians with bad hair." "I mean," she says, "Sheena's got 'world peace,' and Dee is fighting HIV and AIDS . . . for Christ's sake, is it too much for us all to come together and fix this? Look at them! [*She gestures to the audience.*] Aren't we a community? Can't we help a girl out?!" [*The crowd cheers.*] [36]

South Jersey Against AIDS[37] at the time a local independent AIDS advocacy group, got its start at Studio Six in 1981; the kickoff fund-raising party netting $10,000 in forty-eight hours.[38] In her analysis of the ACTUP movement, Deborah Gould describes the importance of emotion in mobilizing the gay community to action in the face of the AIDS epidemic.[39] Efforts to make sense of the many deaths, the loss of sexual expression, the new danger found in the homosexual lifestyle, and the increasing social stigma attached to homosexuality are never without feeling. In fact, "emotion incites, shapes, and is generated by practices of meaning making."[40] Early AIDS activist history recounts the actions taken in the wake of the callous government response to the deaths of hundreds of thousands of Americans, mostly gay and bisexual men, drug users, poor men, and women of color.[41] The Miss'd America Pageant, one such activist response in Atlantic City, required a consolidation of local gay identity.

The Miss'd America Pageant was created in the 1990s as an outlet for gay expression and advocacy in reaction to the devastating impact of the AIDS epidemic, but what it became was something different altogether. It developed into an event where gay and straight residents of Atlantic City might gather together to celebrate their identity as residents of a first-class entertainment capital, and it became a symbol of Atlantic City's continued vibrancy despite its reputation. As the Miss America Pageant continues to be embattled and marginalized in American culture, many residents assert with some irony that the Miss'd America Pageant will instead become the pageant for which Atlantic City is famous.

THE GAY COMMUNITY, THE MISS AMERICA PAGEANT, AND THE BIRTH OF THE MISS'D AMERICA PAGEANT

1970s Atlantic City was the promised land for many of us gays.[42]

The Miss'd America Pageant was the creation of drag queen Sandy Beach and was produced by Gary Hill and John Schultz of the Schultz-Hill Foundation. It started on the deck of the gay club Studio Six / Brass Rail, owned by Schultz. By 2016, the pageant had outgrown Boardwalk Hall (the original site of the Miss America Pageant), then Harrah's Casino ballroom, the House of Blues nightclub, and then the Music Box concert venue at the Borgata Hotel Casino and Spa, finally moving in 2016 to the Borgata's 2,700 person–capacity Event Center[43] According to Hill, the pageant's audience is 70 percent heterosexuals friendly to gays and about 30 percent LGBT people.[44] Sandy Beach, a legendary local drag queen and comedian, recounts fondly its humble and decidedly local beginnings:

> Miss'd America began in 1993. AIDS was a problem everywhere, and . . . we figured, we have [to do something] to help our friends that are dying. SJAA made sure people got their groceries and medication [so we wanted to contribute to the organization]. . . . Being that it was the day after Miss America [when we had the idea for our own pageant], we knew that we had a built-in audience . . . we could get a crowd. The press jumped on it. They knew I would just parody Miss America, not [do] anything to hurt it.[45]

The Miss'd America Pageant began as a locally contextualized event, one in which inside jokes and local knowledge were highlighted and the humor was self-referential.

Sandy Beach also spoke at length about the parodies in the first years of the pageant. In the beginning, Miss'd America pageants all started with skits aimed at lampooning the Miss America Pageant, the local Atlantic City community, and gay culture in general through double entendre and bawdy humor. These skits were all based on the same premise: the drag queens were all going to compete in Miss America, but then something happened, and they "missed" it! Hence, they had their own pageant— "Miss'd America."[46] The absurd shenanigans of the queens followed pop culture and local cues; one year the queens went down with the ship on the *Titanic*, and another year were all gunned down in *Boardwalk Empress*. Each year the pageant's theme commented on events that took place in the Miss America Pageant the night before; it was local humor, based on shared background knowledge and the shared experience of the local LGBTQ community. Sandy Beach recalls the early years: "You could do anything then. I'd make fun of stupid things in AC and never made fun of the city itself, or Miss America. We'd talk about PETA protesting the high-diving horse or Trump's hair . . . never anything . . . mean spirited. We were bawdy though . . . X-rated at times . . . anything goes."[47]

The skits themselves and the antics of the early Miss'd America Pageants might be understood as a kind of reading of Miss America itself.[48] The result was the creation of a strong connection between the drag queens and the main pageant and its performers. This is a measure of not only the affection the LGBT community felt for Miss America and Atlantic City, but also an expression of empathy for both; for like the gay community, both the city and the pageant were under constant attack and constant scrutiny.[49]

After its second year in Boardwalk Hall, the desire by Hill and Schultz to give the Miss'd America Pageant national attention resulted in the firing of Sandy Beach as the creative director and the addition of new rules, restrictions, and format changes that brought Miss'd America more in line with Miss Gay America and other large national and international contests. Sandy Beach recalls: "I think the show is well produced and technically

Figure 3.6. Miss'd America Pageant programs featuring skits, 1993–2004. Photo credit: Paul Dempsey (from the collection of Robert Hitchen and Patti Smith).

very good now . . . it now mirrors Miss America very well. It has an opening number, it has evening gown, it has swimsuit, catchy music for you to walk the runway . . . whereas before I would pick the most ridiculous music as background for a lot of the elements. The pageant was more local and filthy before; we did a lot of dirty jokes. Now it's very PG. They cleaned the show up when I left."[50]

Drag queen Her Royal Highness (HRH) Mortimer shares the same story of what was lost and what was gained as the Miss'd America Pageant transformed: "My mom used to come every year. Once we stopped doing the skits she stopped coming. It had to change because we wanted to make this a bigger thing and the skits were very local. So, in order to get more national attention, we had to make it more generic . . . get rid of the in-jokes that only the locals and personalities involved would get . . . in-jokes about the past pageants. Insider stuff . . . I lament it, but it had to change."[51]

The 2012 restructuring aimed to meet the standards for national pageants and popular culture aesthetics of *RuPaul's Drag Race* (from which contestants began to apply), and to gain recognition beyond the local community. Miss'd America's cultural expression through performance changed; its meaning was now subject to and looking for interpretation from outside the local gay community. Likewise, the production values have improved greatly, as has the spectacle of femininity. Camp presentations have diminished over the years, and real,[52] traditional pageantry presentations have increased. It is safe to say that female representations have become more strongly subject to national rather than local norms for gender performance. In this way, the pageant shifted its political discourse from local concerns to national concerns in the gay community. During the three Miss'd America Pageants observed for this ethnographic study, the pageant themes reflected these broader concerns: "Orlando [Massacre]" (2016), "Patriotism" (2017), "Broadway" (2018), and "Superheroes" (2019). No mention was made of the Miss America Pageant, which now precedes the Miss'd America Pageant by a month (rather than one day). The temporal division is symbolic of the larger dissociation from the pageant that once acted as its muse and of the ever-widening rift between Atlantic City and the Miss America Pageant. The only references made to Miss America that I witnessed came when Miss'd America acknowledged former Miss America Suzette Charles as a judge (2018) and an opening reference to the size of the audience being twice as large as "the one last month in Boardwalk Hall." This was met with boisterous cheers and applause from the audience.

Ticket prices have also increased with the venue changes. What used to be a $5 admission now ranges from $45 to $150 per ticket, contributing to the changing demographic of pageant attendees. The crowd is now mostly white, upper middle class, and straight; local dignitaries and celebrities are in attendance, but many in the local gay community are noticeably absent. These changes have had the impact of weakening gay communal identity as it was expressed through the early performances of Miss'd America, at least as it coalesced around the early days of the pageant. In September 2017, the pageant opened as follows:

> Mimi Imfurst descends from the stage rafters to the tune of "God Bless America." She is dressed like the Statue of Liberty, crowned, with torch in hand. She smiles a demure smile as she scans the audience. She lands, feet on the floor, as the song ends and the music suddenly changes. All at once she rips off her Libertine robes to reveal an American flag–sequined corset and thigh-high patent leather boots. The song is "American Idiot," and as she dances and sings, bounding across the stage, she mocks the state of affairs. Throwing rolls of paper towels into the audience, she mimics Trump and his visit to Puerto Rico after the catastrophic hurricane. She is defiant. The crowd is surprised. Some cheer, some are quiet. Why they react this way is unclear, but as the opening number ends, the mood is boisterous. That's Miss'd America.[53]

While the early Miss'd America performances were bawdy and provocative, the modern pageant has been under pressure to depoliticize the performances to appeal to the more diverse, if not conservative, audience at the Borgata Casino. The performance by Miss'd America 2017 Mimi Imfurst, as described above, may have resulted in the 2018 contestants being advised to "tone down the political content." Reaction from the contestants was swift and negative on Facebook. Their objections are indicative of the important role that drag queens feel they play as activist artists. In particular, Tina Burner posted the following on September 20, 2018:

> A year ago, I competed in a benefit pageant at Borgata Hotel Casino & Spa for @missdamerica_ac. I had an amazing time with my drag family and was pleased to have placed 2nd-Runner Up. I had taken the opportunity on that stage to do an entire political package. With my democratic blue evening gown to my #resist tap production number. As drag queens, we must remember that any time we are given a stage with an audience we have to use it to teach and at the very least provoke a con-

Figure 3.7. Tina Burner, Miss'd America Pageant, in Talent, "Resist," 2018.
Photo credit: Paul Dempsey.

versation. It has come to my attention that this year all the girls were
sent a message and were told "The Borgata Hotel, Casino and Spa has
requested that our contestants refrain from any political performances."
From a brick thrown at Stonewall, to standing at the front lines and
resisting our current administration, drag is everything political. If we
sit there and be silenced, it is a violation of our freedom of speech. Since
Miss'd America is a benefit for The Greater Atlantic City GLBT Alliance,
I would not want to deter anyone from donating to that, but with that
said we shouldn't allow the Borgata to profit from drag on restrictions
of what our drag should be and how we choose to do it . . . as you step
up to that microphone, let your voice be heard with no censorship."[54]

As a charity event, Miss'd America is dependent on donated space and
services. The growth of the pageant has shifted this dependency from local
residents to large venue owners, which in Atlantic City are casinos. The
dependence on large corporate entities has resulted in a greater commodification of the pageant and some loss of control over its content and

messaging. In Foucault's terms, the Miss'd America contestants are becoming subject to the same policing and constraints of the heteronormative beauty pageants on which they comment. These same constraints may also come from other powerful sources. *RuPaul's Drag Race* has also affected modern drag pageantry, in that drag queens are now subject to a level of professionalism where the bar continually rises. Queens now complain about the cost of entering a pageant (which can average from $5,000 to $10,000) and of the necessity for professionally made costumes, backup dancers, designer wigs, and the like. In the early years of the Miss'd America Pageant, queens made their own costumes—often refashioned from thrift store clothing; did their own makeup; and pieced together their talent performance. Camp was valued over polish, message over presentation. National standards for entertainment now trump these local values.

She's Fabulous! Why Gays and Atlantic City Love the Miss America Pageant

My great-grandfather was the mayor of AC in the 1920s; my mom was a dancer in the 40s. I had box seats to Miss America; I had a deep love for the Miss America Pageant. The staff came back every year; they are lifelong friends. Why bite the hand that feeds you?" [55]

While many people see the Miss America Pageant as an anachronism, it is beloved in much of Atlantic City and within the gay community. Each year, for example, locals gather on the Boardwalk, including the gay community at New York Avenue and the Boardwalk, for the annual Show Us Your Shoes Parade, and many continue to attend the pageant, though this number has diminished. Since 1921, the Miss America Pageant has provided an economic boon to Atlantic City, encouraging people to extend their summer holiday into September. In many ways, Miss America is seen as one of the jewels of AC, one that maintains its reputation from the days

when the Boardwalk was glamorous and the Steel Pier had diving horses;
when Atlantic City was "America's Greatest Resort." Despite the fact that
the Miss America Pageant has failed to provide this same economic advantage today, and has suffered various internal scandals, its image has
remained largely positive in Atlantic City until the restructuring in 2018.

The Miss America Pageant's economic relationship to the local community is bolstered by the gay men who have always been a big part of the
pageant's organizational structure. Even as contestants change, these same
men return to the pageant year after year as wardrobe assistants, makeup
artists, hair stylists, choreographers, dancers, and musicians. They patronized the local bars on New York Avenue and supported small businesses,
either because they were gay or because it was the place to be seen. As former Miss'd America winners HRH Mortimer (1995), Morgan Wells (1999),
and Joy Marnier (1998) recounted over dinner:

> HRH: Back when [Miss'd America] was at the Studio [Studio Six] they
> were literally told, all of the [Miss America] contestants . . . don't go
> there . . . you can't go to Miss'd America . . . but the families [of the
> contestants] started coming because they heard about it . . . espe-
> cially the parade show because we would do a big show on the deck
> after the parade . . . and it was packed!
>
> JOY: I mean, the gays all came and the sisters; all the dancers, you
> know, the ones that came every year. They knew us.
>
> MORGAN: They knew *you* more than most, girl!
>
> HRH: [*Laughs.*] Hmmm . . . Morgan would make all the costumes . . .
>
> MORGAN: Yep, we would talk costumes. I remember the three of
> us . . . and for Miss'd America, we did it that one year, and Kate Shin-
> dle (Miss America 1998) came out. She was the reigning Miss Amer-
> ica, and she came to our show.
>
> HRH: She popped out on stage and sang a number, and it was really
> bad, and the place went crazy! She had the Miss America crown and

we were all putting it on, and she was *awesome*. And she said, "How can I not come here? These are my people . . . all my friends are theater people."

MORGAN: Because her platform was AIDS, so she broke the rule, and after that people started coming . . . not just the workers and costumers.[56]

The synergy between the Miss America Organization and the Atlantic City gay community was clearly seen when dismal TV ratings forced the Miss America Pageant to leave Atlantic City and move to Las Vegas (2006–2013). Concomitantly, the Miss'd America Pageant ceased, only to resume in 2009 with a Miss'd America 2010 crowned in a new venue—the now vacant Boardwalk Hall, where Miss America had been contested. The Miss'd America Pageant was reimagined and trademarked as the property of the Schultz-Hill Foundation, supported through the newly formed ACGLBT Alliance, an "organization to promote the social, economic, and political advocacy of the Gay, Lesbian, Bisexual, and Transgender community and GLBT supportive community in our region," as its president, Richard Helfant, noted in 2010.[57] The Alliance, founded as a mechanism for supporting LGBTQ causes in Atlantic County and representing itself as the face of the gay community in Atlantic City, was dedicated principally to the production and expansion of the Miss'd America Pageant and its philanthropic and social agenda. As informants recount, Miss'd America resumed in 2010, despite feeling abandoned by the Miss America Pageant. As Jeff Vassar, head of the Atlantic City Casino and Visitor Association, stated: "Something has been missing from AC for the last five years. We have a runway that needs to be dusted off, that's taking up some space, that needs to be put to good use. It's the home of a crown, fit for a queen."[58] The new MC, *Queer Eye*'s Carson Kressley, alluded to the Miss America Pageant during his opening monologue: "Oh my Gaaaaaad, there's more people here than watched the real pageant on TLC! How much better is Atlantic City than Vegas?"[59] Though in Boardwalk Hall, the traditional

Figure 3.8. Studio Six, Miss'd America Pageant, 1999.
Photo credit: Robert Hitchen.

venue of Miss America, the Miss'd America Pageant retained its original
structure this first year back.[60] As Sandy Beach describes at the pre-pageant
press conference: "The show picks up five years later. Our queens are in
Florida, at the Anita Bryant retirement home for aging beauty queens.
They are reminiscing about the old days, and about how old they have
gotten, and they drink some Grey Goose (sponsor) miracle Mar-a-Lago
(Trump Casino—sponsor) water and become amazingly young again. And
they get a phone call to please come back to Margate, to do a fundraiser
to save Lucy's ass! And that's how we get back to the city."[61]

By the next year (2011), the pageant added a swimsuit competition mir-
roring the structure of the Miss America Pageant and the Miss Gay America Pageant.[62] After Sandy Beach was removed as creative director and
replaced by a professional writer, producer, and director, Mark Dahl, the
Melanie Rice Orchestra replaced homemade tape-recorded tracts, and the
pageant finally lost its local references and most of its local contestants.
The opening skits were also eliminated, as were the ubiquitous references

to Miss America. The Miss'd America Pageant had taken over the official pageant scene in Atlantic City and the venue at Boardwalk Hall; it even had a theme song! (See appendix C.) The pageant had moved into the mainstream, demonstrated when winner Michele Dupree (Miss'd America 2010) was interviewed on the network news show *NBC Philadelphia's Sunday Morning Show*.[63] As the 2013 MC, *Drag Race*'s Michelle Visage commented in an interview with the *Huffington Post* about her upcoming hosting of the Miss'd America Pageant:

> HUFFINGTON POST: What do you think the biggest difference will be between the Miss America pageant and the Miss'd America pageant?
>
> MICHELLE VISAGE: [*Laughs.*] The Miss'd America pageant will be fabulous. The Miss America pageant is predictable.[64]

This repositioning of Miss'd America was an important development in cementing the rift between the Miss and Miss'd America pageants. In the first year of the Miss'd America Pageant, 1994 crown holder Alexia Love remembers the excitement of having a float in the pre-pageant Miss America Parade:

> I remember the first [Miss'd America] pageant. Me and Mortimer were in the back room getting dressed, and we had to do a real presentation, I mean evening gown and some production number, and we were all excited, and I remember, some paper from North Jersey, I think it was the *Star Ledger* . . . [was] interviewing us about the pageant. We thought it was a hoot! It [the venue] was packed—300 to 400 people. I thought the deck was going to collapse. The runway was out there, and all the lights and the people and John [Schultz] and Gary [Hill] . . . it was really exciting. It was crazy. What I really remember about the pageant was the actual float. We were the first gay float on the Boardwalk. We won for best float that year . . . in the parade! I was Tina Turner, Mortimer was Barbara Streisand, Gidget was Bette Midler, Chantee [was] Natalie

Cole, Alexa St. Claire was . . . Aretha Franklin, and Steven Moore was Cher. It was one of the most fun times I ever had on the Boardwalk. Everyone was throwing bottles at us, but we won. It was exciting, and then we went to Studio Six and did a show.[65]

Since its return to Atlantic City, the Miss America Pageant has refused to allow Miss'd America to present a float in the parade, citing a rule that will not allow any other titleholder to march. In 2018, Suzette Charles (Miss New Jersey 1983, serving as Miss America for Vanessa Williams in 1984, and a resident in nearby Ventnor City), advocated for the ACGLBT Alliance with the Miss America Organization, and a float was approved, only to be withdrawn a week later. The withdrawal happened in the wake of the Miss America Pageant redefining itself in response to sexual harassment scandals to become Miss America 2.0—identifying as a contest rather than a pageant; eliminating the swimsuit competition; making evening gown attire optional so that a contestant might wear what she feels "comfortable" in; and taking away the iconic runway and theme song made famous by Bert Parks altogether. In response, the Miss'd America Pageant advertised itself with the slogans "The Pageant with the Swimsuit" and "We Got Your Runway!," positioning itself as independent of and in opposition to the pageant it once revered.

Criticism by local queens and residents was fierce, as was the anger expressed toward the new leadership of the Miss America Organization, in particular, Gretchen Carlson, the face of the revamped pageant. Outrage among the drag queens ranged from "You call that a parade? Where are the floats?!" to "OMG . . . there weren't nobody there. You got no runway; you got no swimsuits; you got no song; you got boring."[66] In 2018, the Atlantic City newspapers overflowed with op-eds criticizing the new "politically suspect" format and changes. The pageant (now contest) had lost its "pageantry"—its entertainment value, its spectacle.

CHAPTER 4

Camp and the Queering of Miss America

The corner of New York Avenue and the Boardwalk in Atlantic City, beach side, is the "girls' side" of the street, the spot where lesbians congregate to watch the parade and cheer as the cars go by carrying the Miss America Pageant contestants. On the opposite side of the Boardwalk, gay men stand in front of the Ripley's Believe It or Not! Museum waiting for the parade to begin. This year, there is added intrigue, since it is the first time an openly lesbian contestant, Miss Missouri, Erin O'Flaherty, is competing for the crown as America's "ideal woman." Many spectators carry rainbow flags; some are dressed in drag, men in full makeup, women donning tee shirts with men's chests and muscular arms printed on them. Others wear rainbow kitsch: plastic sunglasses, boas, crystal studded crowns.

Both men and women flirt with local police as they beg to stand pressed up against the parade route and promise they will behave in return. Drag queen Morgan Wells stands in a gown and headpiece on the men's side. Beside her stands a man, shirtless, with pierced nipples attached to chains. Gay men congregate sorted by age and acquaintance under the marquee of the museum. To their right quietly sits a family with beach chairs and three small towheaded children on their laps; Shoobees (out-of-towners), they gawk at the spectacle before them.

The convertibles carrying the Miss America Pageant contestants in the Shoe Us Your Shoes Parade pass in alphabetical order. They wear costumes whimsically representing their states, with shoes decorated and held up in the air with one leg as they lean back in their seats and wave to the crowds. "Show us your shoes!" is screamed from the New York Avenue crowds as each contestant passes. As they do, most are met with cheers of encouragement and waving rainbow flags, while others receive sometimes not so flattering critiques of their tepid presentations. "You on New York Avenue now honey! You ain't in Kansas anymore!" yells someone in the crowd.

A baton-twirling team from Kentucky approaches. The young girls dressed in rainbow-colored leotards draw near, and the excitement among onlookers builds. They all respond by waving their rainbow flags and chanting, "Twirl girl, twirl! Twirl girl, twirl!" As they jump up and down and continue to wave their flags, the twirlers, a little disconcerted, perform their number. Flags begin waving, and people push in toward the yellow cones along the parade route. Miss Missouri, Erin O'Flaherty, is dressed in a blue-and-white baseball uniform and holding up a pair of bejeweled high-top sneakers. As the convertible nears, the cheers increase. She smiles, but she is demure as she waves. Jean runs toward the car waving her rainbow flag. And though Erin smiles and waves back, she appears a bit awkward with this group of locals looking for some acknowledgment of their shared identity. The crowd chants, "Show us your shoes!"[1]

The Miss'd America Pageant can be interpreted as a queered version of the iconic Miss America Pageant. Writing about the San Francisco theatrical production *The Golden Girls: The Christmas Episodes*, Eleanor Patterson illustrates how the meaning of popular cultural artifacts like television shows can change as they are "rearticulated within queer interpretive communities."[2] This live, interactive drag version of the popular TV show allows the *Golden Girls* to persist, "though recycled and renewed with new ideas and cultural practices as it continues to circulate through culture."[3] Patterson argues that the drag queens' remake of the iconic show is a "politically meaningful site of participatory culture" and solidarity, with an "explicitly queer text."[4] Like *The Golden Girls: The Christmas Episodes*, the drag production of the Miss'd America Pageant can be said to rearticulate and queer the scripts of pageantry and femininity residual in the iconic Miss America Pageant. This chapter explores the "queering" of aspects of the Miss America Pageant as it is reproduced in the contestation of the Miss'd America Pageant, and as the gay community in Atlantic City interacts with and interprets the Miss America Pageant itself.

CAMP: QUEER LANGUAGE IDEOLOGIES AND FOLK WISDOM

To me, a drag queen is always over the top. It [drag] is always larger than life, tongue in cheek. It's not serious, and it IS *serious*. It is a celebration of femininity, but it's not trying to be the most natural woman. What is natural but *boring*? It's [drag] campy, it's what any great performance is about.—Mimi Imfurst[5]

Within gay culture, performance and presentation are seen, when deemed admirable and deserving, through the eyes of camp aesthetic. Camp is central to understanding gay culture and identity, yet, as scholars in many disciplines have noted, difficult to define. Camp is "slippery," having eluded critical and clear definition;[6] or as Helene Shugart and Catherine Waggoner have described it, camp is an evasive phenomenon characterized by the trite statement "You know it when you see it."[7] In part, camp is difficult to define because it appears in so many forms and is understood through a variety of interpretations and disciplines.

Drag can be understood as a quintessential expression of camp. As Mimi Imfurst's quote suggests, drag is at the heart of worthy performance, the antithesis of natural, and the antidote to boring. Mark Booth views camp as a matter of self-presentation, a performance necessitating an audience. As he explains: "If you are alone and bored at home and in desperation you try to amuse yourself by watching an awful old film, you are not being camp. You only become so if you subsequently proclaim to others that you thought Victor Mature was divine in *Samson and Delilah*."[8]

Although camp is not exclusive to gay communication and presentation, interpretations of camp are, according to Rusty Barrett, deeply dependent on the normative citations[9] within LGBT communities, comprising a folk wisdom[10] in gay male culture. From this perspective, gay men learn a set of "essential aesthetic judgments for the evaluation of camp" that play an important role in the "social construction of (gay male) identity."[11] Drag, unlike transvestism, is premised on theatrical structure and style. "There is no drag without an actor and his audience, and there is no drag without drama (or theatricality)."[12] A man who becomes a drag queen has come out in and been socialized in the homosexual community first. He is already a gay man and must come out again as a drag queen. The drag queen, like camp, flaunts her homosexuality on stage, without any apology. As Esther Newton notes in her classic study of drag queens in New York City, drag is inherently expressive of gayness: "Drag symbolizes gayness. The drag queen symbolizes an open declaration, even celebration, of homosexual. The drag queen says for his gay audience, who cannot say it, 'I'm gay, I don't care who knows it, the straight world be damned.'"[13] As Morgan Wells, Miss'd America 1999 and owner of Morgan Wells' Drag Closet,[14] explains: "Yaaaas it's campy! And girl you know it should be. You got to have something to laugh about. And why not? When your friends are all sick and dying and then people are saying it's your fault. When what you supposed to act like is really the drag. The world is already ironic, funny, ridiculous. It's just that some of us can see it, you know . . . and some of us can't. You ain't a drag queen, *no*, you probably ain't *gay* unless you can!"[15]

The ability to see the ironic, funny, and ridiculous nature of the world at any moment is illustrative of this folk wisdom and gay ideological perspective that also include assumptions about gay male superiority in areas of taste and style. Shared as well are values about self-presentation, such as the necessity for passing in certain contexts[16] and the ironic, sometimes parodical nature of these quotidian public presentations of self.[17] Gay men must become versed in this folk wisdom and the language ideologies underlying gay camp communicative interaction in order to be success-ful in gay culture, since fluency in these gains access to gay subculture and protection from the often hostile heterosexual world.

Language ideologies in gay and drag communication and ways of speaking are important products and practices developed and shared in the drag community in Atlantic City. Local queens learned how to per-form drag together as they all worked the same vibrant bar scene, to make costumes, put on productions, and paint their faces.[18] They developed a particular way of communicating with each other, sharing a vocabulary and style of communication, a camp style of speaking that signaled their identity as local drag queens. Communication was based on competition, and humor was based on a kind of reading of those performances. Read-ing can be described as a sometimes-scathing critique of someone's appear-ance, lack of talent, intelligence, hygiene, or, most of all, sexual behavior. Reading is one of the many aspects of communicative interaction that indexes gayness, and as Barrett beautifully illustrates in his research, "gay male subcultures are crucially constituted through language."[19] Reading is a communicative strategy that is learned as part of the evolution of one's identity as a gay man. Miss'd America 2015, Fifi Dubois, talks about how she sees "drag language": "It's fun . . . its campy. . . . Its gay culture. I think it gives us our own dialect, our own language that people can use. It's a way to identify other gay people. Or other drag queens . . . through how we talk."[20] Gay language (e.g., sentimental voice, emphatic stress, dimin-utive affix, marked vocabulary),[21] and stylistic forms like reading and camp in general, serve to index gay identity and gay culture. Indexicality is crit-ical to understanding forms of camp (discussed further in the section below), and is "central to monitoring questions of sexual identity such as 'gaydar.'"[22] Much of gay language establishes identity through forms of indexical disjuncture. Indexical disjuncture uses indexical signs (aspects of communication) that are marked. That is, they are counter to norma-tive expectations of the relationship between form and context.[23] Drag queening is an obvious form of disjuncture, and so are the mocking and insulting characteristics of reading, since their intention is to be properly read as neither mocking nor insulting. This is one reason drag queens often find it curious that feminists critique their presentations as misogynistic. The disjuncture, although referencing normativity, has little to do in their minds with its uncritical acceptance. As Josh Rivers notes, "Drag queens all over the world are engaged in the quotidian negotiation of boundaries between what Michael Lambek terms the 'continuous person,' their 'boy selves,' and the 'discontinuous act of performing' their drag personas."[24] Reading is a recognition of this negotiation, which is how drag identity is properly *werked*.[25] It is a recognition of the fluid (rather than distinct) boundaries between their boy and drag selves. As Evelyn Syde described:

It's not just insulting someone. A good read is well thought out, edu-cated, creative and clever, but in person . . . well, reading does come from the AIDS crisis and the terror that everyone was going through, and it was a way for people to find humor in a desperate situation, so . . . reading and shade are friendly reminders to not take this so seriously, ourselves. At the end of the day we are men in dresses. This is not nec-essarily a living; we are doing it out of love for the most part. [It] is a reminder to humble yourself, and to remember that at the end of the day you are going to go home to your cats.[26]

The sentiment that reading acts as recognition of fallibility is meant to remind queens not to take themselves too seriously, but it is not meant to be hurtful. One reads oneself and people one cares about.

During the 2018 Miss'd America Pageant dress rehearsal, as each con-testant was introduced and came to the microphone out of drag to say something about themselves, HRH Mortimer yelled from the seats, "Whore!!!" When asked later about the purpose of this "reading," he explained: "I say 'whore' because I want to throw them off their game . . . like someone in the audience is like, 'Ohhh . . . you whore! And they find out later it's me, saying, 'I see you.' I make sure to say it with every one that came out. To me 'whore' is not an insult, it's a compliment. It's like recognizing you exist . . . hey, I see you up there on that runway . . . I'm here with you. It's real."[27] In addition to the obvious disjuncture of such communication, the idea of seeing someone for who they are and what they are suggests an insider's knowledge and support of shared culture and the experience of being one and the same as their drag personas, as "queering the boundary between" what Rivers refers to as their stable "boy selves" and the "discontinuous act of performing drag."[28]

As a queer text, the Miss'd America Pageant is undeniably a camp version of the Miss America Pageant. As such, drag queen contestants use camp as an expressive device to affirm gay cultural values and critique the heteronormative culture through irony, parody, and humor. To deny that the world of pageantry is contrived, an exaggerated presentation of the feminine ideal, is tantamount to taking oneself too seriously. So, in their admiration for the Miss America Pageant, drag queens must define beauty queens as camp performers.[29]

HRH Mortimer illustrates the importance of the mastery of camp folk wisdom and the language ideologies and practices that evolve from it when he describes how gay male audiences are so hypercritical, a theme both Newton and Rupp and Taylor explore in their ethnographies on drag:

> There is the three second rule when you walk out on stage: the first second they look at what you are wearing; the second they are like, "Alright I like the song she's doing"; the third second is "That bitch can't lip-sync," so you've got to make sure you know what you are doing when the music stops and you get on that microphone. Gay audiences are so hypercritical . . . but I had a great following for twenty years. You have to know what they want, and what they want is something fabulous.[30]

The rules of camp performance and gay sensibility require that camp queens be self-deprecating, that they point out all of their own flaws, either verbally or through their actions or dress, before the audience does. Failure to do so may result in a reading by the audience.

The pragmatic importance of camp within gay male communities is also described by Michael Bronski, who sees HRH Mortimer's "three second rule" as an example of camp used as a self-defense in the face of potential homophobia, "a first strike wit" in an impossible situation, where wit and irony provide the only reasonable response to the "terror of straight reality."[31] Richard Dyer, likewise, sees camp as a form of "self-defense," "self-identification," and "belonging":

> The fact that gay men could so sharply and brightly make fun of themselves meant that the real awfulness of their situation could be kept at bay—they need not take things too seriously, need not let it get them down. Camp kept, camp keeps, a lot of gay men going . . . it gives you [at the same time] a tremendous sense of identification and belonging. It is just about the only style, language, and culture that is distinctively and unambiguously gay male. . . . Camp is the one thing that expresses and confirms being a gay man.[32]

Camp as noted here is a way for gay men to not take themselves too seriously, so that they can cope with the difficulties of living in a heteronormative world. It is a marker of gayness. To be a successful gay man, you must understand the language, style, and culture of camp.

Many queens also told of the important role of drag in their coming-out process. Drag was a vehicle for their self-identification as gay men, in a world where they might not fit even gay male standards of behavior or attractiveness. This was the case for drag queen Adriana Trenta (Miss'd America 2018), who self-described her boy persona as "skinny, goofy, and balding at twenty,"[33] but in addition, drag offered her a place in and a deeper connection to the gay community, and inspired her activism, helping gay youth:

> Drag totally changed my experience of everything. I did really not understand the concept of gender being a spectrum until maybe a few months into drag when I met these people . . . [and learned about] experiences

that I didn't have and saying, "I didn't know this. Tell me more!" . . . and really being a true ally for people. Drag really taught me that. Drag has given me the ability to connect with the young LGBTQ community, particularly those that are in high school or college. Ultimately, I feel that drag has really brought me closer to the community![34]

Drag queens all spoke about the two-stage process of coming out, both within the gay community and to their family and friends. Adriana Trenta moved to New York City knowing that her parents and sister did not accept her and her homosexuality, attesting to the difficulties inherent in coming out to family. Compounding this rejection was the reveal that occurred when Adriana's parents received notice that her PrEP prescription was ready to be picked up at the pharmacy (she was under twenty-four and was on her parents' medical insurance when they were notified).[35] The realization that their son was a sexually active gay man made the reality of her gayness undeniable and led to further rejection and conflict. When Adriana returned to Atlantic City in 2018 and was crowned Miss'd America 2019, the press that resulted outed her drag identity to her family and friends.[36] Adriana's parents reacted by forcing her into therapy and threatening the withdrawing all financial support if she did not comply. She went to a therapist and took a "big boy job" in finance for a while to appease them, but now dedicates her time and energy to her career in drag performance. She has cut all financial ties with her parents. Adriana explained that midway into her reign "they went crazy when they found the pictures and looked up Adriana [my drag identity] on Facebook! They said they wouldn't accept it [my being a drag queen], that it was sick, and that people weren't cheering for me, they were laughing at me. I was a clown, a faggot clown. . . . Well, this faggot clown is going to march in New York Pride as Miss'd America and compete for the Miss Stonewall crown on the fiftieth anniversary of the struggle. At least it's out now!"[37]

Camp is intimately integrated into gay male culture, as a performative practice with potential for the disruption of heteronormativity.[38] From this perspective, it may be understood as a subversion of gender conventions.[39] Certainly, Miss'd America contestants, unlike their Miss America counterparts, see their performance as a questioning of heteronormative gender conventions, if not a subversion. Many queens, however, are deliberately subversive and see themselves and their role as drag queens as activism. Tina Burner, Margeaux Haze, Mimi Imfurst, Honey Davenport, and Champagne Bubbles all emphasized the serious nature of their drag in activist terms. This subversiveness reveals itself in their activist efforts in society, and also in conflicts they have with the Miss'd America Pageant and other drag venues, where modern commodification of both drag shows and pageants has created a situation that is seen as threatening to drag's integrity and purpose. In addition to advocating for Miss'd America contestants, Tina Burner (Miss'd America Pageant contestant, 2017) has been outspoken about the necessity of drag queens to use their microphones as a platform for social justice. Honey Davenport is outspoken about revealing the inherent racism in gay nightlife. In late September 2018, she appeared at The Monster, a gay bar in Greenwich Village that hosts its own drag shows, took the stage, and announced that she would not be performing: "Yesterday, I was sent a message from the general manager [of this bar] telling me that the advertisement for this party looked like they were promoting an event for Black people and that THAT was bad for business. He said that the two dancers we had on our stage tonight had to be replaced with 'beautiful people.' After six years of literally laying everything I have on the line on this stage, I can no longer do it."[40]

Since then, Honey (Miss'd America 2015) has continued her crusade for racial and gender equality on the national stage, as a contestant on *RuPaul's Drag Race*, season 11. Drag queen Margeaux Haze (Miss'd America contestant 2015 and 2018) is very outspoken as an advocate for LGBTQ rights and the necessity of drag as a platform for social action. Margeaux, who considers herself a performance artist (her day job is working with wigs, makeup, and wardrobe in theater and television), described her talent portion of the 2018 Miss'd America Pageant and why she chose to perform it:

I am working on a piece that is about societal labels; it's one thing to have someone else place it on you, but I think many people start to accept those labels without knowing the damage that they do to themselves and the people coming up behind them. It's a song called "Who You Are." It talks about [how] it's OK not to be OK.... [*She sings:*] "Seeing is deceiving; dreaming is believing. Fight for what you want.... Understand who you are.... Instead of finding the shame in those labels, how about celebrating who you are ... all aspects of your being." I have [a] huge metal neck plate and hanging from that are petals that completely cover my costume. My body is completely covered except for my head. And each of these flower petals have some kind of societal label, whether it be "dyke" or "tranny" or "fag" or "whore" or "femme" or "masculine," and one by one I remove those labels and there is a huge old fashioned trash can, one by one they all go into the trash can to reveal this absolutely breathtaking ball gown underneath, because, because when you peel away all the crap that you let people pile on you, there is something beautiful in every one of us.[41]

The performative dynamic characteristic of camp is arguably best seen in drag but is also found in broader contexts in the gay community.[42] Barbuscio suggests, for example, that the necessity for passing in straight or conventional life "promotes a heightened awareness and appreciation for disguise, impersonation, the projection of personality, and the distinctions to be made between instinctive and theatrical behavior."[43] As Dyer asserts, for example, camp evolved because

gay men have staked out a claim on society at large by mastery of a style and artifice . . . we have had to hide what we really felt (gayness) for so much of the time, we had to master the façade of whatever social setup we found ourselves in—we couldn't afford to stand out in any way, for it might give the game away about our gayness. So, we have developed an eye and an ear for surfaces, appearances, and forms—style. Small wonder that when we came to develop our own culture, the habit of style should have remained so dominant in it.[44]

Farrah Mascara expresses her practice in passing as an act of drag performance when discussing her character:

The way that I act as a male day to day is probably more of a performance—that I've learned overtime to, like, not be feminine or things like that. It does feel more natural to do, you know, my performance as Farrah. Even sometimes when I'm on the phone like all these years I've gotten, "Oh! Mrs. . . . Like, blah blah blah, and I'm like, No. . . ." So you know when you're talking to someone you don't know, you have to deepen your voice a little or, um, you know, like when you go on a job interview you gotta shake the hand a little bit more firm because you're, "Oh, I need to masculine up more for this," so probably my day to day life is more of a performance than what I'm doing as Farah.[45]

Camp may also be seen as a product of the oppression it satirizes, a coping strategy for dealing with the very stigmatization of homosexuality by the heteronormative culture.[46] Susan Sontag, for example calls camp a "solvent of morality [that] neutralizes moralization, sponsors playfulness."[47] And to Barbuscio it is a strategy for "survival in a hostile world."[48] Tina Burner speaks of the "serious responsibility" she has to her community, despite her comedic presentation:

I'm 6'2" out of drag; add six-inch heels and I'm 6'8", hair, I'm over 7 feet tall, so I'm a monster and people *literally* look up to me physically, so they *have* to listen. This isn't television; you can't change the channel when I'm on stage. And I'm not just here to try to win a sparkly hat! It's about having a voice . . . and there are so many people who don't have a voice in this community, and can't speak up—get killed even for looking like me, so I feel like if I have a microphone for two hours during a show, why should I only talk about frivolous things? Why can't I make people think for a second? And doing it in a way that can make people laugh is an easy way to spark up a conversation. Sometimes things are hard to look at, but that's what life is . . . if you are going to live it.[49]

This certainly is the case in the Atlantic City community and elsewhere, where drag queens may be revered on stage while harassed and beaten when out on the streets. Drag as a performance provides a safe space for the expression of gay identity and may also provide an opportunity for reducing the stigma of homosexuality found in heteronormative culture. As Margeaux Haze describes the potential impact of her performance on straight audiences:

If they are open to it, straight people can be moved . . . you know, the straight guy they put in the front row so he can be harassed? You *know* it's coming (and its usually his girlfriend that brings him). It's like a power struggle. . . . And the women and the gays win. We reverse the privilege for a time. We expose the patriarchy with its rules. Not in our house! I think that many [straight people] do end up changing their minds . . . some do, but they have to be open to it, or it's a freak show and that wall won't come down. If it does, though, humor is a useful weapon. It's always political.[50]

Camp may be a practical strategy when interacting with the dominant heteronormative community, but it also is intended to be joyful. Camp in general, and drag performances in particular, should spread love and bring joy, through humor to those who act as audience.[51] An audience that camp itself requires.

The queens I interviewed universally stated that camp, as it is expressed through drag, is meant to be joyful, and they viewed that as the most important role of drag in culture, to bring joy. Love and joy are integral elements of camp folk wisdom even as there are other, varied reasons for performing drag. Whether politically motivated; seen as a vehicle for creativity and for performance; as a method of subversion; as comedy; as self-expression; or as a way to embody their true natures, all the drag queens noted the centrality of love and joy as important components of drag performance. To Alexia Love, it was "all about love all the time." Evelyn Syde expressed it thus: "I just want them [the audience] to have a good time, to feel a little better, and maybe that turns into feelings of warmth and they bring that out into the world. I want them to spread love. I think we all need to take a moment to laugh." [52] And FiFi Dubois put it this way:

> Drag is campy . . . it's telling a story that could be taken seriously but doing it over the top in a way that doesn't necessarily, well, you wouldn't see it in real life. Taking the seriousness out of it, making light of a crazy situation like an abusive mother or your children . . . something that is really sort of depressing and really shouldn't be a good thing, but poking fun at it and making it lighthearted rather than so sad and dreary. Sometimes real life isn't so easy and funny. But everybody likes to laugh, they need to laugh . . . the role of camp in drag for me, well, especially for me . . . if someone tries to do a drag show that is completely serious, it will not work. It fails automatically. [People] want to escape the mundane; they want to escape the nine to five seriousness of life; they want to laugh a little bit, get out of the pressure of it all, so that's it. That's why I think camp is important to drag. It takes you out of the seriousness of your own life for a moment, and allows you to laugh, to get perspective, to decompress, to have fun. That is what drag is supposed to do. Yes, there are straight people who don't get it. They are going to see the clown, but do you know what? If I have to be your clown to get you through your day, then I'm happy to be your clown. But a drag queen is different from a clown in my mind. I guess they laugh with me; I'm in on the joke. A clown you laugh at.[53]

Tina Burner underscores the importance of laughter, in opposition to some of the most iconic measures of drag performance. In a statement that optimizes camp, she notes: "I don't have to do 'death drops' or 'cooter slams.' . . . I just want to be able to have the power to change someone's day or brighten their mood."[54]

What You Got There, Miss Thang? "Show Us Your Shoes" and the Queering of the Miss America Parade

The influence that the Miss'd America Pageant and the gay community have had on the Miss America Pageant over the years is marked. This influence can be seen overtly in the queering of elements of the Miss America Pageant, where traditions have taken on a camp sensibility. Some changes made by the Miss America Organization that move away from or are in opposition to this camp sensibility may also be understood as an influence of gayness, a phenomenon that my analysis terms "de-queering." The most visible example of the queering of the Miss America Pageant is found in the origins of the Show Us Your Shoes Parade, which now takes place on the night before the pageant finals. Formerly known as the Miss America Parade, it originally boasted stylish floats, marching bands, and convertibles showcasing each contestant, who rode on the back of the car wearing an evening gown and white gloves as they were presented to the public like debutantes, waving as they rode down the once-fashionable Boardwalk. Today, contestants wear costumes and decorate their shoes as they are paraded down the Boardwalk in a camp-style spoof of their own past presentations. As the Miss America 2.0 Competition magazine boasts: "A highlight of Miss America competition week has always been the infamous 'Show Us Your Shoes' Parade featuring the 51 Miss America candidates and 51 pairs of one-of-a-kind handmade wearable art/shoe creations, each celebrating the spirit of their candidate['s] home state with costuming and spectacular fun!"[55] The event is described as camp at its finest: "highlight," "infamous," "one-of-a-kind," "art/shoe creations," "costuming," and "spectacular fun." If you needed further evidence of the campiness of the parade, you need only look to the quote at the top of the glossy two-page spread featuring the clenched, perfectly white smile of Cara Mund, Miss America 2018, parading. It reads, "Give a girl the right shoes, and she can conquer the world," quoting Marilyn Monroe, an icon of the gay community.[56]

Figure 4.1. Drag Kings and Queens, "Show Us Your Pride," New York Avenue reunion, 2018. Photo credit: Paul Dempsey.

Sontag, and more recently others, have recognized a variety of *pop camp*, a stylistic appropriation of authentic camp sensibility, devoid of resistive potential.[57] The Show Us Your Shoes Parade of the Miss America Pageant may be seen as such a spectacle. How this transformation happened can be understood as a process of queering where gay styles of communicative interaction were appropriated in response to the interactions of the Miss America contestants with the onlookers from the gay community on the Boardwalk at New York Avenue.

In the 1980s Studio Six hosted a drag parade show on the night of the Miss America parade. It quickly turned into an event where Miss America Pageant contestants' families came to cheer satirical portrayals of the contestants. The bars were standing room only. "They saw the love we had for Miss America . . . we didn't make fun of them, we made fun of ourselves," recalled HRH Mortimer, who performed each year in the drag parade show with other local queens.[58] Sandy Beach recalls the parade's origins, and relates the story of its queering:

> Show Us Your Shoes [was] started on New York Avenue by a bunch of people hanging out at my friend Joe Rizkowski's apartment for a party. We were looking over the balcony into the cars and saw the girls were wearing bedroom slippers and socks with these gorgeous gowns on . . . then we just tried to embarrass them [by yelling,] "Show us your shoes!" so they'd have to show us their bedroom slippers and their bare feet. It was just one of those chants that started on New York Avenue, and the next year we had signs . . . and then tee shirts, and watches, and oh, the queens were all out. It went from this little thing and then it traveled up and down the Boardwalk. Two years later, the pageant people, who hung out on New York Ave, got wind of it and started decorating the girls' shoes, so when the girls did show them off, they got a crowd reaction. We'd hoot and holler . . . the shoes just got more outrageous every time they came down the Boardwalk . . . and then it just became this parade.[59]

The yelling of "Show us your shoes!" is an example of the communicative style of reading. According to drag language ideology, the drag queens read the Miss America contestants both to express their camaraderie with and affection for them, and to make sure that they didn't "take themselves too seriously." The Show Us Your Shoes Parade is now trademarked by the Miss America Pageant, and the shoes are displayed in Boardwalk Hall each year, highlighted as part of Miss America's public relations campaign. This co-opting of the phrase "show us your shoes" restricts its referencing by the local community, but to this day on New York Avenue and the Boardwalk, contestants still meet catcalls and respond in kind. Gay presence on New York Avenue has diminished since the demise of the bars and clubs, although crowds saw a slight resurgence in 2016, when the first openly gay contestant, Erin O'Flaherty (Miss Missouri), competed for the crown, and again in 2018 when the old Saratoga Club reopened as a Cajun

Figure 4.2. Erin O'Flaherty, Miss Missouri, Show Us Your Shoes Parade, New York Avenue and the Boardwalk, 2016. Photo credit: Paul Dempsey.

restaurant and the New York Avenue community had a "reunion." The Show Us Your Shoes Parade was also an important part of the festivities during the Las Vegas years, and each year a video is produced for the pageant, previewing the Show Us Your Shoes footwear entries.[60]

Suffice to say that Show Us Your Shoes is beloved, and it is *camp*; whether it is pop camp, a stylistic appropriation of authentic camp sensibility, and denuded of subversive potential is a more complicated question. The appropriative nature of the Show Us Your Shoes Parade is bolstered by two realities: though over a dozen newspaper articles and locally broadcast stories about the parade have been published (see bibliography), and the parade is described on the official Miss America website, not one of these stories mentions the gay community or drag queens as having contributed to its evolution. From the Marching.com official page: "The parade started decades ago as a simple procession of contestants on the boardwalk and has grown to become a deeply rooted family-friendly multigenerational parade. The reigning Miss America leads this extraordinary event, which takes place just one day prior to the crowning of the new Miss America."[61] And from Atlanticcitynj.com, the official Atlantic City booster page of the Casino Reinvestment Development Authority (CRDA): "One of the most popular and beloved traditions in Miss America Pageant history is also returning: the Show us Your Shoes Parade. Although the exact origin seems to be debatable, most accounts agree that it began in the 1970s and was related to individuals on a hotel balcony overlooking the parade route. From that viewpoint they noticed that some of the contestants riding in the convertibles wore casual footwear or no footwear at all. "Show us your shoes" started as a teasing refrain and quickly caught on."[62] And from Casinoconnection.com: "Another great tradition is the catch phrase "Show us your shoes," which rings out from the crowd as contestants cruise by on the back of convertibles. The slogan has been around since the 1970s and has grown so popular that it has become the parade's signature name."[63] And finally, from the Miss America Organization website itself:

> "The parade is a highlight of Miss America competition week," said Regina Hopper, Miss America Organization President & CEO. "The people of Atlantic City and fans of Miss America from across the country get the opportunity to come together to have fun and enjoy this great tradition!" . . . Parade Producer Todd Marcocci and his talented team at Under the Sun Productions have returned to create this unique parade: "We are beyond thrilled to have the opportunity to produce the Miss America Show Us Your Shoes parade, the most unique parade in the nation. . . . No other parade exists like this one."[64]

In each of these accounts, the essential and important role of the gay community in general, and the drag community in particular, has been erased. Nowhere on the Miss America Organization website is the history of the parade explained, though the history of the pageant is retold in great detail. In fact, the overall impression of these accounts—and a myriad of others—is that the parade is a "fun," "family-friendly affair," produced by Under the Sun Productions or DSW Shoes and rumored to have been

Figure 4.3. Calle Walker, Miss Alabama, Show Us Your Shoes Parade, New York Avenue and the Boardwalk, 2016. Photo credit: Paul Dempsey.

inspired by individuals yelling "Show us your shoes." Though campy, the parade is anything but resistive of mainstream heteronormative notions of gender, as it has been co-opted. Nonetheless, and despite such tacit denials, it has been queered. As described on Atlanticcitynj.com: "In past years, contestants have worn anything from army boots to ski boots, flip flops to swim fins, bunny slippers to designer shoes. For the 90th anniversary of Miss America, the 'DSW Show Us Your Shoes Parade' included a Robin Leach interview with each contestant about a second pair of shoes she created to showcase her personal theme."[65]

Drag queens HRH Mortimer and Alexia Love explain the origins of the parade:

HRH: They [the Miss America Organization] fought it for so long . . . they would tell them [the contestants], "When you get by New York Ave they are going to be screaming 'Show us your shoes' . . . do *not*

do that." It was this big thing . . . and of course we would scream like
crazy, and if they didn't show us their shoes . . .

ALEXIA LOVE: We would boooo, and then one might throw up a leg
and we'd be like, "Yehhhh, werk that, girl!"

HRH: So it took years for them to actually start doing the funny
shoes. When I first moved here as a kid, I would stand right here on
New York Ave for the parade, and all the drag queens would be out,
and it was fabulous, but they [the contestants] would not show
their shoes . . . when they said they were going to name the parade
the "Show Us Your Shoes" I was like, "Are you kidding?" You fought
it for years. . . . It was too funny. It started at the boarding house
right over Ripley's Believe It or Not.

ALEXIA LOVE: Yes, it did, it went on for years . . . and now they think
they made it![66]

Despite the appropriation, trademarking, and virtual rewriting of history
to exclude the queer origins of the parade, the Show Us Your Shoes Parade
remains popular in the gay community in Atlantic City, and the parade is
still seen through the lens of its camp history. The ethnographic data I col-
lected suggests that the parade is interpreted as denuded pop-camp or
true camp with resistive potential based on the audiences who participate
in and interpret the event through their own symbolic lenses. To some,
the parade is just fun; to others it pokes fun at the absurd images of ideal
femininity and the normative restriction placed on women and their bodies. Once again, "camp is in the eye of the beholder."

CHAPTER 5

Show Us Your Shoes,
Not Your Midriffs

Mimi Imfurst stands at the top of the risers as she enters wearing a twelve-foot-long purple bejeweled velvet octopus stole, its arms wrapped around her torso and dragging down the steps behind her. Hair high in a platinum blonde bouffant, her lips bright red, Mimi cocks her head, turns, and drops the stole coyly, revealing a sparkling black velvet swimsuit and gold and purple shell accessories. She struts, turns her back to the audience, and winks; a finger goes to her lips, as if to say, "OH my, I'm so exposed." She seems oblivious to her fatness. In fact, she shows a confidence in her superior form, her extra-large body. Hands on her hips, accentuating her ample frame, Mimi walks down the runway. Stopping at the end, she licks her lips slowly, turns, and walks back to center stage, moving her hips slowly to the music. "Mimi Imfurst, contestant number 1" is announced, along with her measurements, "seventy-two, forty-eight, seventy-two." The crowd cheers and applauds, and she bends over slowly, pausing, bottom to the audience to retrieve her stole.

As Mimi is escorted away by Speedo-clad male dancers, the next contestant begins to descend. Farrah Mascara steps gracefully, one stilettoed foot after the other, in a sequined red robe. As she reaches the stage her robe falls away, revealing a red cut-out sequined swimsuit, fishnet stockings, and giant lobster-clawed hands. She moves her thumbs, pinching the air. Flashing an open-mouthed toothy smile, she shakes her head side to

side, her huge hair just seconds behind. Farrah struts from one side to the
other as she makes her way down the runway, ending in a figure eight,
pinching claws held high. She shimmies and jiggles her large body, putting one claw to her mouth in feigned embarrassment. "Miss Farrah Mascara, contestant number 2! Her favorite food is chicken nuggets, her
favorite color, the rainbow."

Farrah squeals and grabs the arm of one of her escorts as the next contestant appears at the top of the risers in a gold lamé robe cinched around
her waist. Tina Burner descends in sparkly white platform shoes and
reveals her swimsuit, white and skirted, with a gold belt and anchor, and
gold tasseled epaulets on the shoulders. Tina's ginger hair is coiffed 1950s
style, and she holds a captain's nautical cap, posing, one knee bent, arms
by her side, wrists flexed, head cocked to one side. She walks shyly to the
top of the runway and puts one white-gloved hand to her mouth as she
knocks her knees together and giggles. "Tina Burner, contestant number 3!
Her favorite perfume is fishy."[1]

Werk It Gurrl! Pageantry as Camp

The drag subculture in Atlantic City admires the Miss America Pageant
in part because of their interpretation of its pageantry as an exaggerated
performance of femininity, as an act of creativity, or, simply put, as precisely what they themselves do—camp. They empathize with Miss America contestants; pageant performances are interpreted as staged executions
of femininity at its finest. Sandy Beach describes this star performance
quality in her comparison of the pageants: "It all boils down to talent. You
have to have, in either profession . . . the wow factor . . . it does not matter
if they are a Miss America contestant or a Miss'd America contestant . . .
like Vanessa Williams; that night that she won, you knew when she fin-
ished that song, she was your new Miss America. When I saw Kitty Hiccups (Miss'd America 2011) do her "I Wanna Be a Rockette," dancing down

that runway, doing high kicks, you knew that was star quality and she was going to be the Miss'd America."[2]

Drag pageant queens and beauty pageant queens share an admiration of pageantry and the experiences and values that underlie it. As Rupp and Taylor note, drag queens are interested in billings and publicity, in lighting and makeup and stage effects, in timing and stage presence. The quality by which they measure performers and performances is talent. Certainly, talent and stage presence are important aspects of both beauty and drag pageants. Drag queens admire and often model themselves on established performers, both in their performances and in their offstage lives;[3] in particular, drag performers' special but not exclusive idols are female entertainers.[4] These performers are usually gay icons (with a high camp factor). They encapsulate gay style, manner, and folk wisdom. Many queens spoke of their female icons as inspirations, or actually used them as their drag personalities. Drag queen Shi-Queeta-Lee, a veteran actor and female impersonator, emulates her icons in her drag persona: "I love Tina Turner, Whitney Houston, Mary J. Blige, and Diane Ross. They are my icons and my muses. I can't be nobody else, or don't want to. I live in DC and even got to perform at the White House for the Obamas. What a thrill; I tell you I was channeling them [her icons]. They are larger than life. They didn't let anything keep them back."[5]

Drag queen Jenna Tall (Miss'd America contestant 2015–2018) spoke of the importance of her role models in the development of her drag career:

Everyone, when they're growing up has a role model, and I don't know, when I was a little boy growing up, I always gravitated towards female role models for whatever reason. Probably I knew I was gay at a very young age. I guess that was the beginning of it . . . they are all just sewn into me . . . and just really, really beautiful actresses. And then it sort of turned from, the world of acting and things like that into just really famous drag personalities like Sasha Colby, Erica Andrews . . . I don't know, that's just who I pull reference from . . . they are so over the top and powerful.[6]

The emphasis in both Jenna and Shi-Queeta-Lee's accounts is on the powerful and larger than life characteristics of their "gay icons." They are women who have "overcome adversity," "never given up," and are "absolutely fabulous!" Likewise, drag queen Adriana Trenta (Miss'd America 2019) so admires pop star Ariana Grande that she named her drag persona after her, and performs to her music in talent competitions.[7] Drag queens' idols were almost exclusively women, although not always celebrities. Drag queen Farrah Mascara spoke at length, for example, about the inspiration given to her by the strong women in her life like her mother and aunts who raised her.[8] These were the models for her drag persona. And drag queen Cha Cha spoke passionately and emotionally about his mothers and sisters, and the way they have overcome misogyny, abuse, and incarceration as models for his drag persona and performance.[9]

Although the Miss America Pageant emphasizes the authenticity of the contestants and protects that authenticity ("she's just the girl next door, but smart and talented") with a variety of rules and regulations, drag queens make a distinction between the women competing in the pageant and the pageant persona you see on stage. They believe that, like themselves, the Miss America contestants present a well-manicured performance on stage. Miss America contestants are viewed by drag queens as performers, and admired as such, rather than as representations of real women. However, although one need only search the web for the many sites, courses, and manuals tutoring contestants on every aspect of pageant performance, beauty queens do not necessarily see their presentations as constructed personas. They aim, as do drag queens, to let the audience see "who they are," although for drag queens, who they are is decidedly and deliberately different from their boy selves. When comparing the two pageants, drag contestants often expressed the view that Miss America contestants were just like them, but for certain institutional constraints. As Adriana Trenta explains:

> I think that what pageants in the female-identifying world are missing is that senses of creativity. I mean we are given a blueprint of what we are supposed to do, but it is really up to us to color in or outside the lines and do what we want to do. I really wish that the (cis)pageant scene would take a step back and realize that it's not about the category.... Or when they are doing talent and they get to do a song that is performed a million times before, usually off-key, and it's like society is telling them what they think is talent and what they think is beauty and what they think is.... *Let these women tell you* what they think beauty is! Let these women earn their title as Miss so and so ... *of course!* That's what I get to do in a pageant. Half the fun of the pageant is hearing the themes and going, "Okay! What *can* I do with this?" [*Becomes very animated.*] ... The creativity that can come from themes and that can come from a sense of "No holds barred! Anything goes!" It really is an eye-opening experience, and I really wish that the pageant scene would ... I think that they lack the creativity ... I guess it's more about empty traditions rather than creativity. The artistry needs to be reignited and it really needs to be shaken up. I feel ...

> (Laurie: So you feel that Miss America should be more like a drag pageant!?)

> "*Yaaaassss!* Give them all *lace fronts!*[10] Give them ... give them the ability to do a themed presentation. Give them the ability to do a creative swimsuit that does not have to be fully functional as a bathing suit.[11]

In Adriana's view, the Miss America contestants are being denied the freedom to express their creativity in performance. Whether it is their performance in swimsuit, or talent, or any other aspect of presentation, the failure of the Miss America Pageant is in its excessive rules and restrictions. If beauty pageant contestants are objectified, according to drag queens, it is because they do not have control over their performance, over their interpretation of femininity. Their lack of agency is judged by drag queens to be evidenced in the uniform shapes, styles, and presentations of the women's bodies and the utilitarian, uniform nature of their clothing. Their swimsuits, for example, according to Adriana, are potentially for swimming. But practicality is not part of a drag queen's vocabulary, especially in the swimsuit competition, where tucking and taping and shaving and padding are all essential aspects of creating a believable presentation of an almost naked female body.

It isn't simply about the swimsuit, however; creativity and freedom of expression are important values for performance in all aspects of drag culture. Drag queen Shelby Late (Miss'd America contestant, 2018), a wigmaker in her boy life, found the Miss America Pageant "sorta flat, but the same as us," musing, "Hmmm . . . it would be so cool if they [Miss America contestants] could change their hair to enhance their costuming . . . can't imagine not being able to match your hair to your dress."[12]

The drag community also shares discourses of achievement and choice expressed by female beauty pageant contestants. There is an admiration for the guts and poise these performances entail, and a premium is placed on professionalism, as drag and pageantry are seen as legitimate careers in entertainment. Presentation skills and confidence are also seen as positive outcomes of the experience of pageant competition. Pageant girls are not to blame for the failure of beauty pageants and their tawdry reputation. It is instead the heteronormative world that objectifies women and stigmatizes gay men. This reality allows gay men to empathize with beauty pageant contestants despite their very different worlds. For drag queens, this empathy is even more pronounced, for they have the opportunity to experience what it is like to be a woman, to be the object of the male gaze, to be stigmatized and subject to violence, even by those in the gay community.

Despite all that they share, there are significant ways in which drag and beauty pageants part ways. The ability to cross boundaries, break rules, and act out to challenge the audience to "think outside the box"[13] are all part of camp sensibility, significant attributes of gay icons and important ways in which drag pageant queens and beauty queens differ.

The Body on Display: The Feminine Body as Object and Subject in Pageantry

Seriously, I have a lot of respect for those girls. They go 24/7 and then they walk flawlessly across the runway in those heels. The composure is astounding! Man, I know what hell that is. They are amazing. Just amazing.[14]

As a way of understanding how the body is interpreted and controlled through culture, it is instructive to look at the ways that the Miss America Pageant and the Miss'd America Pageant perform and value femininity. No matter how trivial it may appear, the Miss America Pageant is a significant enactment, rich in symbolic meaning. Until 2018, and the move to Miss America 2.0, both the Miss America Pageant and the modern Miss'd America Pageant contested the same elements (swimsuit, evening gown, talent, interview). Each element of the pageant is a corporeal display, meant to clarify and affirm an aspect of ideal femininity that is contested in the wider cultural discourse. Though the Miss America Pageant and the Miss'd America Pageant have the same overall structure, of ethnographic interest are the ways in which each pageant differs, and what these differences reveal.

The Feminine Body as Object: The Swimsuit Competition

Victoria "Porkchop" Parker comes out for the swimsuit competition eating a fried pork chop. Her fat body is a point of pride, celebrated and squeezed into her tight, high-cut suit as she struts along the stage. She turns to reveal writing on the buttocks of her swimsuit, which reads "Made in America." Her defiance of body norms and female eating etiquette is marked as she smiles and chews with an open mouth. Licking her fingers, she tilts her chin and nods coyly toward the audience.[15]

The next year, Victoria "Porkchop" Parker, fifty pounds heavier, wore a swimsuit emblazoned with the Muppet Miss Piggy's face and wore a Kermit the Frog doll hanging off her back. As she stated in her interview with comedian Randy Rainbow, "You see, when you are big, and you are beautiful, and voluptuous, you flaunt it, and last year I was a size 24 . . . you got to work with what you got; that would have scared a lot of big girls, but not me."[16] This attitude is in marked contrast to the experience of Miss America contestants, whose bodies are thin, sporting an extremely narrow range of normal. The swimsuit competition is, in particular, where all aspects of bodily presentation are managed. Fitness is emphasized, so much so that the competition segment's name was changed to both reflect this emphasis and deflect accusations of objectification. As Crystal Lee, a former Miss America contestant, attests in an op-ed to the *Los Angeles Times*: "Backstage at Boardwalk Hall in Atlantic City, the scene before the swimwear segment looked like a Pilates class. The other Miss America finalists were doing sit-ups on the cold ground, holding wall sits, and squeezing in burpees and pushups as a last-ditch effort to accentuate their muscle tone. I was standing in my sponsored, custom-tailored black bikini and high heels, mentally preparing for my 15 seconds in a swimsuit on national TV."[17] Lee experienced the swimsuit competition as empowering, despite what she described as the preparation regimen for contestants, which included measuring for coverage and gluing suits to their butts and breasts with Good Grip adhesive. As Rita states of her experiences as a contestant in the Miss America Organization: "I competed for Miss Mass in 2003. . . . The two-piece, yeah, they went around with rulers, and it was strict. They measured everything, how much skin you could show, how wide the straps could be."[18] In contrast, drag queen Savannah Savonier describes her experience competing in the Miss'd America Pageant:

> We do have a more realistic view of what our bodies are . . . we get to be not a cookie cutter, we control the amount of femininity that we are presenting to the audience. The Miss America Pageant has become so blocked. When they [the contestants] are in swimsuits, they all have the same set of hips, and they go ahead and get breast implants to make sure they are the right cup size. We don't have to do that . . . we can be one thing one day or even one act, and another thing the other. . . . I can do what I like . . . I can serve up rack of lamb in swimsuit and come back serving lamb bites in evening gown [*laughs*].[19]

Sarah Banet-Weiser observes that "the swimsuit competition is an event that is about physical and moral disciplining of women's bodies. . . . It requires contestants to wear swimsuits that are designed to never come in contact with water and are strictly regulated in terms of how many inches of skin may be exposed . . . and it is precisely this disciplining that makes the swimsuit competition an absolutely necessary element of the Miss America Pageant; because it is the performance of the female object, a performance that is then juxtaposed to the interview and talent competitions, which are the performances of the female subject."[20] The Miss America Organization realized the importance of swimsuit as juxtaposition to the subject focused competition segments as the pageant moved to reform and rebrand itself in 2018. The swimsuit competition, whether deemed empowering or objectifying, has always been controversial and at the center of the debates over the meaning of the Miss America Pageant. The objectification and commodification of women's bodies are epitomized in the pageant. However, it is in the swimsuit competition that the contradictions inherent in the meaning of the pageant are laid bare.[21]

In 1921, moral conservatives protested the display of women's bodies in swimsuits,[22] and believed that beauty pageants themselves were obscene. In 1943, the newly victorious Miss America, Jean Bartel, refused to be

Figure 5.1. Mimi Imfurst, Miss'd America Pageant, in Swimsuit, 2016.
Photo credit: Paul Dempsey.

Figure 5.2. Sapphira Cristal, Miss'd America Pageant, in Swimsuit, 2018. Photo credit: Paul Dempsey.

crowned in her swimsuit ("unless she is swimming," she stated), which at the time was the practice of the pageant.[23] By 1948, contestant activism and other ongoing criticism from conservatives resulted in the two-piece suit being banned from the pageant, and the crowning to be performed in evening gown attire.[24] Miss America 1951, Yolande Betbeze, refused to wear a swimsuit during her reign, leading to the loss of the Catalina Corporation as a pageant sponsor and the birth of the rival Miss USA Beauty Pageant.[25]

In 1954, the Miss America Pageant was first televised, and the widened gaze enabled by mass media set the controversy ablaze once again. The swimsuit most famously became the focus of feminist protest against the Miss America Pageant in 1969. Rejecting the lack of equality for women in the United States, the New York Radical Women, a second-wave radical feminist organization, waged the now infamous protest and bra burning against the Miss America Pageant on September 7, 1968, in Atlantic City. The group had as its stated mission a "dismantling of the patriarchy." Although the organization, begun in 1967 on the Lower East Side of Manhattan, lasted only a few years, its direct actions helped define the feminist movement and pioneered crucial elements of modern feminism.[26]

Although bras were never burned, symbols of misogyny and patriarchal oppression were disposed of in a "freedom trash can." As Roxane Gay notes, the protesters presented a "Womanifesto," detailing their positions against antifeminist symbols, among them "the degrading Mindless-Boob-Girlie Symbol." In particular, these feminists framed the Miss America swimsuit requirement as a symbol of women's oppression, "to highlight the ways women are enslaved by beauty standards."[27]

The protesters also claimed that the Miss America Pageant was a racist event, since a woman of color had never won, and there had never been a black or Native American (a "true Miss America") contestant.[28] New York Radical Women also protested the "military-industrial complex"[29] and the consumeristic nature of corporate sponsorship of the pageant. They rejected the overvaluing of beauty as a measure of a woman's worth, and that the contestants were forced to be the impossible, "both sexy and wholesome, delicate but able to cope, demure yet titillatingly bitchy . . . inoffensive, bland, apolitical," yet intelligent and knowledgeable, and so proclaimed, "*No more Miss America!*"[30] The criticism of the competition as objectifying and oppressive to women has continued to this day.

In an informal survey taken in Convention Hall in 1970, the *Press of Atlantic City* asked pageant-goers whether they believed the swimsuit competition should be eliminated. The overwhelming sentiment was in favor of keeping swimsuits as part of the pageant. As the *Press* noted, one gentleman said that he believed "They [the swimsuits themselves] should be cut out . . . and let them [the contestants] go nude." He was only kidding, but Shelley Osbourne of Margate opined, "I believe the girls should

Figure 5.3. New York Radical Women, Miss America Pageant protest, Atlantic City Boardwalk, 1968. Photo credit: AP.

be required to show poise at all times . . . even in a bathing suit." Convention Hall guard Abe Weiss suggested, "With all the female impersonators in this town . . . it seems to me the people would appreciate seeing the real thing for a change." Mr. Bizub from Patterson New Jersey said, "I'm against over-exposure on the boardwalk . . . but I think bathing suits belong in the pageant." And finally, one Texas pageant-goer enthusiastically asserted that he was as much in favor of bathing suits in the Miss America Pageant as he was of miniskirts![31] Pageant-goers in the 1970s overwhelmingly opposed the elimination of the swimsuit competition, despite the contradiction it posed to a scholarship pageant. In 2018, nothing much had changed. Miss America 2.0 based its new branding on the elimination of the swimsuit competition, along with other changes aimed at promoting the subject presentation of women and eliminating those aspects that might be interpreted as objectifying. According to surveys, pageant-goers overwhelmingly opposed the changes, and some Miss America state-level organizations refused to abide by the new regulations, only to have their charters and funding rescinded.

Banet-Weiser explains the contradiction as follows: "The pitting of the swimsuit competition's *object* against the interview's *subject* reflects the popular sentiment of being sexual and serious at the same time . . . the pageant attempts to accommodate the contradictions of constructing oneself as a feminine subject in US culture."[32] Miss America contestants themselves have a decidedly different view about their presentation in pageantry. By and large, ex-contestants see the pageant as empowering rather than objectifying. In particular, they point to the poise and confidence that the swimsuit competition experience instills in contestants. As 2014 runner-up Crystal Lee contends: "Walking out in a bikini before a crowd cheering my name gave me a rush and sense of courage I never thought possible. I know I will never again be able to get that feeling. . . . Letting contestants don the bikini was inherently feminist because women made that choice for themselves. . . . Critics love to lambast pageants for being objectifying and degrading. But ask contestants like me. We'll tell you we were baring our midriffs because we wanted to."[33]

In contrast, the Miss'd America Pageant, though it displays examples of ideal normative feminine beauty, remains undisciplined. This allows for contestants like Victoria "Porkchop" Parker, Michele Dupree, Cleo Phatra, and Miss'd America 2017, Mimi Imfurst (described in the opening scenario), to revel in the spotlight during the swimsuit competition in their fat bodies. These displays are examples of camp and elicit comic responses from the audience but are also interpreted as a satirical critique of narrow feminine norms.

Shelby Late, a personal trainer in her boy persona, explains the difference between the Miss America Pageant and the Miss'd America Pageant as a difference in the presentation and judgment of the actual versus the performed body. She describes the object presentation of Miss America and the way that her curvy body is constructed:

I can be what I want. I can be completely different in talent versus swim-suit, because it's all a character, so the character can change. In Miss America, they are themselves. They are selling themselves, whereas I am a character. I don't care how the audience perceives me, as male or female. I think it [my character] is a heightened expression of a human, male or female; it's obvious. It's not meant to be real [*laughs*]. I don't think I can confuse anybody, yeah . . . I think it's clearly a lot of makeup, but it's not clowning out there; it is still based in reality, because physi-cally, Shelby is curvy, she's got some hips. That's because I work out a lot, so I'm definitely a bit of a muscle queen, so Pattaya [drag mother] and I have worked on finding the right proportions for my shoulders, which has resulted in a curvy girl.[34]

Though an obvious exaggeration, Shelby Late is also real. She has Shelby's boy identity as part of her essential physical as well as psychological iden-tity. So, a muscular man with big shoulders became a curvy girl.

In 2014, the swimsuit portion of the Miss America pageant was renamed the "physical fitness" portion, and many local feeder pageants no longer required contestants to wear high heels during their parade in front of the panel of judges. But, of course, these moves served only to highlight the contradiction apparent in wearing a swimsuit in a competition for scholarships.

When the Miss'd America Pageant first began, there were no swimsuit or evening gown competitions. The pageant was based instead on the skits, talent portion, and interview. The first year the pageant was contested, a winner was not crowned. This makes sense when one considers that the contest was local, and that the function of the pageant was to assert com-munity resilience and identity, celebrate local personalities, and help those who were suffering from the scourge of HIV/AIDS. It was focused on the interpretation of the bodies on stage as subjects, many well known and beloved. As the pageant changed to include swimsuit and evening gown competitions, and expanded to a national audience, the ambiguity of this object presentation had to be resolved. For many drag queens, the forced objectification was managed through camp presentations, which simultaneously celebrated the female form and displayed its subjugation through absurd presentation. Drag critiques heterosexual masculinity and its policing of female bodies through mockery, not the female form itself.

THE FEMININE BODY AS OBJECT: THE EVENING GOWN COMPETITION

Cha Cha emerges from backstage. Her gown is green and blue, made of silk, sequins, and peacock feathers. Her dark brown hair is styled in a tall bouffant, curls falling down over her face and shoulders. Her bare arms lift two long rods by her sides as a huge peacock tail fans out behind her. She struts across the stage, sparkling and powerful.[35]

The evening gown competition is a display of feminine comportment. It is meant to symbolize through the formal presentation of the body the training in etiquette that a debutante might display after finishing school. Where else would one wear an evening gown? As such, it is an overt display of class consciousness. In the Miss America Pageant, gowns are often created by famous designers and are meant to express the understated elegance of the upper middle class. As former beauty pageant contestant Rita remembers: "My first dress was borrowed . . . I played the piano . . . that's what I knew. Girls would spend thousands of dollars on designer dresses made for them. I went to discount stores or had them made when I visited the Philippines. That always made me feel bad; I mean it always felt like it highlighted the differences between the haves and have-nots."[36] Rita went on to discuss the ways that wealth and privilege were held up as ideals of decorum and comportment; ideals which she felt she might not fully meet as the daughter of immigrants from the Philippines. Later, when the changes to evening gown for Miss America 2.0 were announced, Rita was asked about elimination of the evening gown competition. Surprisingly, Rita was torn about new format. She felt that the new rules might make the competition more affordable to disadvantaged contests, but bemoaned the loss of pageantry that seemed to accompany the proposed changes: "I always felt like the system was designed for rich girls to succeed, not girls like me. . . . You know, the ones who could afford the expensive gowns, hire personal trainers, private hair dressers, make-up artists, and have an endless supply of resources at their disposal. Having said that, I also liked the elegance and glamour of the evening gown competition. I mean, who wears a crown with business attire, and why have a contest without the pageantry? Girls can just take a test for that!"[37]

According to the Miss America Organization website, the changes to the evening gown competition are meant to give participants the freedom to express their self-confidence in evening attire of their choosing, all while discussing how they will advance their social impact initiatives. Contestants should dress like they are going for a job interview or giving a TED Talk. The changes to the evening gown competition have served to redefine ideal womanhood; now, she is career-minded and should show her power not through her appearance, but through her professionalism and career-minded comportment. Whether this succeeds in giving women agency in competition, or simply polices ideal womanhood in a new way remains to be seen.

In the Miss'd America Pageant, the evening gown component is generally viewed as an opportunity to be glamorous, although more campy queens do give comedic interpretations of glamour or play off uber femme or other gay icons.[38] Because gowns provide the most coverage of the body, they present the greatest opportunity for creating the illusion of femininity.[39] As with the Miss America Pageant, evening gowns are the costliest investment a drag queen must make to participate in pageantry, especially because in drag, glamor is taken to exaggerated levels. Drag queens take pride in their ability to do their own tailoring, stoning,[40] and beading. Considering the ever-rising costs of queening in general and pageantry in particular, queens express pride in their self-sufficient skills, problem-solving

Figure 5.4. Savannah Savonier, Miss'd America, in Evening Gown, 2016.
Photo credit: Paul Dempsey.

abilities, and cost-saving strategies. Local drag queen Jenna Tall, for example, got into drag because it combined all her talents—female impersonation, dancing and choreography, sewing and beading, doing hair and makeup. "It just seems like a perfect outlet to be able to accomplish all my loves and passions," she said. "I always wanted to be a person who was very self-sufficient. I sort of either already knew how to do the general stuff or I learned very quickly because it gets expensive when you gotta outsource everything."[41] Sewing and beading, as well as doing hair and makeup, all part and parcel of the evening gown competition, are essential skills learned within drag families and are part of the shared knowledge and practices of the community of practice in Atlantic City; this was especially true in the early days of the Miss'd America Pageant.

More seasoned queens may have a crew of helpers who work tirelessly at the tasks once accomplished independently. *Drag Race* alumna Mimi Imfurst came to compete for the Miss'd America title in 2016 with a crew of assistants, many of whom are drag performers in their own right. Drag queen Cleo Phatra, herself the popular host of a weekly drag variety show, *Gaybill*, in Philadelphia, came to assist Mimi with wardrobe, hair, and makeup. Noah, a baby queen and fanboy, assisted also, as a gofer and general helper. Some queens have speech and talent coaches, some have managers; this in addition to their drag families,[42] self-constructed families whose members support each other and assist in the skill building and nuts and bolts of pageant competition.

THE FEMININE BODY AS SUBJECT: THE TALENT COMPETITION

The lights go up, and Cha Cha appears on stage in front of a scaffold with various props. She looks full-figured in her orange prison jumpsuit. There appear to be beer cans rolled in her teased hair and a purple comb stuck in the knots. She looks ahead in disgust, broom in one hand, and in heavy Spanish-accented English she complains about the cleaning, chomping on gum. She finishes her monologue, "He had it coming!" She takes off her orange suit, and another costume emerges from beneath it, along with another character, and another, each representing a wrongly incarcerated female. The next contestant, Shi-Queeta-Lee, charges out on the stage in a red-sequined flapper dress. She *is* Tina Turner. Her backup singers dance and lip-sync in unison. Shi-Queeta-Lee has played everyone from Beyoncé to Michelle Obama. She lip-syncs and dances a soulful rendition of "Proud Mary" before breaking into its second refrain. She is met with a standing ovation from the audience.[43]

In addition to singing and dancing in homage to Broadway or pop divas, overt expressions of ethnicity and political dissonance are par for the course in drag performance. Cha Cha's talent performance was motivated by personal experience in Mexico, where her mother and sister were jailed, victims of their husbands' oppression. She states:

> My sister and my mom, they were both in jail for things they didn't do; their husbands put them there . . . the pageant gave me an opportunity to express this, to finish it. The number is about women's struggle; it is a struggle I can relate to. I came from Oaxaca as an immigrant. I didn't speak English. I have struggled. Life isn't fair always. . . . The first girl [in my performance] was about following the rules. . . . I didn't do that; like, I wasn't straight. I really felt, for maybe one second, what it's like to be a woman . . . what it's like to live in a man's world. Injustice, I know that too in some ways.[44]

Cha Cha's experience makes for a decidedly expressive portrayal of gender—the act's creation and performance speak to the inextricable integration of race, class, and gender. Her internal motivations for performing each character throw into question Judith Butler's assertion that gender is always wholly performative, rather than expressive, cognitive, or instrumental. Cha Cha's performance has complex motivations that speak to her unique experiences in her body and in relationship to the female bodies that she knows intimately.

Figure 5.5. Margeaux Haze (Powell), Miss'd America Pageant, in Talent, "Labels," 2018. Photo credit: Paul Dempsey.

In contrast to the performances in Miss'd America, the talent competition in the Miss America Pageant shows a glaring lack of expression of personal identity, most particularly when these identities are nonnormative. Vanessa Williams, the first black Miss America, for example, sang the show tune "Anything Goes" in her talent competition. Her choice of songs was unremarkable in that it could have been performed by any of the other contestants and did not signify her identity as a black woman. What is remarkable about the talent portion of Miss America in general is its uniformity and apolitical content. As Lauren Cox writes in *Hollywood Life*: "Unfortunately for the contestants of the 2017 Miss America pageant, their [demonstrated] talents were just not enough to excite their fellow people. As many of the contestants danced, sang, and twirled batons to impress the judges, the internet went wild with overwhelming boredom—especially when the only contestant holding an instrument was eliminated and not allowed to perform.... There were some really incredible performances during the talent portion, but many of them appeared to be very similar."[45]

THE FEMININE BODY AS SUBJECT: THE INTERVIEW

In the Miss America Pageant, the interview is the most perilous competition. Here, contestants are asked to assert who they are as a subject in a thirty-second answer to a question chosen through lottery. These questions are sometimes political in nature, and they afford contestants an opportunity to highlight their social platform but also to potentially falter by expressing an unpopular opinion.[46] The challenge is for the contestants to express these opinions in a way that also meets the assumed qualities of ideal femininity, as one pageant coach explains:

> While it is perfectly fine to have your own opinions, here is where expressing them like a queen comes into play, since during your reign you will be around a variety of different people with different views. To answer this question, if you feel it necessary, state your view first, 'While I feel that . . .' but then state the opposing side, 'I understand that . . .' Close with, 'As a result . . .' or 'However . . .' Stating both sides to the view is important and you won't sound 'stuck up,' or 'spoiled.' With everything going on in the world, be prepared for lots of questions that face a lot of opposition. It is your job to be a queen and handle it with grace and class, and the way to do that is by recognizing and acknowledging all sides before offering a solution.[47]

In the 2016 Miss America Pageant finals, when asked which women should be on the new ten-dollar bill, Miss Colorado, Kelley Johnson, responded that Ellen DeGeneres was her choice: "I think that woman is so amazing. Not only is she kind; not only is she intelligent; not only is her entire platform speaking of tolerance and equality for all and kindness, but she is able to be funny without insulting people."[48] Miss Colorado's answer sums up the qualities with which any Miss America should be identified: kindness, intelligence, tolerance, and tact. She may have opinions, but not any that might offend someone. In this way, the woman as subject is highly disciplined, and successful contestants learn the rules accorded to the content and form of one's speech.

The Miss America interview portion exists in marked contrast to the expressive quality of drag contestants' presentations as female bodies, displaying feminine behaviors. Platforms for Miss'd America Pageant contestants have included trans rights (vis-à-vis discrimination in the gay community), AIDS activism, the creation of a gay teen shelter, and various campaigns against political candidates who espouse antigay rhetoric. Chantel Rashae, a 2013 contestant, unabashedly presented her personal talents by themselves as a way to give back to the community. This bold assertion of self-worth (as subject) is typical of drag queens, who openly proclaim their "fabulous qualities,"[49] in opposition to their reading of their opponents' (other queens') failings.

And the Winner Is . . . The Marked Body: Performing Gender in a Cultural Space

In both beauty and drag pageants, women's bodies are presented and marked with important social and cultural meaning. This meaning is an expression of the core values of the community in which they are situated. The Miss America Pageant began in 1921 as part of the Fall Frolic, a way to get people to stay at the beach for one more week, extending the summer season. Criticized by religious organizations for being too risqué, and associated with the sordid side of resort business, the pageant did not gain its wholesome reputation until 1945, when it crowned the first Jewish Miss America, Bess Myerson. That cultural moment graphically symbolized the American opposition to Nazi fascism and extermination of European Jews; it made Myerson a particularly powerful representation of American values. Myerson's crown was quickly tarnished—she was asked to change her name to something that sounded less Jewish (Beth Merrick),

Figure 5.6. Adriana Trenta, crowning of Miss'd America, 2018.
Photo credit: Paul Dempsey.

but she refused. Her victory tour was cut short due to lack of sponsorship
and because many hotels had discriminatory policies barring Jews, leaving her without a place to stay as she toured.

In the 1930s, Renee Slaughter, pageant director for thirty years, instituted Rule 7, officially requiring that contestants be "white and in good
health." This edict was not repealed until 1940, although the first black contestant did not compete on stage in any role other than house slave in a
production number until 1970. Black female bodies were finally valorized
when Vanessa Williams became the first black woman crowned Miss
America in 1984, even though she faced criticism for not being black
enough. "There were a lot of people who had issues. . . . I was too light. My
eyes were the wrong color. My hair wasn't the right texture and [I was]
getting criticism for being who I was,"[50] Williams stated. She was also the
target of persistent racist hate mail and death threats, which she documented in her memoir, *You Have No Idea*. Williams's reign was cut short
after nude photos of her were published without her consent in *Penthouse*

magazine. Her body became a symbol of her lack of qualification for the
title. Her ex post facto naked body was enough to disqualify her for the
Miss America crown.

In contrast to the discrimination found in the early policies of Miss
America, the Miss'd America Pageant crowned its first black queen, an
Atlantic City local named Alexia Love, in 1993, for a 1994 reign. Almost
half of the Miss'd America Pageant winners have been drag queens of
color, and many more people of color participate as contestants. The visibility of diversity is bolstered by the overt expression of racial and ethnic
identity performed in the Miss'd America Pageant, in all aspects of competition. In the Miss America Pageant, nonnormative identity markers in
the contestants are generally ignored or erased. Contestants of color act
as placeholders—brown and black and yellow faces in the crowd who
behave and dress and perform just like their white counterparts. This same
expectation is seen in the case of nonnormative sexuality and religion. The
lack of queer visibility in Miss America was noted by all who were involved
in some way in the Miss'd America Pageant. As Jeff Wilson, former emcee
of Miss'd America during the early days at Studio Six, noted:

> Recently I thought there was an opportunity they really lost out on.
> They had one of their former winners marry her girlfriend legally, Deir-
> dre Downs . . . she was 2005, and I believe she was the first Miss Amer-
> ica to graduate from medical school . . . brilliant and talented and I just
> thought that's something . . . I mean that's all inclusive, but it all just
> got shuffled away. I thought that would have been a good opportunity
> for them to say, hey, look, we are *all inclusive*, we are the *modern woman*,
> we are *every woman*, and . . . you know, the fact that you are with
> another woman doesn't make you less. But again, they totally chose not
> to endorse, or even look at that. . . . . . I think it was the same year as Erin
> [O'Flaherty]. . . . And again, they didn't go *very* far with that . . . they
> went further with the girl that had the tattoos on her than they did
> with Erin.[51]

The Miss America Organization is aware of the criticisms surrounding its lack of diversity and its antifeminist image. In addition to presenting Miss America as a "scholarship competition" rather than a beauty pageant and renaming the swimsuit competition a "fitness" competition, diversity has become a touchstone issue for Miss America public relations. Negotiations of race and sexuality can be clearly seen in an advertisement for the Miss America Pageant in 2017. The ad describes the intentions of the Miss America Pageant to paint itself as having changed in its presentation of women and touts its inclusiveness. The video, posted by the online version of *People* magazine, *People > bodies*,[52] opens with the title "Miss America 2017 is coming," and goes on to say: "This year's contestants include . . . Arianna Quan, the first Asian-American contestant, Miss Michigan [pictured in the video], . . . Erin O'Flaherty, the first openly gay Miss America contestant [pictured], . . . and Sierra Jackson, Miss D.C., who raises awareness for military families [pictured; she is African American]." The fact that only these three contestants were highlighted, and not a "typical" looking contestant, speaks to the Miss America Organization's awareness of the desire for the pageant to reform its reputation from being outdated and irrelevant. Much as with its adoption of liberal feminist language, the Miss America Pageant is looking for a way to manage the incongruence between its usual heteronormative whiteness and the value society places on diversity.

The Miss'd America Pageant, on the other hand, has never suffered from a lack of contestant diversity in the competition. Contestants who are gender-nonconforming or undergoing gender transition may also compete, and have, as long as they have not undergone transition surgery. Since its reinvention on the national stage, however, Miss'd America has also been criticized—for lacking enough people of color on the judges' panel, for not including any ex-winners as judges, and for continuing to exclude fully transitioned transgender contestants. These criticisms may indicate a shift by the Miss'd America Pageant toward national, heteronormative standards absent in the more local context, within the gay community, where interpersonal relationships and a shared common experience, rather than national racial or gender divisions, more clearly define gay identity.

The rescinding of Vanessa Williams's crown in light of her nude modeling, and the regulations that require Miss America to have never been married or pregnant, clearly illustrate that women's bodies are sexually regulated by the Miss America Organization. We should not be surprised at these examples, though, as women's bodies have always been contested grounds when it comes to sexual behavior. The fact that reading in the drag community and drag's satirical presentations during performances are often focused on body shape, sexual promiscuity, and hygiene are most likely a reflection of this same fierce policing of aspects of the female body and its comportment. The Miss'd America Pageant, however, lampoons this policing, relishing presentations of women's bodies as diverse, both in dimension and race, as well as sexually active, even sexually promiscuous. In drag pageants, women's bodies are not disciplined in Foucault's sense. In fact, drag pageants act in opposition to this Foucauldian discipline by embracing violations of female chastity and upper-middle-class comportment. The freedom with which these social rules are violated speaks to a critique of patriarchal heteronormative culture, where men's physical presentations are less subject to critique. Beauty pageants in general, and the Miss America Pageant in particular, present the female body marked in such a way to uphold heteronormative patriarchal gender norms: female, and in binary opposition, male. Women's bodies in the Miss'd America Pageant and other drag pageants, by contrast, are in opposition to the narrow normative female gender performance, and similarly normative male—an expression they cannot or will not perform.

Conclusion

DRAG QUEENS AND BEAUTY QUEENS

Sandy Beach walks out onto the small stage, gold lamé top, red lipstick, and blonde wig just a bit askew. She's hobbling a bit, her hip not what it used to be. The spotlights shine in her eyes as she adjusts her hair and squints to see who might be in the audience. The crowd claps and cheers. Her monologue speaks about the old days, how great it is to be back hosting a show in Atlantic City at Club Unique, and the president she calls "Fat Nixon." She makes an off-color joke, because "it's never too soon," and in response to the moans turns her back and pretends to fart.

Sapphira Cristal dances her way around the room. Avoiding low-hanging lights, she high-kicks and does splits between tables and chairs. She stops to air-kiss friends and collect tips—dollar bills placed in her bra or plucked out of audience members' outstretched hands. Though she's a trained opera singer, she lip-syncs as she dances, her mouth movements as exaggerated as her painted face.

Morgan Wells's costume is extravagant, as always—with electric lights and other moving parts. In heels she appears eight feet tall. She lip-syncs and winds her way around the audience as her costume transforms, piece by piece removed, until she wears only a sequined swimsuit. The crowd cheers as she "makes it rain," throwing her tips up in the air and watching them fall to the floor of the stage around her.

Jenna Tall enters the small, half-full bar on Tennessee Avenue with a loud "Heeeey y'all, what up bitches? You here for this fucking show?" She states the rules for all the uninitiated. No touching, no kissing, no heckling. Just throw money, lots of money. "You got money, don't you? And tip the bartenders!" The small crowd—straight women, some couples, and a few gay men—applauds. The stage is small, a venue that boasts a weekly gay event—a tea dance[1] and drag show—every Sunday, beginning at 3 p.m. The music starts and she begins her opening number.

Mortimer sits at the VÜE, the bar at the top of the Claridge Hotel. He is dapper as always, wearing his signature bow tie and glasses. His ginger hair is neatly cropped. He sips a dirty martini and leans back in his chair. He confides that he may come out of retirement to do a drag bingo for charity, or maybe just for fun, but for now he has a "big boy job" managing the bar. He laughs at the things he remembers and bemoans the things that have changed and the things that never will.[2]

Atlantic City, Miss America, and the Miss'd America Pageant: A Symbiosis

The story of the Miss America Pageant is in many ways the story of Atlantic City. Atlantic City has always doggedly struggled to redefine itself in the face of changing social and economic realities, and challenges to its identity and mission, just like Miss America. Both the Miss America Organization and Atlantic City seek financial stability, notoriety, and popularity as a successful venue for quality entertainment. Both have fought back in the face of irrelevancy. More recently on the scene, the Miss'd America Pageant was born and has evolved out of an important, yet marginalized population of Atlantic City, the gay community, and the reality that their community was being threatened—marginalized because of homophobia, important because of their essential role in the entertainment industry at the center of the tourist economy, threatened by the consequences of the AIDS epidemic.

Like other marginalized communities, the gay community is anything but a footnote to the city's history. Gays have a long history in Atlantic City, as does the sex tourism that exploited them. Unlike the midway of the Centennial Exhibition in Chicago,[3] the gay community in Atlantic City was not a manufactured sideshow fashioned for the benefit of tourism. It was a community of people who created a neighborhood for themselves, who lived, worked, loved, and celebrated their culture on the streets of New York Avenue and the winding Snake Alley. Their community was also a destination for people from Philadelphia, New York, and Washington, D.C.—large cities with residents in search of gay social life and vacationing. Heterosexual tourists looking for an experience of the exotic were onlookers to this authentic locale. Drag in Atlantic City also has a long history, one that is tied to the gay revelers who flocked to the bars and clubs on New York Avenue. In fact, the gayborhood persisted after Atlantic City began to decline.[4] While Atlantic City's official tourist industry was failing in the 1970s, the ethnographic accounts presented here tell of a thriving and boisterous gay nightlife during that same period, one that was overlooked by city planners.[5] These descriptions of gay life are not simply nostalgic, though the feeling of nostalgia is certainly deep for residents, gay and straight locals alike. The nostalgia itself is a testimony to the existence of a real community, one that has gone through a process of diminution.[6] No one has nostalgia for the midway. The recounting of queer history, like the ethnographic narratives depicted in this book, depends largely on the health of intergenerational relationships, since queer history is unofficial history, omitted from standard written chronicles. Gay culture has also been left unrecognized partly because of the loss of community created by the AIDS epidemic. Having decimated a generation of the gay community in Atlantic City, AIDS has threatened the recounting (restoration) of this history, making intimate stories like the ones in this book ever more precious. As drag queen Margeaux Haze (née Powell) lamented: "After the AIDS crisis we lost a huge chunk of our community in the middle, and there's an older LGBT community and drag community that are trying to help the younger generation along, but those conversations aren't happening in the right way, and they are not being heard in the right way, like your parents are trying to tell you what to do, and, and, it's a shame . . . the gap is so wide because we lost so many of that generation . . . that information would have been more conversational . . . to them."[7]

Gay language and culture have always impacted popular culture and entertainment, and in Atlantic City, the nightlife on New York Avenue and the drag queens who performed there and elsewhere in the city have greatly influenced the culture of this tourist town. Of particular note is the way that the gay community has "queered" the Miss America Pageant, and how in response the Miss America Organization has (1) demonized, (2) denied, (3) co-opted, and then finally (4) rejected this queering. What will be interesting to witness going forward is how this rejection of the entertainment value of pageantry as campy by the Miss America Organization will play on the national level. So far, their stance has failed to ignite more interest in the pageant. Perhaps the impact of the mainstreaming of drag and drag competitions is to forever change how we view such pageants and competitions. Increasingly, audiences understand that drag pageants and drag shows are essentially valuable as theater, and read them as metaphor, not through the lens of realness.

Miss America 2.0: The De-queering of Miss America

It is easy to critique or disregard the Miss America Pageant without understanding the phenomenon it has become; either through rose-colored memoirs on the one hand, or feminist critiques on the other. One way to understand this iconic national pageant is through its relationship with Atlantic City culture and the local gay community that championed it, even as its national popularity waned. The Miss America Pageant has been directly influenced by its parodic sister, the Miss'd America Pageant, but the influence has also been in many ways indirect. The Miss America Pageant has undergone many changes over the years in response to changes in American culture, views of the feminine ideal, and women's changing roles. The reforms to Miss America in recent years, however, have had the most profound impact on the pageant, and may, according to many, lead to its demise. This is ironic, considering that according to the Miss America Organization, these changes, self-branded as Miss America 2.0, have been made as a way to address the criticisms leveled against the pageant. Miss America has long been considered irrelevant by many, but continues to hold a certain fascination for parts of American society. As Kate Shindle, Miss America 1998, says of her reign: "Even in the late 1990s, after Miss America has been pronounced dead, extinct, irrelevant more times than anyone can probably count, I am newsworthy. Children climb over each other at assemblies to touch me. Or the crown. I can't always tell which."[8] Nowhere is this fascination and support as steady and as long-lived as in Atlantic City. But as Shindle also notes in her memoir, "Uneasy lies the head that wears the crown," for in bearing its weight, winners must bear the decades of "stereotypes, expectations, scandal, myths, media scrutiny, public skepticism,"[9] and, most recently, leadership choices that have resulted in the pageant slowly and painfully falling apart.[10]

In the midst of the crisis to make itself relevant, the Miss America Organization has removed the theatrical elements of the pageant by which it was beloved as campy by the gay community. The loss of the swimsuit competition, the runway, the theme song popularized by Bert Parks, and the word "pageant," along with the dramatic alteration of the evening gown competition, have sucked the camp out of the event, and drawn the incongruency of the pageant into a harsh focus, forcing viewers to ask the question, "Why are we watching a *scholarship contest*?" This questioning affirms what the Miss America Organization has always denied—that the competition was, and to most still is, essentially a beauty pageant. As former first runner-up Crystal Lee lamented in an op-ed to the *Los Angeles Times*, dropping the swimsuit category was a great loss to the competition. Co-opting the language of feminism, she views the changes as a sexist imposition by feminists, and a loss of agency for contestants:

The swimsuit] delivered a powerful message: that beauty and brains are not mutually exclusive and that you can be a feminist and flaunt your body. Letting contestants don the bikini was inherently feminist because women made that choice for themselves. Future participants will be forced into a new form of sexism, one that emerges out of today's popular feminist narrative. It may be driven by contemporary ideas, but it disguises the same familiar barriers and judgments surrounding women's decisions. Critics love to lambast pageants for being objectifying and degrading. But ask contestants like me. We'll tell you we were baring our midriffs because we wanted to."[11]

Echoing the narrative of choice, agency, and empowerment held by women and girls in the pageant world, Lee clearly illustrates the importance of beauty to the Miss America Pageant's identity, to pageant contestants, and to American heteronormative notions of ideal femininity. Brains and beauty, not brains alone, mark the ideal woman. She is the product of an addition of intelligence, not of the loss of her value as an object of sexual arousal. She is still the chaste girl next door, but in heels and a bikini of her own choice. Regardless of one's position on the value of pageantry, critics and supporters alike can agree on one thing: the changes adopted with the reforms of Miss America 2.0 in 2018 have extracted the last bit of life from the iconic pageant and brought the symbolic meaning of pageantry and its core elements under an unwanted microscope.

The value of individual choice so important to pageant culture is found in the specific alterations made to the evening gown competition. Evening gowns are now optional, and the contestants are asked to dress in whatever they feel most comfortable.[12] Despite these new options for personal presentation and expression, every contestant in Miss America 2019 chose to wear an evening gown. Choice is also emphasized with regard to the social responsibility platform, originally adopted in 1990. In an attempt to front-load the personalities and platforms of the contestants in the competition, the newly titled "Social Impact Initiative" was the subject of discussion at each point in the 2.0 competition. Previously, the contestants' platform was announced only during the swimsuit competition and again in the interview portion. Note that before, in swimsuit, as with Barnum's Circassian Beauties, the contestants did not speak. Instead, the host narrated their walk across the stage. Now, absent this problematic (objectifying) portion of the program, contestants are free to speak throughout the pageant, and talk they have, endlessly repeating themselves. In making the contestants simply subjects, their object value as entertainers was completely sidelined.

The final loss of entertainment value was the purging of the iconic runway and theme song. The removal of these ritual elements further served to make the pageant reality rather than spectacle. Fans sat stunned in Boardwalk Hall, either out of boredom, despair, or simple confusion. "What happened to the pageantry?" some asked.[13] It was certainly no longer a pageant.

The pageant's period of greatest popularity has been attributed by most historians of Miss America to the leadership of Lenora Slaughter (served 1935–1967) first as executive secretary and then as organizer of the pageant. She transformed the Miss America Pageant by first and foremost building interest in the embattled pageant within the Atlantic City community itself.[14] Slaughter aimed to rebrand the pageant from a mere "flesh parade" to a respectable way for young women to aspire to an education and a successful career. She re-established the Boardwalk Parade; instituted scholarship awards and a talent competition;[15] shifted focus from swimsuits to evening gowns, which she termed "elegant wear"; and most importantly, created an army of local sponsors and volunteers from Atlantic City's high society. Slaughter capitalized on the support and direct involvement of local volunteers, leveraging their credibility and sparkling reputations in order to transform the reputation of the Miss America Pageant. The Hostess Committee, for example, was composed of Atlantic City's high society "ladies of the house," who were, and still are, charged with chaperoning the young contestants, ensuring their respectability. Throughout the years, residents of Atlantic City by and large have been supportive of the Miss America Pageant and celebrate its contestation each year, even as it is largely ignored in the rest of the country. To many residents of Atlantic City, Miss America is family, part of the city's storied history and identity; both the city and the pageant are a spectacle, both are a little shady, and both are embattled, struggling to survive in changing times.

My research for this book revealed many stories of the involvement of important local families in the Miss America Pageant over the years. Grandmothers, mothers, and sisters served as hostesses and on other committees; fathers served on the Miss America Pageant board, supported the organization by donating cars for the parade, or acted as local business sponsors or judges. Kate Shindle (Miss Illinois 1998) is herself a Miss America blueblood hailing from Brigantine Beach, across the bridge from Atlantic City. Her mother served as the head of the Hostess Committee, chaperoning contestants; her father worked pageant security and later was on its board of directors; and Shindle and her brother helped set up Convention Hall every year before the contestants arrived. All in all, everyone in Atlantic City social circles participated in some important way in the pageant. For them, the Miss America Pageant was the most important event of the year, and they were all an integral part of it: "Few people outside the zone between Philadelphia and the Atlantic Ocean . . . really understand the yearly arrival of the Miss America Pageant in Atlantic City . . . where I come from it's the Super Bowl and the Academy Awards rolled into one—but instead of watching it from afar, everyone you know is involved in making it happen . . . the entire community mobilizes to put on the big show—volunteering, driving contestants around, going to the parade. . . . Living as we do, a stone's throw away from Atlantic City, it's highly likely we will be in the pageant at some point."[16]

Local businesses played a major role in the pageant by providing volunteers, sponsorship, and services. The Miss America crown itself and its history provide a concrete illustration of the strong association that the residents and businesses of Atlantic City have for the Miss America

Pageant. Since 1920, the crown had been made by Schoppy's, a small trophy store in Linwood, New Jersey, just west of Atlantic City. When the pageant moved to Las Vegas in 2006, Schoppy's lost the contract to make the crown. Upon the pageant's return to Atlantic City in 2012, the contract was not renewed. As Dave Talerico, the manager of Schoppy's, told the *Press of Atlantic City*: "Taking the pageant out of Atlantic City was like taking the Packers out of Green Bay or taking the Mummers out of Philadelphia. It means more to us. It's part of our local identity."[17]

As previously described, the gay community in Atlantic City enjoyed special social and instrumental connections with the employees who returned every year to produce the pageant; in addition, many gay locals also had experiences volunteering or otherwise supporting the production. Jeff Wilson speaks about his heartfelt connections to the pageant:

> I grew up in Miss America. My mother was a chaperone for Miss America for years. . . . I grew up with my mom volunteering in the pageant so it was always a part of my life. As soon as I could volunteer myself, I was on the parade committee and special services which is the . . . ummm . . . they took care of the formers [former winners] when they would return as far as getting them into different appearances or book signings, or if they needed shopping done. We hosted them personally for the whole week or two that they were here. They [the Miss America Pageant] thought they were their own thing, but the city knew it was theirs, I mean AC, we were Miss America . . . even to this day it survives on the shoulders of its volunteers, but even more so back in the day. The city turned itself over to Miss America—the firemen, the police, the emergency management, people in droves volunteered to be chaperones, to be escorts, to do anything for the girls. I mean Miss America! [*Laughs.*] The city . . . I mean *she was ours*, and Miss'd America became ours, you know, unique, in itself, again, without being offensive. Again, over the years, sadly enough, Miss America lost a lot of that. I think Miss America may have started taking herself a little too seriously, and some-

times I am concerned that Miss America may have lost a lot of opportunities to maintain the level it used to have, its viewership, its regard.[18]

The feeling of ownership or community that Atlantic City locals associate with the Miss America Pageant is magnified in the gay community, where the Miss America Pageant represented friendship, fellowship, and support. All the drag queens who performed on New York Avenue in the old days spoke about the camaraderie built on shared experiences with the Miss America Pageant and later the Miss'd America Pageant. Wilson went on to describe the vibrant social scene on New York Avenue and the support for the Miss'd America Pageant shown by Miss America employees:

> You had a lot of the pageant people [attending the Miss'd America Pageant] because you know of course . . . the people who were supporting the [Miss America] contestants were the stylists, the hair and makeup people, the costume designers and gown designers, and it [Miss'd America] was their chance to come and blow off some steam, and . . . come and see just a fun parody of Miss America, and I will tell you, there was a time when I was volunteering for . . . the Miss America Organization, and it was the sort of thing where the big wigs [at Miss America] would say, you know, don't go there [to see the Miss'd America Pageant], because they are making fun of us . . . but, it was like, it wasn't like anyone was making fun of Miss America; it was just AC's sorta twist on it, and it was in no way meant to be offensive or derogatory to Miss America, or the contestants, or the organization in the local pageants; it was a celebration of Atlantic City and a way to decompress . . . it was the end of the season, and so it was also you know, for all of us living there it was a time, you know, to just exhale from all the craziness.[19]

So strong were these feelings of ownership and connection that the lighting designer and stage manager of the original Miss'd America Pageant, Joe Lazarus (née Lillian Larue), stated with certainty that the reason Miss'd America ceased when the Miss America Pageant moved to Las Vegas was because they felt "betrayed": "They forgot who they were. They took themselves too seriously. What was the point of doing an homage to an organization that had abandoned us? We lost who we were when they left, or at least we thought we did."[20]

Since this book was written, significant changes have happened in the Miss America Pageant. Gretchen Carlson, the mastermind of Miss America 2.0 and a contentious figure, has been fired from her position as pageant organizer. The community of Atlantic City, now weary of the way the pageant has been managed, the incremental exclusion of community members from volunteering positions, the great cost incurred by the city to run the pageant, and dwindling crowds, has left the fate of the pageant uncertain. In September 2019, the Casino Redevelopment Administration reported the absurdity of "the MAO [being given] $4.325 million last year to put on a show in a city that's considered a food desert,"[21] highlighting the lack of viability of large subsidies and the need for private sector solutions if the Miss American Pageant were to be renewed for 2020. On July 24, 2019, the Miss America Pageant announced it would be leaving Atlantic City for the Mohegan Sun Casino in Connecticut.[22]

MISS'D AMERICA: IS AC "COMING OUT"?

The future of the Miss'd America Pageant and the gay community in Atlantic City is likewise at a crossroads. As the Miss America Pageant takes leave of the city, having all but purged itself of the vestiges of its gay roots,[23] the Miss'd America Pageant has an opportunity to reimagine itself. Released from its honorary drag mother, Miss'd America could rise to iconic status in Atlantic City as the Miss America Pageant once did. The pageant has now moved to a new home at the Hard Rock Hotel and Casino just steps away from New York Avenue on the Boardwalk.[24] The Schultz-Hill Foundation (owners) has taken over the running of the pageant, and the ACGLBT Alliance has been dissolved. There is talk about potentially broadcasting the pageant on national television, and even creating a Miss'd America Parade.

At the same time, drag is having a resurgence of sorts in Atlantic City programming.[25] Three casinos have regular drag productions, most catering to bachelorette parties and straight crowds, featuring queens from *RuPaul's Drag Race*.[26] The impact of *Drag Race* on drag performance and drag culture is significant and largely beyond the scope of this book. The movement of drag into popular entertainment and popular culture can certainly be attributed in large part to the immense popularity of this reality show. The popularizing of drag has directly impacted the Miss'd America Pageant as much as its original muse, Miss America. Drag is no longer a local phenomenon, with local references. Queens are less campy and more polished; competitions are now costly, and therefore serious business. RuPaul's queens are now competing in Miss'd America, or Miss'd America contestants have gone on to compete on *Drag Race*.[27] Talent is now professionalized, and the pageant is likewise professionally produced and directed, a far cry from the skits enacted by local queens on the deck of Studio Six, on Mt. Vernon Avenue, with performances inspired by and beholden to local references, the gay community, the Miss America Pageant, or the crisis of AIDS.

Miss'd America is now a national pageant, and as such must answer to the larger gay and drag communities, rather than showcasing local concerns. For some, this engenders a feeling of remorse; to others it serves as a coming-out party. The way that drag in particular, and gender in general, are defined has changed significantly in recent years. Transgender queens, genderqueer queens, nonbinary queens, and bioqueens are challenging the definition of traditional drag and pressing for opportunities to compete. Drag queen Cherry Poppins related the sentiment of most young queens, who see drag as an art form separated from older premises about gender: "People associate drag with gender for some reason and I get the distinction; I see the confusion. Drag is an art form, it does not matter where on the spectrum you fall or what gender you express or feel; you are doing the art form. It's not a 'men dressing up as women' competition, it's a 'drag' competition. Drag is drag. Drag is performance with a transformation. It's testing boundaries. Dressing up as something you are not. It's growing and changing like any art form, it's undefinable."[28] Nicole Onoscopi adds: "I think gender should be removed from drag. It is an art form, it is traditionally a female presenting art form, but now that people are coming to the realization that gender is fluid and it's not black or white, I think that it is time that we re-evaluate what the rules are."[29]

Like its "drag mother," the Miss'd America Pageant will have to struggle with these changes to remain relevant. And although it continues under the umbrella of a local charity, supporting local causes in the LGBTQ community in Atlantic City, the growing movement of the pageant toward a national audience and standards of pageantry will be a challenge to maintaining local support and connections.

In the meantime, at street level, Atlantic City may be experiencing a second coming out of its own. Local queens, many having moved to Philadelphia, are returning to Atlantic City to perform. The New York Avenue Reunion (Show Us Your Pride) and the reopening of the old Saratoga Club as the restaurant Bourré in September 2018 has birthed a monthly drag brunch featuring local queens, hosted by former Miss'd America 2004, Brittany Lynn. In August 2019, the gay Club Unique opened in the Showboat Hotel, featuring a weekly drag show, "Putting on the Glitz," hosted by Sandy Beach. Rhythm and Spirits, a club on Tennessee Avenue, now hosts a weekly (gay) tea dance and drag show on Sundays, and there are plans to reopen the Rendezvous as a gay club with weekly drag shows on New York Avenue.

Living in Atlantic City, one sees the Miss America Pageant as one might a wayward child; and while the pageant may be brow-beaten and tarnished in the remainder of the United States, in Atlantic City it has retained its luster, a reminder of the days when Atlantic City was "America's Playground," one of the greatest resorts in the world, where people strolled the Boardwalk in their Sunday finest, the home to beauty queens and diving horses. With the Miss America Pageant leaving for a new home, and the rise of the popularity of drag pageantry, will the Miss'd America Pageant now rise to take its place as the iconic symbol of the glitz and showmanship that lies at the heart of Atlantic City's identity?

Winners of the Miss'd America Pageant

(SERVING AS MISS'D AMERICA FOR THE FOLLOWING YEAR)

Studio Six, New York Avenue (show in September, the Sunday after the Miss America Pageant) *(host Jeff Wilson, creative director Sandy Beach)*

1992 (no booklet-pageant)

1993 "Dream Squirrels" (no winner)

1994 Alexia Love "Casino: Not the Same Pageant without U at Studio Six"

1995 HRH Mortimer No theme

1996 Kiki Panadu / Lillian Larue "Sunstroke Blvd and Other Musical Tragedies"

1997 Chunkie Marinara "The Hunchback of Notta Dame: And Other Musical Mishaps"

1998 (Lemon Fresh) Joy Marnier "Hercurlers! And Other Hair-Raising Myths"

1999 Morgan Wells "Mule-Anne: And Other TiTanic Tales"

2000 Ms. Ten'e (Long) "TarzAnne: In the Swimsuit Adventure"

2001 Chlamydia Liverpool "Divas on Survivor Island"

2002 Miss Sheena "Expect the Unexpected: Ten Years of Mayhem and Merriment for a Good Cause"

2003 Claudia Dumont "Forever Blonde: A Satirical Look at TV
Reality Shows"

2004 Brittany Lynn "Gigli: The Musical"

2005 Andrea Lamour "Fair-In-Height 5'11"

–*No Miss'd America Pageant 2006–2009. (Miss America was produced
in Las Vegas from 2006–January 2013, and only returned to Atlantic
City in September 2013.)*

*In 2010, Miss'd America is taken over by the Shultz-Hill Foundation, run
by the ACGLBT Alliance, and expanded to attract a national contestant
pool. The rules are aligned with the Miss America Pageant and Miss Gay
America, to include swimsuit and evening gown portions. Sandy Beach is
"removed" from the process after 2011, although there are attempts to make
amends for this rift in later years. The show moves back to Saturday, but
sometimes is held weeks after the Miss America Pageant.*

Boardwalk Hall (show now in January)

2010 Michele LaCroix Dupree "This Isn't It!"

(host Carson Kressley)

2011 Kitty Hiccups "Boardwalk Empress" (host Suzanne
Westenheoefer)

2012 Sable Scities No theme

(host Michelle Visage)

Showboat, House of Blues

2013 Victoria (Porkchop) Parker "Circus"

(host Carson Kressley)

*The Miss America Organization returns to Atlantic City in September 2013
for the Miss America Pageant 2014.*

Harrahs, ProBar

2014 Honey Davenport "The 70s"

(host Carson Kressley)

Borgata, Music Box

2015 Fifi DuBois "SciFi"

(host Carson Kressley)

Borgata Event Center
   (host Carson Kressley)
   2016 Mimi Imfurst "Showgirls"
   2017 Pattaya Hart "America"
   2018 Adriana Trente "Broadway"
Hard Rock Casino & Hotel Soundwaves Theater
   (host Carson Kressley)
   2019 Sapphira Cristal "Superheroes"

In 2020, the ACGLBT Alliance is disbanded. The pageant is now run soly by the Schultz-Hill Foundation, and there are plans to expand its national visibility while maintaining its charter as a "drag pageant for men."

Drag Queens Interviewed in Field Notes, with Dates

Sandy Beach (Robert Hitchen),* September 28, 2017; January 16, 2018

Champagne Bubbles (Stephen James Markley), September 23, 2016; September 21, 2018

Tina Burner (Kristian Seeber), October 6, 2017

Cha Cha (Aaron Barrera), September 23, 2016; January 6, 2017

Sapphira Cristal (O'Neill Nichol Haynes), October 6, 2017; September 21, 2018

Honey Davenport (James Heath-Clark), September 21, 2018

Vias D'Kline (A. J. Makibbin), September 21, 2018

Fifi Dubois (James Mullady), March 12, 2019

Pattaya Hart (Methawee "Plu" Sayampol), October 6, 2017; October 7, 2017

Margeaux Haze (née Powell) (Hason Hayes), September 21, 2018

Mimi Imfurst (Braden Maurer-Burns), September 23, 2016

Lillian Larue (Joe Lazarus), July 18, 2019

Shelby Late (Ian Joseph), September 21, 2018

Shi-Queeta-Lee (Jerry VanHook), September 23, 2016

Ms. Ten'e (Long) (Ten'e Long), December 3, 2017

Alexia Love (AJ Jones), February 19, 2019; April 14, 2019

Brittany Lynn (Ian Morrison), December 3, 2017; April 14, 2019

(Lemon Fresh) Joy Marnier (Audwin King), December 3, 2017;
　　April 14, 2019

Farrah Mascara (Nicholas Makara), September 23, 2016

Morgan Morgan (Michael Edwards), October 6, 2017

HRH Mortimer (Mortimer Spreng),* September 22, 2016; March 3,
　　2017; April 14, 2019

Nicole Onoscopi (Cole Smith), September 21, 2019

Cleo Phatra (Bobby Goodrich), September 23, 2016

Cherry Poppins (Michael Samhat), September 21, 2019

Savannah Savonier (Jabarri A. "Ajae" Smith), September 23, 2016;
　　October 6, 2017

Roxi Starr (Larry Cook), September 23, 2016

Stasha Storm (Alexi Morales), September 23, 2016

Evelyn Syde (Benjamin Gaddis), September 21, 2018

Jenna Tall (Ashton Shawer), September 23, 2016

Adriana Trenta (Kevin Swanson), October 6, 2017; September 21, 2018

Boxxa Vine (Aaron Johnson), September 21, 2019

Morgan Wells (John Stanton),* December 3, 2017; April 14, 2018

Whendy Whaxwood (Ryan Viramontes), September 21, 2019

---

* Re-interviewed throughout the research process for clarification.

Original Miss'd America Theme Song

(LYRICS BY SANDY BEACH [ROBERT HITCHEN],
ORIGINAL MUSIC BY BERNIE WAYNE)

Boy have we missed America

That sense of fun we used to have

We're having a good time now in Atlantic City

To be a winner, you don't have to be pretty

She may even turn out to be

Your cousin from Schenectady

Boy have we missed America

The good times now, are here to stay

We picked a true beauty

She took the crown by storm

God knows what she's stuffed in her Maidenform

So there she is

Wearing big hair she is

Don't say it isn't fair she is

She's missed America

Notes

Note: The section headings in this chapter are derived from the drag and local lexicon of Atlantic City. The current marketing catchphrase for the resort community is "Do AC." The phrase "down the shore" is used by locals—New Jersey and Philadelphia residents—to describe a trip the beach. One does not go "to the beach" for a holiday, but "down the shore." "Gurl" is a term of endearment and solidarity used among drag queens or drag queens and their friends or allies. The phrase "how this bitch is turned out" is the way local drag queens describe the creation and running of a drag show like the Miss'd America Pageant. "Tea" is drag lingo for information, but often refers to gossip, or information that is disguised, and then revealed.

1. What is now known as Boardwalk Hall was previously called Convention Hall. When the new Convention Center was built in Atlantic City, in 1997 Convention Hall was renamed Boardwalk Hall to avoid confusion. In common parlance, Convention Hall now designates the large arena-like room where events like the Miss America pageant, stadium football, and concerts occur. Some literature and individuals use the names interchangeably in interviews and in print. However, most residents distinguish Convention Hall from the new Convention Center. In writing this book I use the name Boardwalk Hall unless naming it otherwise through direct quotation.

2. Field notes, August 2017.

3. Enoch "Nucky" Johnson, the Mob Museum, https://themobmuseum.org /notable_names/enoch-nucky-johnson/. Enoch Lewis "Nucky" Johnson inspired the Nucky Thompson character in the HBO television series Boardwalk Empire. He was the son of the powerful sheriff of Atlantic County and, following in his

father's footsteps, was elected Atlantic County sheriff in 1908. Johnson's approach was to rule Atlantic City with money and influence rather than violence: "Johnson ruled with a velvet hammer. His power was such that he never needed violence to get his way," Nelson Johnson, author of *Boardwalk Empire*, wrote in "Atlantic City's Next Gamble," an opinion piece for the *New York Times* in 2014. He personally profited from Prohibition and was under constant investigation by anticorruption reformers and the press. Johnson was eventually forced to resign but remained a powerful force in the Republican Party in Atlantic City until his death in 1968.

4. N. Johnson, *Boardwalk Empire*, 89.

5. Ralph Hunter, Atlantic City African American History Museum, personal communication, January 6, 2018; Henrietta Shelton, Chicken Bone Beach Historical Foundation, personal communication, October 16, 2018.

6. Simon, *Boardwalk of Dreams*, 6.

7. Simon, *Boardwalk of Dreams*, 46. The "midway" is a reference to the area that used to lie on the outskirts of the Victorian era Columbian Exposition held in 1893, what became known as the World's Fair. Though the exposition itself was a celebration of scientific discoveries and the advancements achieved in European (white) society, the midway offered more exotic attractions, eroticism, freaks of nature, and ofttimes criminality. People went to the midway to view the other, to gawk at the spectacle of the uncivilized. For a history of popular entertainment and the role of the midway and its "freak displays" in understanding culture, see Bogden, *Freak Show*. For a history of the racial aspects of the midway, see Bederman, *Manliness and Civilization*.

8. Simon, *Boardwalk of Dreams*, 46.

9. N. Johnson, *Boardwalk Empire*. For a history of the African American community in Atlantic City, see N. Johnson, *The Northside*.

10. According to the strict regulations, the Miss America Pageant forbids contestants from participating in potentially unsavory behavior. A fuller discussion of the code of conduct is found in chapter 3. The current policy can be found on the Miss America website (www.missamerica.org).

11. The AIDS epidemic resulted in the increased stigmatization of homosexuality worldwide in the 1980s and 1990s. This increased stigmatization of the gay "lifestyle" and increased homophobia in Atlantic City are reflective of this larger phenomenon. For a discussion of AIDS-related stigma among heterosexuals, see Herek, "Illness, Stigma, and AIDs," 103–150, and Herek and Glunt, "An Epidemic of Stigma," 886–891. For a description of stigmatization within the gay community, see S. Sengupta et al., "HIV Interventions to Reduce HIV/AIDS

Stigma," 1075–1087, and Peter Smit et al., "HIV-Related Stigma within Communities of Gay Men," 405–412.

12. Ritual enactments like pageantry may be understood as *revitalization movements* in anthropology. A revitalization movement is an inherently political movement, since it is an attempt to regain a sense of power or self-determination by a culture under significant stress or threat. Revitalization movements coalesce around a common value or practice that becomes a symbolic expression of that culture or subculture. In this case, drag performance can be seen as such a ritual enactment, and Miss'd America as a particular expression of Atlantic City's gay subculture.

13. *RuPaul's Drag Race* is a VH1 reality competition that premiered in 2009. Since then, *Drag Race* has been hugely popular, spawning a renaissance of drag performance in both the LGBTQ and the heterosexual community. Drag performance is now a part of popular culture rather than exclusively gay culture, largely due to the popularity of the show.

14. The Miss America Pageant was rebranded in 2018 by chairman Gretchen Carlson as Miss America 2.0 (Miss America Pageant Program 2019). This resulted in significant changes to the pageant's philosophy and structure, including the elimination of the swimsuit (fitness) competition, the runway, and the iconic theme song "There She Is, Miss America." The song was written in 1955 by Bernie Wayne, and most famously sung by Bert Parks each year.

15. From 2005 to 2013, the Miss America Pageant was held in January in Las Vegas, Nevada, rather than in Atlantic City. In 2014 the pageant returned to Atlantic City and moved back to its original date in September, the first weekend after Labor Day. Traditionally, Miss Americas selected in September are named Miss America for the following year.

16. "Cisgender" (sometimes cissexual, often abbreviated to simply cis) designates people whose gender identity matches the sex that they were assigned at birth.

17. Sandy Beach, field notes, 2019.

18. See appendix A, which lists the winners of the Miss'd America Pageant, the venues in which the it was held, and the hosts; and Appendix B, which lists the drag queens interviewed.

19. Printed program for the Miss'd America Pageant 2000, private collection of Robert Hitchen (Sandy Beach).

20. The Atlantic City Gay Lesbian Bisexual and Transgender (ACGLBT) Alliance is a nonprofit organization composed of individuals and businesses who support gay business and promote social justice for LGBTQ+ individuals in Atlantic City. The Alliance sponsors social events and currently runs the Miss'd America Pageant as its signature event. Proceeds from the event support local LGBTQ

causes, including MANNA (an organization feeding those infected with HIV/ AIDS), SJAA (the South Jersey AIDS Alliance), and an LGBTQ Activism Scholarship at Stockton University).

21. Fiona Moore, "One of the Gals Who's One of the Guys," 107.

22. See Barrett, *From Drag Queens to Leathermen*; Geczy and Karaminas, *Queer Style*; and Shaw and Ardener, *Changing Sex and Bending Gender*.

23. Bucholtz, "Editor's Preface," xv.

24. The term "boy name" was also used interchangeably with "birth name" by drag queen informants. Appendix B has a list of drag queens and, in some cases, members of their entourage who were interviewed for this book.

CHAPTER 1 — PAGEANTS AND PAGEANTRY

1. Field notes, September 10, 2017, Boardwalk Hall, Atlantic City.

2. The term "queered" refers to the queer origins of a practice, or the changes made to the practice originating in gay culture.

3. Shugart and Waggoner, *Making Camp*.

4. Esther Newton, "Role Models," 46.

5. King O'Riain, *Pure Beauty*; King O'Riain, "Making the Perfect Queen," 74–83.

6. For a discussion of the importance of studying popular culture, see C. Cohen, Wilk, and Stoeltje, "Introduction: Beauty Queens on the Global Stage";." Block, *Fan Phenomena*; Block, *Popular Culture Supplement*; Hancock, "Interview," 25–29; Hancock, Johnson-Woods, and Karaminas, *Fashion in Popular Culture*.

7. Brzuzy and Lind, *Battleground*; and C. Cohen, Wilk, and Stoeltje, *Beauty Queens on the World Stage*.

8. Miller, *Ancient Greek Athletics*, 140; and Crowther, "Male Beauty Contests in Ancient Greece, the Euandria and Euexia," 285–287.

9. Miller, *Ancient Greek Athletics*, 122.

10. Miller, 140.

11. Miller, 122.

12. Brzuzy and Lind, *Battleground*, 8; C. Cohen, Wilk, and Stoeltje, *Beauty Queens on the World Stage*.

13. Frost, "The Circassian Beauty and the Circassian Slave," 249.

14. Frost, 250.

15. Frost, 250.

16. Bogden, *Freak Show*, 238.

17. Frost, "The Circassian Beauty and the Circassian Slave," 251.

18. "Whiteness" is defined as a set of characteristics and experiences generally associated with having white skin and being a member of the white race. Anthropologists believe that race is a social construct, and as such, whiteness is a category

constructed in opposition to other socially constructed racial groups of color (nonwhite). Because whiteness is defined as the hegemony and people of color as the "other," whiteness comes with many privileges. Historically, the "exotic" presentation in freak shows was displayed in opposition to and to help define whiteness itself.

19. Bogden, *Freak Show,* 239.

20. Frost, "The Circassian Beauty and the Circassian Slave," 257.

21. Bogden, *Freak Show,* 26—28.

22. Prentice, *Miracle at Coney Island;* and for a fuller description of the quasi-scientific nature of these displays, see Prentice, *The Man Who Ran a Carnival Attraction That Saved Thousands of Premature Babies.*

23. "Ripley's Believe It or Not!: A Century of Strange."

24. Eltman, "A.C. Exhibit Pioneered Incubators for Premature Babies."

25. Riverol, *Live from Atlantic City,* 13. As this book was being edited, Atlantic City revoked its financial support for the Miss America pageant, and the organization moved its annual contest to The Mohegan Sun casino (Connecticut) in January of 2020. The pageant, although televised, received dismal ratings.

26. Quoted in Gay, "Fifty Years Ago, Protesters Took on the Miss America Pageant."

27. For books, see Watson and Martin, *There She Is, Miss America;* Oppliger, *Girls Gone Skank;* for dissertation, see Riverol, "The Miss America Pageant; and for articles, see Dow, "Feminism, Miss America, and Media Mythology," 127—149; Weintraub and Eisenberg, "The Shape of Things to Come," 246–247.

28. Shindle, *Being Miss America,* 18.

29. Gay, "Fifty Years Ago, Protesters Took on the Miss America Pageant."

30. *Miss America* (video). PBS, 2001.

31. Shindle, *Being Miss America,* 13.

32. Thursby, "Jean Bartel Dies at 87."

33. Gay, "Fifty Years Ago, Protesters Took on the Miss America Pageant."

34. For a more complete analysis of the ongoing feminist critique of beauty pageants, see Bordo, *Unbearable Weight;* Bordo and Jaggers, *Gender/Body/Knowledge;* Brzuzy and Lind, *Battleground;* Dow, "Feminism, Miss America, and Media Mythology," 127–149; Gay, "*Fifty Years Ago, Protesters Took on the Miss America Pageant*"; B. Roberts, *Pageants, Parlors, and Pretty Women.*

35. Brzuzy and Lind, *Battleground,* 35.

36. Banet-Weiser, *The Most Beautiful Girl in the World,* 64.

37. Carroll, "Miss America 2018 Pens Letter on Being Silenced."

38. See Hamlin, "Beauty Pageants and American Politics"; Hinojosa and Carle, "From Miss World to World Leader," 24; Hoad, "World Piece," 56–81; Jewel, *From*

Mammy to Miss America and Beyond; Oliver, *Queen of the Virgins*; K. Roberts, "Speech, Gender, and the Performance of Culture," 261–279.

39. C. Cohen, Wilk, and Stoeltje, *Beauty Queens on the World Stage*, 2.

40. Rousselle, "*Miss America Contestants Were Asked Politically Charged Questions.*"

41. Beranac, "10 Political Pageant Interview Questions."

42. United Press International, "*Beauty Queen Abdicates.*"

43. Rousselle, "*Miss America Contestants Were Asked Politically Charged Questions.*"

44. Rice, "Why Interview Miss America Contestants about Political Views?"

45. Banet-Weiser, *The Most Beautiful Girl in the World*, 2.

46. Banet-Weiser, 3.

47. See Foucault, *The History of Sexuality*; J. Butler, *Gender Trouble*; J. Butler, *Bodies That Matter.*

48. C. Cohen, Wilk, and Stoeltje, *Beauty Queens on the World Stage*, 8–11.

49. V. Williams and H. Williams, *You Have No Idea.*

50. Miss America Organization website, https://www.missamerica.org/ (viewed September 11, 2017).

51. Miss America Organization website, https://www.missamerica.org/ (viewed September 11, 2017).

52. Wilcox, "Is It Miss . . . or Myth America?,"?" C20–21.

53. Winfrey, "Miss America Pageant to Ignore Casino Gambling."

54. Shindle, *Being Miss America*, 69–70.

55. Kerr, "Penthouse Says Nude Photos Are Those of Miss America." Nude pictures of Vanessa Williams were published in the July 1984 edition of *Penthouse*. Subsequently, she was forced to resign as Miss America two months before the end of her reign.

56. Yan, "Vanessa Williams Gets Miss America Apology 32 Years Later."

57. Banet-Weiser, *The Most Beautiful Girl in the World*, 6.

58. Banet-Weiser, 7.

59. Williams and Williams, *You Have No Idea.*

60. Erin O'Flaherty, personal communication, September 22, 2018.

61. Whitestone, "An Interview with Heather Whitestone Callum."

62. Rita, field notes, 2016.

63. Miss America Organization website, https://www.missamerica.org/ (viewed January 31, 2020).

64. Erin O'Flaherty, field notes, 2016.

65. See Bogden, *Freak Show*; Lipsitz, *Time Passages*; Thomson, ed., *Freakery*, 1996; and Thomson, *Extraordinary Bodies*, 1996.

66. Miss America Organization website, https://www.missamerica.org/ (viewed September 11, 2017).

67. Deford, *There She Is*, 3.

68. See Napikoski, "What's Wrong with Beauty Pageants?," 2020, for a summary analysis of feminist critiques of beauty pageants, in particular, the Miss America Pageant.

69. See Shindle, *Being Miss America*; G. Carlson, *Getting Real*.

70. Banet-Weiser, *The Most Beautiful Girl in the World*, 14–15.

71. Shindle, *Being Miss America*, 29.

72. Rita, field notes, 2016.

73. A transgendered individual is a person whose sense of personal identity and gender does not correspond with the sex assigned to them at birth.

74. The Miss America Pageant has four main categories within its structure. Miss Gay America, Miss'd America, and many others have designed their pageants around this four part structure, while other drag pageants have incorporated selected pieces. The original contestation of the Miss'd America Pageant did not include swimsuit. Instead, the pageant opened with a parodical skit in which all the drag contestants participated.

75. Gillespie, "Miss Gay America Is Trying to Keep Drag Pageants Alive." The following are the most important drag pageants and the year they were first held: Miss Gay US of A, 1979; Miss Continental, 1980; Universal Show Queen, 1984; National Entertainer of the Year, 1991; Miss'd America, 1992; Miss National, 1994; Miss Gay International, 1999; All American Goddess, 2007.

76. Mimi Imfurst, field notes, 2016.

77. Evelyn Syde, field notes, 2018.

78. Goldstein, "Why Does Ru Paul's Drag Race Demonize Pageant Queens?"

79. Goldstein.

80. D'Addario, "Ru Paul's Aggressive Tirade in Defense of the Term 'Tranny.'"

81. Missed America Pageant, field notes, 2016—2018.

82. Although the definition of drag was an important aspect of all interviews with drag queens over the course of research for this book, the topic was fronted during interviews in 2018 and 2019, after transgender exclusion in the Miss'd America Pageant was challenged by former Miss'd America winner Honey Davenport. At the time of this writing, the pageant has kept its restrictions but has worked to clarify its policy.

83. Gillespie, "Miss Gay America Is Trying to Keep Drag Pageants Alive."

84. Alexia Love, field notes, 2018.

85. Fifi Dubois, field notes, 2018.

CHAPTER 2 — ATLANTIC CITY, DRAG CULTURE,
AND A COMMUNITY OF PRACTICE

1. Field notes, September 24, 2016.

2. For other definitions of drag and drag queens, see Rupp and Taylor, *Drag Queens*; Newton, *Mother Camp*.

3. This book is focused on drag queens rather than the equally interesting phenomenon of drag kinging. Those who research drag kings point to the many differences between these seemingly parallel forms of gendered performance. Certainly, drag queens have played a political role in the gay rights movement and in gay bars that is different from that of drag kings, and the stylistic aspects of their performance are also quite different. For an interesting comparative analysis of drag kinging and queening, see Horowitz, "The Trouble with 'Queerness.'"

4. R. Baker, *Drag—A History*, 13.

5. David L, "Communities of Practice."

6. Wenger, *Communities of Practice.*

7. David L, "Communities of Practice."

8. David L, "Communities of Practice."

9. Sandy Beach, field notes, 2017.

10. Alexia Love, field notes, 2018.

11. HRH Mortimer, field notes, 2016.

12. Actor, comedian, and drag queen Sandy Beach (Robert Hitchen) wrote, directed, and performed in the original Miss'd America Pageants at the nightclub Studio Six. Others credit John Schultz, owner of Studio Six, as its originator.

13. Originals, field notes, 2019.

14. Originals, field notes, 2019.

15. Originals, field notes, 2019.

16. Originals, field notes, 2019.

17. Originals, field notes, 2019.

18. Originals, field notes, 2019.

19. Originals, field notes, 2019.

20. Drag queens who are cis-women are termed "bio-queens" or "faux-queens." Transgender queens are sometimes referred to as "trans-femmes" or "trans-queens" in the drag community. There are also "genderfuck queens" or "anti-queens," who commonly identify as sexually ambiguous with fashion, gender identity, sexual identity, and/or sexual lifestyle. For an explanation of styles of drag queens, see P. Turner, "The 11 Most Common Styles of Drag."

21. Schacht and Underwood, *The Drag Queen Anthology*, 9.

22. According to Johnson, "Negotiating Style and Mediating Beauty," in Bantut pageantry, drag queens and the drag kings who support them maintain the gendered dynamics and power of men and women in Bantut society, respectively. This bolsters the often-stated position that drag queens assume the privilege of man within gay culture.

23. Hopkins, "'Let the Drag Race Begin,'" 140–141.

24. Adriana Trenta, field notes, 2017.

25. According to Iovannone, "Dancing on My Own," the "normate gay" refers to gay men who are slim, toned, white, cisgender, and able-bodied, and who express their gender in conventionally masculine ways, or who are seen as "straight acting." Gay male culture has many labels to define bodies, or types, that deviate from the ideal: hairless, muscled, slim, well-groomed, and attractive. Though alternate models of the physical ideal exist (for instance, bears, radical faeries, etc.), the focus on physical attraction and perfection is central to acceptance in gay male culture.

26. Stoeltje, "The Snake Charmer Queen," 11–30.

27. Stoeltje, 16.

28. Farrah Mascara, field notes, 2016.

29. Alexia Love, field notes, 2018.

30. Field notes, audience interviews, September 24, 2017.

31. Field notes, audience interviews, September 22, 2018.

32. See Newton, *Mother Camp*; Steven P. Schacht, "Four Renditions of Doing Female Drag," 157–180; Tewksbury, "Gender Construction and the Female Impersonator," 27–43.

33. Evelyn Syde, field notes, 2018.

34. Evelyn Syde, field notes, 2018.

35. Evelyn Syde, field notes, 2018.

36. Miss'd America Pageant, field notes, September 2016.

37. Anthropologists who study power make a distinction between *authority* and influence. While authority is the ability to express agency over oneself and others that is formalized by the social and political structure, influence is the possession of informal power. Influence is therefore seen as illegitimate or manipulative, lacking formal cultural validation. In the United States and most Western cultures, women traditionally have very limited access to formal authority and more frequently wield power through influence.

38. Miss'd America, field notes, September 2017.

39. Rupp and Taylor, *Drag Queens*, 31.

40. Stasha Storm, field notes, 2016.

41. Savannah Savonier, field notes, 2016.

42. Foucault, *Discipline and Punish*, 124–125.

43. Foucault, 135.

44. Johnny, field notes, 2016.

45. Sapphira Cristal, field notes, 2016.

46. Roxi Starr, field notes, 2016.

47. Jackie Beat and Sherry Vine, field notes, 2016.

48. Virginia Slimp (pseudonym), field notes, 2016.

49. Banet-Weiser, *The Most Beautiful Girl in the World*, 11–12.

50. J. Butler, *Gender Trouble*, 140.

51. Farrah Mascara, field notes, 2016.

52. Cha Cha, field notes, 2016.

53. Cleo Phatra, field notes, 2016.

54. The theory of performativity was first proposed by Judith Butler in *Gender Trouble* (1990) and *Bodies That Matter* (1993). It contends that there is no gendered self (subject); instead, gender is constructed through a repetitive performance of gender through stylized repetition of acts, a miming of the dominant conventions of gender. All gender is therefore "drag" in that, as RuPaul famously states in his memoir *Letting It All Hang Out* and later the song "Born Naked" (2014),"We are born naked, and the rest is drag." Drag, Butler claimed in *Gender Trouble* (188–189), is subversive in that it questions the normality of heterosexual scripts about gender, although she later admits that not all drag is subversive: "Drag is subversive to the extent that it reflects on the imitative structure by which hegemonic gender is itself produced and disputes heterosexuality's claim on naturalness and originality" (*Bodies That Matter*, 85

55. Cleo Phatra, field notes, 2016.

56. Cha Cha, field notes, 2016.

57. Cha Cha, field notes, 2016.

58. Halladay, "A Lovely War," 19–34.

59. Bérubé, *Coming Out under Fire*.

60. Rhyne, "Racializing White Drag," 183.

61. McCune, "Transformance," 151.

62. Spruill, "Ad/Dressing the Nation," 91.

63. Swarr, "Moffies, Artists, and Queens."

64. Rhyne, "Racializing White Drag."

65. *Shoobee* is a local word for tourist. It derives from the fact that day trippers to the beach used to bring their change of clothing in shoe boxes. This is a term found only in this region. In northern New Jersey shore towns, tourists are known pejoratively as *bennies*.

66. Jeff Wilson, field notes, 2019.

67. Evelyn Syde, field notes, 2018.

68. Cha Cha, field notes, 2017.

69. Pattaya Hart, field notes, 2017.

70. Newton, "Note to Reader," in *Mother Camp,* xx.

71. Merleau-Ponty, "The Body in Its Sexual Being."

CHAPTER 3 — NEW YORK AVENUE

1. HRH Mortimer (Mortimer Spreng), field notes, October 3, 2019.

2. Stegner, *A Sense of Place,* 2.

3. Austin, *How to Do Things with Words.*

4. J. Butler, *Bodies That Matter,* vii.

5. Certeau, *The Practice of Everyday Life,* 123.

6. Rupp and, *Drag Queens,* 59; Sisson, "How Gay Bars Have Been a Building Block."

7. Rupp and Taylor, *Drag Queens,* 12.

8. Simon, "New York Avenue," 309–312.

9. Simon, 310.

10. John Schultz, field notes, 2019.

11. "New York Avenue in the 1970s" Facebook page.

12. HRH Mortimer, field notes, 2016.

13. Jeanie, field notes, 2016.

14. Robert, field notes, 2017.

15. John Schultz, field notes, 2019

16. Frank, field notes, 2017.

17. John Schultz, field notes, 2019.

18. Simon, "New York Avenue," 303–304.

19. Simon, 304.

20. Simon, 300.

21. The same can be said for the relative neglect of African American history in Atlantic City, along with myriad other vibrant local histories. For a look at African American history in the region, see N. Johnson, *The Northside.*

22. Simon, "New York Avenue," 301.

23. Frank, field notes, 2016. The reoccupation of marginal spaces by gay communities is well documented. In Atlantic City this "undesirable" character stemmed from the city's economic demise as well as its racism, which increased with the influx of African Americans from the South.

24. Simon, "New York Avenue," 300.

25. Pendergast, "City Reborn," 1.

26. Jeanie, field notes, 2016.

27. Warren, "Suspicious Fire Guts $1.5 M Building."

28. Sandy Beach, field notes, 2016.

29. John Schultz, field notes, 2019.

30. The plan to redevelop the area around New York Avenue is named the Orange Loop because it is where the orange properties are on the Monopoly board game. The plan does not focus on reinvigorating the old neighborhoods (gay and black) but on the development of a new neighborhood.

31. HRH Mortimer, Joy Marnier, and Morgan Wells, field notes, 2017.

32. Georgette Watson, SJAA, personal communication, 2018.

33. Sandy Beach, field notes, 2016.

34. HRH Mortimer, field notes, 2016.

35. Alexia Love, field notes, 2018.

36. Miss'd America Pageant videos from Studio Six, 2003.

37. The SJAA was originally formed locally as South Jersey Against AIDS, Inc., spearheaded by John Schultz, and strongly supported by many in the local community. The independent organization was one of the first HIV/AIDS support organizations to be formed in the United States. SJAA later joined with the New Jersey state-funded South Jersey AIDS Alliance (SJAA). In 2019, the SJAA still provided services for those living with HIV/AIDS and education and prevention services in Atlantic City along with its outreach arm, OASIS. The SJAA is located on Gordon's Alley just off the Boardwalk in Atlantic City, one block from New York Avenue.

38. Don Guardian, personal communication, 2019.

39. Gould, *Moving Politics*, 10.

40. Gould, 15.

41. Gould, 45.

42. Robert, field notes, 2019.

43. In September 2019, the pageant moved to the Hard Rock Casino and Hotel.

44. Gary Hill, field notes, 2019.

45. Sandy Beach, field notes, 2016.

46. Miss'd America Pageant owner John Schultz remembers the name Miss'd America originating as a way to entice Miss America production staff to the show. Since they were always behind the scenes and "missed" the Miss America Pageant, Miss'd America provided production staff and contestants a way to view the show the following night. Sandy Beach and others involved in performing in the show remember the origins differently. They recall that the name originated as a spoof on the queens themselves, who were supposed to compete in the "real" pageant (Miss America), but because of extenuating circumstances "missed" it. The gag was always written into the skit that opened the Miss'd America Pageant through 2010, its first year in Boardwalk Hall.

47. Sandy Beach, field notes, 2016.

48. Reading is a way to "call attention to who someone is" so that they do not get "too full of themselves." Drag queens often use reading to put an uppity queen in their place. The Miss America Pageant, when seen as "taking itself too seriously," was a perfect target for reading.

49. The feminist protest of 1968–1969, modern critiques from liberal feminism, the failure of the casino industry, and the corruption of local government are all examples of the scrutiny faced by the Miss America Pageant and its home in Atlantic City.

50. Sandy Beach, field notes, 2016.

51. HRH Mortimer, field notes, 2016.

52. "Realness" in the gay/drag world refers to the ability to "blend" or "pass" as the opposite sex, or as heterosexual. With realness, camp sensibilities are muted. Realness was a strong cultural value among trans women in the ballroom scene in the 1980s. "The idea of realness is to look as much like your straight counter-part as possible," said Dorian Corey in the film *Paris Is Burning* (1990).

53. Miss'd America Pageant, field notes, 2018.

54. Tina Burner, Facebook post, September 20, 2018. To see Tina Burner's "political" in all categories of competition in 2017, see "Miss'd America 2017 (Tina Burner)" (YouTube video, 2017).

55. Sandy Beach, field notes, 2016.

56. HRH Mortimer, Morgan Wells, Joy Marnier, field notes, 2017.

57. Miss'd America Coming Home (Richard Helfant)" (YouTube video, 2009).

58. Miss'd America Coming Home" (YouTube video, 2009).

59. "Raw Video: There He Is! Miss'd America" (YouTube video, 2010).

60. Although the Miss'd America Pageant was held in Boardwalk Hall, it took place in the smaller Adrian Phillips Ballroom, not Convention Hall, where the Miss America Pageant was held.

61. "Miss'd America Coming Home (Sandy Beach)" (YouTube video, 2009). "Lucy the Elephant" is a famous landmark in Margate, New Jersey. A huge elephant that once served as a hotel, it is now a tourist destination beloved by locals, and often in need of saving from demolition.

62. Swimsuits were first worn in 2000. "TarzAnne: In the Swimsuit Adventure." This I discovered when I watch a portion of the pageant at John Schultz's home, from his personal collection.

63. Michele Dupre, *NBC Philadelphia Sunday Morning*, February 1, 2010.

64. Visage, "Michelle Visage Talks Miss'd America Pageant."

65. Alexia Love, field notes, 2018.

66. Field notes, 2018

CHAPTER 4 — CAMP AND THE QUEERING OF MISS AMERICA

1. Show Us Your Shoes Parade, field notes, September 9, 2018.

2. Patterson, "The Golden Girls Live."

3. Acland, introduction to *Residual Media*.

4. Patterson, "The Golden Girls Live," 2.

5. Mimi Imfurst, field notes, 2016.

6. Cleto, "Introduction: Queering the Camp," 2.

7. Shugart and Waggoner, *Making Camp*, 21.

8. Booth, *Camp*, 17.

9. As defined in Barrett, *From Drag Queens to Leathermen*, normative citation is a verbal or visual signal that expresses as identity, like homosexuality. Examples of normative citations might be an article of clothing (piercing in one ear, bandana), a physical gesture, a way of walking, or the use of camp language (shading, reading, using "gay" slang).

10. As cited in Harvey, "Camp Talk and Citationality," 1145–1165. Folk wisdom is a commonly held belief within a subculture—a shared worldview.

11. Barrett, 22.

12. Newton, *Mother Camp*, 37.

13. Newton, 64.

14. Morgan Wells' Drag Closet is the online store of costume designer and drag queen Morgan Wells. Wells's designs are purchased by many in the drag industry and have appeared on both *Project Runway* and *RuPaul's Drag Race* television shows. Morgan Wells (John Stanton) resides near Atlantic City, where she continues to perform in drag.

15. Morgan Wells, field notes, 2017.

16. Passing is the act of being convincingly "straight" (heterosexual) in public social interactions.

17. Cleto, "Introduction: Queering the Camp," 30.

18. Miss'd America Pageant, field notes, 2016–2018.

19. Barrett, *From Drag Queens to Leathermen*, 3.

20. Fifi Dubois, field notes, 2015.

21. Ochs, "Linguistic Resources for Socializing Humanity," 411.

22. Barrett, *From Drag Queens to Leathermen*, 9.

23. Barrett, 17.

24. Rivers, "Me but Not Me."

25. To "werk" is to play a role to perfection. One werks a dress on the runway, or a look on the street. A drag queen doesn't just walk on stage; she must walk on stage and werk her look. "Werking" is the performance of gender.

26. Evelyn Syde, field notes, 2018.

27. HRH Mortimer, field notes, 2018.

28. Rivers, "Me but Not Me."

29. As this analysis will later note, once Miss America 2.0 became a contest rather than a pageant, removing many of the vestiges of pageantry, drag queens and many local gay male admirers noted that the pageant was ruined because they now "take themselves too seriously."

30. HRH Mortimer, field notes, 1995.

31. Bronski, *Culture Clash*, 46.

32. Dyer, "It's Being So Camp as Keeps Us Going," 110.

33. Adriana Trenta, field notes, 2017.

34. Adriana Trenta, field notes, 2018.

35. PrEP, pre-exposure prophylaxis, is a drug available to be taken as prophylaxis for those at very high risk for HIV. Taken daily, the medicine can prevent HIV from taking hold and spreading throughout the body.

36. To be outed is to be publicly revealed as gay (or as a drag queen) by someone or something without your consent. In this case, Adriana Trenta was outed as a drag queen to her parents through the media.

37. Adriana Trenta, field notes, 2019.

38. See Barbuscio, "Camp and the Gay Sensibility," 40–57; Barrett, *From Drag Queens to Leathermen*; Booth, *Camp*; Cleto, "Introduction: Queering the Camp."

39. J. Butler, "Performative Acts and Gender Constitution," 519–531; Robertson, *Guilty Pleasures*.

40. Honey Davenport as quoted in Fairchild, "Watch This Drag Queen."

41. Margeaux Haze, field notes, 2018.

42. Barrett, *From Drag Queens to Leathermen*; Newton, *Mother Camp*; Rupp and Taylor, *Drag Queens*.

43. Barbuscio, "Camp and the Gay Sensibility," 45.

44. Dyer, "It's Being So Camp as Keeps Us Going," 114.

45. Farrah Mascara, field notes, 2016.

46. Cleto, *Camp Aesthetics*; Dyer, "It's Being So Camp as Keeps Us Going"; Newton, *Mother Camp*; Sontag, "Notes on 'Camp,'" 275–292.

47. Sontag, "Notes on 'Camp,'" 275–292.

48. Barbuscio, "Camp and the Gay Sensibility," 132.

49. Tina Burner, field notes, 2018.

50. Margeaux Haze, field notes, 2018.

51. See also Goodwin, *More Man Than You'll Ever Be*.

52. See also Goodwin, *More Man Than You'll Ever Be*.

53. Fifi Dubois, field notes, 2018.

54. Tina Burner, field notes, 2017.

55. MA2.0 program, 2018, 15.

56. MA2.0 program, 2018, 14–15.

57. See Booth, *Camp*; Malinowska, *The Aesthetics of Camp*; Robertson, *Guilty Pleasures*; Ross, "Uses of Camp," 308–329; Sontag, "Notes on 'Camp,'" 275–292.

58. HRH Mortimer, field notes, 2016.

59. Sandy Beach, field notes, 2016. Alternative stories of the origins of the chanting of "Show us your shoes" exist. Most versions feature one particular drag queen or another as the first to coin the phrase (attributions also go to Tree Top in other accounts). John Schultz retold the origins of the chant differently. He remembers that it was the brainchild of Bobby Johnson, who worked for him for many years and invented the chant when he crafted signs to hold up at the parade out of the Rendezvous bar. Whatever the exact origins, it remains the case that the chant originated in the gay community on New York Avenue and was chanted by the drag queens who occupied the apartments that framed New York Avenue and the Boardwalk. The chant spread down the Boardwalk from New York Avenue. After the first year of the chant, there were signs, megaphones, tee shirts, watches, and other paraphernalia with "Show us your shoes" printed on them before the parade was trademarked.

60. "Show Us Your Shoes Parade Preview: 2014 Miss America Competition" (YouTube video)

61. Marching.com, "Miss America Show Us Your Shoes Parade, Atlantic City."

62. From Atlanticcitynj.com, 2010, the official Atlantic City booster page of the Casino Redevelopment Authority, the group responsible for the redevelopment of the tourism industry in Atlantic City through redistribution of casino revenue.

63. Rossiello, "Show Us Your Shoes Parade."

64. Miss America Organization website, www.missamerica.org (2017).

65. Atlanticcitynj.com, https://www.atlanticcitynj.com/atlantic-city-stories/details.aspx?story=Here-she-comes-Miss-America.

66. Alexia Love and HRH Mortimer, field notes, 2017.

CHAPTER 5 — SHOW US YOUR SHOES, NOT YOUR MIDRIFFS

1. Miss'd America Pageant, field notes, 2016–2017.

2. Sandy Beach, field notes, 2016.

3. Rupp and Taylor, *Drag Queens*, 98.

4. Rupp and Taylor, 97.

5. Shi-Queeta-Lee, field notes, 2016.

6. Jenna Tall, field notes, 2016.

7. Adriana Trenta, field notes, 2017.

8. Farrah Mascara, field notes, 2016.

9. Cha Cha, field notes, 2017.

10. Lace fronts are the wigs worn by drag queens, so called because they are partially lined with lace. Human or synthetic hair is tied by hand to a sheer lace base, which goes over the front of the scalp. Lace front wigs are more popular among drag queens than full lace wigs because they are less expensive and sturdier in construction; the remainder of the wig is made out of a less fragile material which is less susceptible to tearing. Drag queens say they also prefer lace front wigs because they are versatile, allowing them to choose where to part and style their hair. Lace fronts are usually attached with glue and tape, applied to the front hairline. Once applied, the lace or lace front wig can stay in place for weeks at a time, but more importantly for drag queens, it can withstand the rigors of performance— sweating, dancing, even swimming.

11. Adriana Trenta, field notes, 2018.

12. Shelby Late, field notes, 2018.

13. Margeaux Haze, field notes, 2018.

14. HRH Mortimer, field notes, 2016.

15. Miss'd America Pageant, field notes, 2012, viewed tapes.

16. "Behind the Tiara: Randy Rainbow with Victoria (Porkchop) Parker" (YouTube video, 2013).

17. Lee, "My Bikini Moment in Miss America."

18. Rita, field notes, 2016.

19. Savannah Savonier, field notes, 2016.

20. Banet-Weiser, *The Most Beautiful Girl in the World*, 26–27.

21. As Melissa Dribben writes in the *Chicago Tribune*, the reinstatement of the two-piece swimsuit in 1997 brings into harsh focus the foibles of the Miss America Pageant and its inability to paint itself as a wholesome scholarship pageant while remaining interesting to its audience—an audience that wants a beauty pageant.

22. Gay, "Fifty Years Ago, Protesters Took on the Miss America Pageant."

23. Thursby, "Jean Bartel Dies at 87."

24. The two-piece swimsuit did not return to the Miss America Pageant stage for almost fifty years, until 1997.

25. Shindle, *Being Miss America*, 27–28.

26. The New York Radical Women coined concepts like "consciousness-raising" and slogans such as "Sisterhood Is Powerful" and "The Personal Is Political." They wrote formative essays and books about sex and gender roles and misogyny that laid the foundation for women's studies.

27. Gay, "Fifty Years Ago, Protesters Took on the Miss America Pageant."

28. The first black contestant for Miss America was Cheryl Adrienne Browne Hollingsworth, Miss Iowa 1970, and the first to be crowned Miss America was Vanessa Williams in 1983. Asian, Latino, Deaf, and Gay contestants have all recently competed and won since the lifting of Rule 7. After his daughters expressed their desire to become Miss America, the Philadelphia entrepreneur J. Morris Anderson created Miss Black America in 1968 so his children's ambitions would not be thwarted by American racism. The 1968 winner, Saundra Williams, reveled in her win. "Miss America does not represent us because there has never been a black girl in the pageant," she said afterward. "With my title, I can show black women that they too are beautiful." In 1971, Oprah Winfrey participated in Miss Black America as Miss Tennessee. The pageant, which continues today, is the oldest pageant in the country for women of color. Gay, "Fifty Years Ago, Protesters Took on the Miss America Pageant."

29. Protests surrounded the role of Miss America as a "death mascot" by entertaining the troops fighting wars overseas. In addition, the corporate sponsorship of Miss America has also been a rallying point around which the New York Radical Women focused its protests.

30. Gay, "Fifty Years Ago, Protesters Took on the Miss America Pageant."

31. Cramer, "Pageant Swimsuits Favored."

32. Banet-Weiser, *The Most Beautiful Girl in the World*, 25.

33. Lee, "My Bikini Moment in Miss America."

34. Shelby Late, field notes, 2018.

35. Missed America Pageant, field notes, 2016.

36. Rita, field notes, 2016.

37. Rita, field notes, 2019.

38. The term "uber femme" means different things in different communities. It can mean an overly flamboyant homosexual man or a butch lesbian. Among the drag queens interviewed, it was a reference to movie actresses and celebrities who portrayed unusually beautiful and strong women. Most often, these women openly express(ed) their sexuality, in opposition to social mores. Uber femmes (Mae West, Bette Davis, Beyoncé, Madonna) are gay male icons, and are sources of inspiration for drag personas.

39. By "illusion of femininity" I am referring to the ability to appear to be a woman. Sometimes this is directed toward "realness"—to pass for a woman—and sometimes to exaggerated characteristics of the female body that are viewed as camp expressions. In either case, the goal is to present oneself as not male.

40. *Stoning* is what drag queens call the process of enhancing costumes by placing rhinestones on them. Shoes, gowns, stockings, and bathing suits are all subject

to stoning as a way to make them more glamorous. In drag pageantry, the most common article of clothing that must be stoned is the evening gown. Shiny, sparkly, or glittery clothing is considered more beautiful. Rhinestones are attached with glue, sewn in place, or punched into fabric.

41. Jenna Tall, field notes, 2016.

42. *Drag families* are composed of *drag mothers* and their *drag children*. Traditionally and still in many cases today, drag families serve as support systems where biological families have been either unaccepting of their gay children or unavailable. A drag mother is a strong figure who is able to create and keep a "house" based on both her own success as a drag queen and as a support and mentor for her children. Drag mothers and older drag sisters may act as an important support mechanism outside of drag performance. Drag families sometimes carry on the last name of their drag mothers or drag houses. Davenport, Powell, and LaBeija are all examples of drag houses named after drag mothers. Drag children interviewed for this book spoke of their mothers as "saving them from the streets," "teaching me how to be a strong and responsible black, gay man," and "teaching me how to do everything, on and off the stage." Drag mothers interviewed bragged about the children that were coming up to "blow people away." Some drag families are known for their talent (for example, in this book, Pattaya Hart [dancer] is the drag mother of Adriana Trenta [dancer], Shelby Late [singer], and Sapphira Cristal [singer]. Drag families are especially influential in communities of color, where family support is more likely absent. In more loosely structured drag families, a drag queen can have more than one drag mother. Not all drag queens are members of drag families or identify with drag families. Some of the queens identified themselves as *drag orphans* but expressed admiration for certain queens who taught them things, or whom they admired and emulated.

43. Miss'd America Pageant, field notes, 2016.

44. Miss'd America Pageant, field notes, 2016.

45. L. Cox, "Fans Totally Unimpressed with Talent."

46. The *pageant platform* (now known as the *social impact initiative*) is a cause that each Miss America contestant chooses to volunteer her time for, to bring awareness to the cause, raise money, or implement a program she has created that will help address a social ill. The platform is in addition to the more recently implemented Miss America Serves, a program started in 2015 as a group effort to which all pageant contestants contribute, assisting a different charity each year.

47. Hamilton, "The 10 Toughest Pageant Questions."

48. Miss America Pageant, field notes, September 13, 2015.

49. Miss'd America Pageant Video, Private collection, John Schultz.

50. V. Williams and H. Williams, *You Have No Idea*.

51. Jeff Wilson, field notes, 2019.

52. "Meet Miss America 2017" (*People>bodies* video, Accessed August 2016). https://people.com/bodies/miss-america-first-openly-gay-contestant-hopes-to -break-another-ceiling/

CONCLUSION

1. A tea dance is a gay afternoon dance party. For more about the interesting history of the tea dance, see Kohler, "The Very Gay and Interesting History of the Almost Lost Tradition of the Sunday Tea Dance."

2. Sandy Beach, Sapphira Cristal, Morgan Wells, Jenna Tall, and HRH Mortimer, field notes, 2019.

3. See Simon, *Boardwalk of Dreams*, for a discussion of the African American and gay neighborhoods off the Boardwalk as "midway" spaces.

4. For a full description of the economic viability of New York Avenue in the 1970s, see Simon, "New York Avenue."

5. Simon, "New York Avenue," suggests that the city may have had a more prosperous future if city planners and local and state governments had invested in gay tourism, as was later the case in Rehoboth Beach, Delaware, and Asbury Park, New Jersey, which rose in popularity with vacationing gays subsequent to the demise of New York Avenue.

6. One indication of a strong community of practice is a period of nostalgia about its evolution.

7. Though many have written about the far-reaching impact of the AIDS epidemic on the gay community, many older drag queens interviewed for this book lamented the "generational divide" created by the impact of the AIDS epidemic.

8. Shindle, *Being Miss America*, 10.

9. Shindle, 12.

10. Shindle, 13.

11. Lee, "My Bikini Moment in Miss America."

12. Miss America Organization website, www.missamerica.org.

13. Miss America Pageant, field notes, September 9, 2018.

14. For more complete analysis of the history of the Miss America Pageant, see Deford, *There She Is*; Ric Ferenz in the video documentary "Miss America," *American Experience* 2002 (PBS); Osbourne, *Miss America*; Riverol, *Live from Atlantic City*; Shindle, *Being Miss America*.

15. Jean Bartel (Miss America 1943) was credited with suggesting that the pageant award scholarships, a suggestion that was incorporated into the pageant two years later by Slaughter.

16. Shindle, *Being Miss America*, 68.

17. DeRossier, "How the Miss America 'Crown'ing Glory Has Evolved."

18. Jeff Wilson, field notes, 2019.

19. Jeff Wilson, field notes, 2019.

20. Joe Lazarus, field notes, 2019.

21. Carroll, "Miss America Not Returning to Boardwalk Hall."

22. Carroll, "Miss America Leaving Atlantic City . . . Again." The new location of Miss America is somewhat ironic, since part of the behavioral codes of the Miss America Organization stated that contestants could not be photographed on a casino floor. For a discussion of the restrictions created at the advent of casino gambling, see Winfrey, "Miss America Pageant to Ignore Casino Gambling."

23. Because Miss America will now be held in Connecticut in December, the fate of the Show Us Your Shoes Parade is uncertain. The elimination of the parade would mark the purging of the most obvious manifestation of "camp" (gay culture) still remaining in the pageant.

24. The move of Miss'd America from the Borgata Hotel and Casino to the Hard Rock Casino was precipitated by a growing "discomfort" about the exclusion of transgender contestants from the pageant. This issue goes to the heart of redefinitions of "drag performance," and will undoubtedly prove to be a challenge for Miss'd America as it moves forward.

25. Zoppo, "Atlantic City's Dormant Drag Scene," and Amorosi, "Atlantic City Is Again Becoming a 'Drag.'"

26. *Diva Royale*, a weekly revue of celebrity female impersonators at the Tropicana Hotel and Casino, caters to bachelorette parties. *The Spice Girls Drag Brunch* was held on June 22, 2019, at the Golden Nugget Casino. *Dragapalooza*, a musical revue, was held at the Hard Rock Casino on August 10, 2019. The Borgata Hotel and Casino has regularly held drag queen revues twice a year. All of these productions feature *RuPaul's Drag Race* queens.

27. Victoria Porkchop Parker (2013) and Mimi Imfurst (2016) both appeared on *RuPaul's Drag Race* prior to winning Miss'd America. Alexis Michelle and Honey Davenport were first runner-up 2015 and Miss'd America 2014, respectively, before appearing on *Drag Race*.

28. Cherry Poppins, field notes, 2019.

29. Nicole Onoscopi, field notes, 2019.

Bibliography

Ackroyd, Peter. *Dressing Up: Transvestism and Drag, the History of an Obsession.* New York: Simon and Schuster, 1979.

Acland, Charles. Introduction to *Residual Media*, edited by Charles Acland, xii–xxvii. Minneapolis: University of Minnesota Press, 2006.

Amorosi, A. D. "Atlantic City Is Again Becoming a 'Drag:' Miss'd America Pageant Aside, There Is a Long Off-and-On History of Drag in and out of the Casinos." *Metro*, September 23, 2018. https://www.metro.us/news/atlantic-city-again-becoming-drag.

Amusements section. *New York Times*, May 31, 1920.

Argetsinger, Amy. "It's Not Just about Bikinis: Inside the Battle for the Future of Miss America." *Washington Post*, July 25, 2018.

Arriola, E. R. "Faeries, Marimachas, Queens, and Lezzies: The Construction of Homosexuality before the 1969 Stonewall Riots." *Columbia Journal of Gender and Law* 5(1) (1995). https://doi.org/10.7916/cjgl.v5i1.2378.

Associated Press. "Miss America Hopefuls Show Their Shoes in Boardwalk Parade." AP, September 8, 2018. https://www.gazettextra.com/entertainment/miss-america-hopefuls-show-their-shoes-in-boardwalk-parade/article_da1542b0-39c2-5433-a406-a7f92acf90a5.html.

Atlantic City Board of Education. *Annual Reports.* Atlantic City, NJ, 1902–1959.

Atlantic City Board of Trade. *Annual Directory.* Atlantic City, NJ, 1939–1947.

Atlantic City Press. "All's Fair in Love, War Talks for Pageant." *Atlantic City Press*, July 23, 1970.

Austin, J. L. *How to Do Things with Words.* Cambridge, MA: Harvard University Press, 1975.

Babuscio, J. "The Cinema of Camp (aka Camp and Gay Sensibility)." In *Camp: Queer Aesthetics and the Performing Subject; A Reader*, edited by F. Cleto, 117–135. Ann Arbor: University of Michigan Press, 1999.

Bailey, William A. "The Importance of HIV Prevention Programming to the Lesbian and Gay Community." In *AIDS, Identity, and Community: The HIV Epidemic and Lesbians and Gay Men*, edited by Gregory M. Herek and Beverly Greene, 210–225. Thousand Oaks, CA: Sage Publications, 1995.

Baker, Paul. "Polari, a Vibrant Language Born out of Prejudice." *The Guardian*, May 24, 2010.

Baker, Roger. *Drag: A History of Female Impersonation in the Performing Arts*. London: Cassell, 1994.

Balogun, Oluwakemi M. "Cultural and Cosmopolitan Idealized Femininity and Embodied Nationalism in Nigerian Beauty Pageants." *Gender and Society*, March 26, 2012.

Banet-Weiser, Sarah. *The Most Beautiful Girl in the World: Beauty Pageants and National Identity*. Los Angeles: University of California Press, 1999.

Banner, Lois W. *American Beauty*. New York: Knopf, 1983.

Barba, Eugenio. Introduction to *The Secret Art of the Performer*, edited by Eugenio Barba and Nicola Savrese, translated by Richard Fowler. London: Routledge, 1991.

Barbuscio, J. "Camp and the Gay Sensibility." In *Gays and Film*, edited by R. Dyer, 40–57. London: BFI, 1977.

Barkly, Sandra Lee. *Femininity and Domination: Studies in the Phenomenology of Oppression*. New York: Routledge, 1990.

Barnes, Natasha B. "Face of the Nation: Race, Nationalisms and Identities in Jamaican Beauty Pageants." *Massachusetts Review* 35 (3/4) (1994): 471–492.

———. "Representing the Nation: Gender, Culture, and the State in Anglophone Caribbean Society." PhD diss., University of Michigan, 1995.

Barrett, Rusty. "The 'Homo-genius' Speech Community." In *Queerly Phrased: Language, Gender and Sexuality*, Anna Livia and Kira Hall, eds. 181–201. New York: Oxford University Press, 1997.

———. *From Drag Queens to Leathermen: Language, Gender and Gay Male Subcultures*. New York: Oxford University Press, 2017.

Bauerline, Valerie "Miss America's Finances Uncertain as It Fights for Relevance." *Wall Street Journal*, August 3, 2019. https://www.wsj.com/articles/miss-americas-finances-uncertain-as-it-fights-for-relevance-1533288600.

Bauman, Richard. *Verbal Art as Performance*. Prospect Heights, IL: Waveland Press, 1977.

Bederman, Gail. *Manliness and Civilization: A Cultural History of Gender and Race in the United States, 1880–1917*. Chicago: University of Chicago Press, 1995.

Beranac, Nusreta. "10 Political Pageant Interview Questions." *Insider Monkey*, June 28, 2017.

Bergman, David. *Camp Grounds: Style and Homosexuality*. Boston: University of Massachusetts Press, 1993.

Berkowitz, D., and L. L. Belgrave. "She Works Hard for the Money": Drag Queens and the Management of Their Contradictory Status of Celebrity and Marginality." *Journal of Contemporary Ethnography* 39 (2010): 159–186.

Berkowitz, D., L. Belgrave, and R. A. Halberstein. "The Interaction of Drag Queens and Gay Men in Public and Private Spaces." Journal of Homosexuality 52 (2007): 11–32.

Berlant, Lauren. *The Queen of America Goes to Washington City: Essays on Sex and Citizenship*. Durham, NC: Duke University Press, 1997.

Bernard, Diane. "Swimsuits Are Gone from Miss America, but the Relationship Was Always Complicated." *Washington Post*, September 9, 2018. https://www.washingtonpost.com/news/retropolis/wp/2018/09/09/swimsuits-are-gone-from-miss-america-but-the-relationship-was-always-complicated/?utm_term=.c2a2935b5b66.

Bérubé, Allan. *Coming Out under Fire: The History of Gay Men and Women in World War II*. New York: Free Press, 1990.

Billings, Sabrina. "Speaking Beauties: Linguistic Posturing, Language Inequality, and the Construction of a Tanzanian Beauty Queen." *Language in Society* 38 (5) (2009): 581–606.

Bishop, C. J., M. Kiss, T. G. Morrison, D. M. Rushe, and J. Specht. "The Association between Gay Men's Stereotypic Beliefs about Drag Queens and Their Endorsement of Hypermasculinity." *Journal of Homosexuality* 61 (2014): 554–567.

Block, Marcelline. *Fan Phenomena: Marilyn Monroe*. Durham, NC: Intellect, 2015.

———. *Popular Culture Supplement*. Durham, NC: Intellect, 2019.

Bogdan, Jennifer. "Miss America Pageant Will Get $7.3M to Return to Atlantic City." *Press of Atlantic City*, April 15, 2013.

Bogden, Robert. *Freak Show: Presenting Human Oddities for Fun and Profit*. Chicago: University of Chicago Press, 1988.

Booth, Mark. *Camp*. London: Quartet Books, 1983.

Bordo, Susan. *Unbearable Weight: Feminism, Western Culture, and the Body*. Berkeley: University of California Press, 1993.

Bordo, Susan, and Allison M. Jaggers, eds. *Gender/Body/Knowledge: Feminist Reconstructions of Being and Knowing*. New Brunswick, NJ: Rutgers University Press 1989.

Bourdieu, P. *Language and Symbolic Power*. Cambridge, MA: Harvard University Press, 1991.

Boustany, Nora. "The Beauty Queen Exiled for a Smile." *Washington Post*, May 19, 1994.

Britton, A. "For Interpretation: Notes against Camp." In *Camp: Queer Aesthetics and the Performing Subject; A Reader*, edited by Fabio Cleto, 136–142. Ann Arbor: University of Michigan Press,1999.

Bronski, Michael. *Culture Clash: The Making of Gay Sensibility*. Boston: South End Press, 1984.

Brzuzy, Stephanie, and Amy Lind, eds. *Battleground: Women, Gender, and Sexuality*. Westport, CT: Greenwood Press, 2008.

Bucholtz, Mary. Editor's preface to *From Drag Queens to Leathermen: Language, Gender, and Gay Male Subcultures*, by Rusty Barrett, xv–xvi. New York: Oxford University Press, 2017.

———. "You da Man: Narrating the Racial Other in the Linguistic Production of White Masculinity." *Journal of Sociolinguistics* 3(4) (1999): 443–460.

Bucholtz, Mary, and Kira Hall. "Theorizing Identity in Language and Sexuality Research." *Language in Society*. 33 (4) (September 2004): 469–515.

Butler, Judith. *Bodies That Matter*. New York: Routledge, 1993.

———. Gender Trouble: Feminism and the Subversion of Identity. New York: Routledge, 1990.

———. "Performative Acts and Gender Constitution: An Essay." *Phenomenology and Feminist Theory Theatre Journal*. 40 (4) (December 1988): 519–531.

Butler, Paul. "Embracing AIDS: History, Identity, and Post-AIDS Discourse." *JAC* 24(1) (2004): 93–111.

Canby, Vincent. "Film: Miss . . . or Myth? On Beauty Pageants." *New York Times*, September 16, 1987.

Carlson, Gretchen. *Getting Real*. New York: Viking Press, 2015.

Carlson, Marvin. *Performance: A Critical Introduction*. New York: Routledge, 1996.

Carroll, Lauren. "Miss America Leaving Atlantic City . . . Again." *Press of Atlantic City*, July 24, 2019.

———. "Miss America Not Returning to Boardwalk Hall." *Press of Atlantic City*, April 11, 2019.

———. "Miss America Ratings Continue to Plummet." *Press of Atlantic City*, September 10, 2018.

———. "Miss America 2018 Cara Mund Pens Letter on Being 'Silenced.'" *Press of Atlantic City*, August 17, 2018. https://www.pressofatlanticcity.com/missamerica /miss-america-cara-mund-pens-letter-on-being-silenced/article_68b1d407-7716 -540b-a02a-d15816a915c9.html.

———. "Schoppy's Matriarch Was Integral Part of Miss America." *Press of Atlantic City*, January 4, 2019.

Casino Connection. "Miss'd America Pageant Takes Place September 21." *Casino Connection* 10(12) (2013). http://casinoconnectionac.com/issue/vol-10-no-12 -september-12-2013/article/miss-d-america-pageant-takes-place-sept-21.

Certeau, Michel de. *The Practice of Everyday Life*. Berkeley: University of California Press, 1984.

Chauncey, G. *Gay New York: Gender, Urban Culture, and the Making of the Gay Male World, 1890–1940*. New York: Basic Books, 1994.

Chira, Susan. "First Black Miss America Finds Unforeseen Issues." *New York Times*, April 13, 1984.

———. "To First Black Miss America, Victory Is a Means to an End." *New York Times*, September 19, 1983.

Chow, Yiu Fai. "Moving, Sensing Intersectionality: A Case Study of Miss China Europe." *Signs: Journal of Women in Culture and Society* 36(2) (2011): 411.

"Circassian Beauty Exhibit." The Lost Museum, City University of New York, 2018. https://lostmuseum.cuny.edu/archive/exhibit/star.

Cleto, Fabio, ed. *Camp: Queer Aesthetics and the Performing Subject; A Reader*. Ann Arbor: University of Michigan Press, 1999.

———. "Introduction: Queering the Camp." In *Camp: Queer Aesthetics and the Performing Subject: A Reader*, edited by Fabio Cleto, 1–42. Ann Arbor: University of Michigan Press, 1999.

Cohen, Colleen Ballerino, Richard Wilk, and Beverly Stoeltje, eds. *Beauty Queens on the World Stage: Gender, Contests, and Power*. New York: Routledge, 1996.

———. "Introduction: Beauty Queens on the Global Stage." In *Beauty Queens on the World Stage: Gender, Contests, and Power*, edited by Cohen, Wilk, and Stoelje. New York: Routledge, 1996.

Cohen, Richard. "Pageant of Hypocrisy." *New York Times*, July 25, 1984.

Coles, Charlotte. "The Question of Power and Authority in Gender Performance: Judith Butler's Drag Strategy." *eSharp* (University of Glasgow), no. 9 (2007): 1–18.

Cox, Lauren. "Fans Totally Unimpressed with Talent." *HollywoodLife*, September 11, 2016.

Cox, Lauren and Richard Fay. "Gayspeak, the Linguistic Fringe: Bona Polari, Camp, Queerspeak and Beyond." In *The Margins of the City*, edited by S. Whittle, 103–127. Aldershot: Arena/Ashgate Publishing, 1994.

CRDA. "Here She Comes Miss America." *MYAC, CRDA*, September 2013. http:// www.atlanticcitynj.com/atlantic-city-stories/details.aspx?story=Here-she -comes-Miss-America.

Craig, Maxine Leeds. *Ain't I a Beauty Queen? Black Women, Beauty, and the Politics of Race*. Oxford: Oxford University Press, 2002.

Cramer, Robert. "Pageant Swimsuits Favored." *Atlantic City Press*, September 13, 1970.

Crawford, M., G. Kerwin, A. Gurung, D. Khati, P. Jha, and A. C. Regmi. 2008. "Globalizing Beauty: Attitudes toward Beauty Pageants among Nepali Women." *Feminism and Psychology* 18 (1) (2008): 61–86.

Crowther, Nigel B. "Male Beauty Contests in Ancient Greece, the Euandria and Euexia." *AC* 54 (1985): 285–291.

Csordes, Thomas J. "Embodiment as a Paradigm for Anthropology." *Ethos*18 (1) (March 1990): 5–47.

D'Addario, Daniel. "Ru Paul's Aggressive Tirade in Defence of the Term 'Tranny.'" *Salon*, May 27,2014. https://www.salon.com/2014/05/27/rupauls_aggressive _tirade_in_defense_of_the_term_tranny/.

David L. "Communities of Practice (Lave and Wenger)." In *Learning Theories*, July 16, 2014. https://www.learning-theories.com/communities-of-practice-lave -and-wenger.html.

Davis, Kathy. "Remaking the She-Devil: A Critical Look at Feminist Approaches to Beauty." *Hypatia* 6 (Spring 1991): 21–43.

Davis, Kathy. *Reshaping the Female Body: Dilemma of Cosmetic Surgery*. New York: Routledge, 1995.

Deake, David. "Gay Activist or Beauty Queen?" *Theater Week*, August 3, 1991.

de Beauvoir, Simone. *The Second Sex*. Translated by H. M. Parshley. New York: Vintage, 1974.

Deford, Frank. *There She Is: The Life and Times of Miss America*. New York: Viking Press, 1971.

Denetdale, Jennifer Nez. "Chairmen, Presidents, and Princesses: The Navajo Nation, Gender, and the Politics of Tradition." *Wicazo Sa Review* 21(1) (2006): 9–28.

deRossier, John. "How the Miss America 'Crown'ing Glory Has Evolved." *Press of Atlantic City*, August 3, 2016.

Dow, Bonnie J. "Feminism, Miss America, and Media Mythology." *Rhetoric and Public Affairs* 6(1) (2003): 127–149.

Dribben, Melissa. "Miss America Pageant Bares the Truth with Move to 2-Piece Swimsuits." *Chicago Tribune*, July 25, 1997.

Dugan, Kimberly B. "Just Like You: The Dimensions of Identity Presentations in an Antigay Contested Context." In *Identity Work in Social Movements*, edited by Jo Reger, Daniel J. Myers, and Rachel L. Einwohner, 21–46. Minneapolis: University of Minnesota Press, 2008.

Dworkin, Susan. *Miss America 1945: Bess Myerson's Own Story*. New York: Newmarket Press, 1987.

Dyer, Richard. "It's Being So Camp as Keeps Us Going." In *Camp: Queer Aesthetics and the Performing Subject: A Reader*, edited by Fabio Cleto, 110–116. Ann Arbor: University of Michigan Press, 1999.

Eltman, Frank. "A.C. Exhibit Pioneered Incubators for Premature Babies." *Press of Atlantic City*, August 3, 2015.

Erlanger, Steven. "There She Is: Valley Girl Wins the Heart of Siam." *New York Times*, October 19, 1988.

Ewen, Stuart, and Elizabeth Ewen. *Channels of Desire: Mass Images and the Shaping of American Consciousness*. New York: McGraw-Hill, 1982.

Fairchild, Phaylen. "Watch This Drag Queen Call Out Racism in Spectacular Fashion." Medium.com, September 13, 2018. https://medium.com/@Phaylen /watch-this-drag-queen-call-out-racism-in-spectacular-fashion-a308521655d2.

Fein, Esther B. "Miss America Denies Giving Consent to Run Nude Photos." *New York Times*, July 23, 1984.

———. "Miss America Gives Up Her Crown." *New York Times*, July 24, 1984.

———. "Support Awaits Miss America at Home." *New York Times*, July 22, 1984.

Feinberg, Leslie. *Transgender Warriors: Making History from Joan of Arc to Ru Paul*. Boston: Beacon Books, 1996.

Fleisher, Julian. *The Drag Queens of New York: An Illustrated Field Guide*. New York: Riverhead Books, 1996.

Foucault, Michel. *Discipline and Punish: The Birth of the Prison*. Translated by Alan Sheridan. New York: Pantheon Books, 1977.

———. *The History of Sexuality*. Translated by Robert Hurley. New York: Pantheon, 1978.

Fox, Richard Wightman. "The Miss America Pageant: A Scholarship Organization." *Z Magazine*, December 1990.

Fried, Gregory. "A Freakish Whiteness: The Circassian Lady and the Caucasian Fantasy." *Mirror of Race*, March 15, 2013. http://mirrorofrace.org/circassian/.

Frost, Linda. "The Circassian Beauty and the Circassian Slave: Gender, Imperialism, and American Popular Culture." In *Freakery: Cultural Spectacles of the Extraordinary Body*, edited by Rosemarie T. Garland Thompson, 248–263. New York: New York University Press, 1996.

Funnel, Charles. *By the Beautiful Sea*. New York: Knopf, 1975.

Gallop, Jane. *Thinking through the Body*. New York: Columbia University Press, 1988.

Garber, Marjorie. *Vested Interests: Cross-Dressing and Cultural Anxiety*. New York: Routledge, 1997.

Gay, Roxane. "Fifty Years Ago, Protesters Took on the Miss America Pageant and Electrified the Feminist Movement." *Smithsonian Magazine*, January 2018.

Geczy, Adam, and Vicki Karaminas. *Queer Style*. New York: Bloomsbury, 2013.

Geertz, Clifford. "Blurred Genres: The Refiguration of Thought." In *Local Knowledge: Further Essays in Interpretive Anthropology*. New York: Basic Books, 1983.

Germann, Olivia. "Gender Performance: From the Freak Show to Modern Drag." *Digital Literature Review* (Ball State University) 3 (2016): 66–76. http://bsuenglish.com/dlrOLD/past/issue3_germann.pdf.

Gettleman, Jeffrey. "There She Isn't: Miss America Pageant Leaves Atlantic City." *New York Times*, August 26, 2005.

Gilbert, Sandra. "Costumes of the Mind: Transvestism as Metaphor in Modern Literature." *Critical Inquiry*, 1980, 391–417.

Gillespie, Tyler. "Miss Gay America Is Trying to Keep Drag Pageants Alive." *Vice*, October 9, 2017.

Giroux, H. A. *Impure Acts: The Practical Politics of Cultural Studies*. New York: Routledge, 2000.

Glassberg, David. *American Historical Pageantry*. Chapel Hill: University of North Carolina Press, 1990.

Goddard, Richlyn. "Three Months to Hurry and Nine Months to Worry: Resort Life for African Americans in Atlantic City, NJ (1850–1940)." PhD diss., Howard University, 2001.

Goffman, Erving. *Frame Analysis*. Garden City, NY: Doubleday, 1974.

———. *The Presentation of Self in Everyday Life*. Garden City, NJ: Doubleday, 1959.

———. *Stigma: Notes on the Management of Spoiled Identity*. Englewood Cliffs, NJ: Prentice-Hall, 1963.

Golden, Janet. "About Those Boardwalk Baby Incubators." *Metropolis*, October 8, 2010.

Goldman, William. *Hype and Glory*. New York: Random House, 1990.

Goldstein, Kayla. "Why Does Ru Paul's Drag Race Demonize Pageant Queens?" *Wussy*, May 10, 2016.

Goodwin, J. P. *More Man Than You'll Ever Be: Gay Culture and Acculturation in Middle America*. Bloomington: Indiana University Press, 1989.

Gould, Deborah B. *Moving Politics: Emotion and ACTUP's Fight against AIDS*. Chicago: University of Chicago Press, 2009.

Gray, Daphne. *Yes, You Can, Heather! The Story of Heather Whitestone, Miss America 1995*. Grand Rapids, MI: Zondervan Publishing House, 1995.

Haag, Matthew, and Cara Buckley. "Miss America Ends Swimsuit Competition, Aiming to Evolve in 'This Cultural Revolution.'" *New York Times*, June 5, 2018. https://www.nytimes.com/2018/06/05/business/miss-america-swimsuit.html.

Halberstam, Judith. *Female Masculinity*. Durham, NC: Duke University Press, 1998.

Hall, Stuart. "Notes on Deconstructing the Popular." In *People's History and Social Theory*, edited by Raphael Samuel, 227–241. London: Routledge and Kegan Paul, 1981.

Halladay, Laurel. "A Lovely War: Male and Female Cross-Dressing and Canadian Military Entertainment in World War II." In *The Drag Queen Anthology: The Absolutely Fabulous but Flawlessly Customary World of Female Impersonators*, edited by Steven P. Schacht and Lisa Underwood, 19–34. New York: Harrington Park Press, 2004.

Halliday, M.A.K. "Anti-Languages." *American Anthropologist* 78 (3) (1976): 570–584.

Hamashima, Mariko. "Beauty in the Indigenous Pageant: The Cultural and Social Relevance of Miss Samoa." Independent Study Project (ISP) Collection. 1486, 2012. https://digitalcollections.sit.edu/isp_collection/1486.

Hamilton, Mary. "The 10 Toughest Pageant Questions and How to Answer Them." *The Pageant Planet* (TPP), June 26, 2016.

Hamlin, Jennifer. "Beauty Pageants and American Politics." *Origins* (blog). Ohio State and Miami University, September 9, 2016.

Hancock, Joseph H. II. "Interview." In *Fashion, Style & Popular Culture*, 2–3, Wilmington, NC: Intellect Books, 2013. https://www.scribd.com/document/134040528/Intellect-Fashion-Supplement

Hancock, Joseph H. II, Toni Johnson-Woods, and Vicki Karaminas, eds. *Fashion in Popular Culture: Literature, Media, and Contemporary Studies*. Chicago: University of Chicago Press, 2013.

Harris, Daniel. "The Aesthetics of Drag." *Salmagundi*, no. 108 (Fall 1995): 62–74.

Harvey, Keith. "Camp Talk and Citationality: A Queer Take on 'Authentic' and 'Represented' Utterance." *Journal of Pragmatics* 34 (2002): 1145–1165.

––––––. "Describing Camp Talk: Language/Pragmatics/Politics." *Language and Literature* 9(3) (2000): 240–260.

Haynes, Karima A. "Miss America from Vanessa Williams to Kimberly Aiken: Is the Crown a Stumbling Block or Steppingstone?" *Ebony*, January 3, 1994, 42–46.

Herek, G. M. "Illness, Stigma, and AIDS." In *Psychological Aspects of Serious Illness*, edited by P. Costa and G. R. Vanden Bos, 103–150. Washington, DC: Proceedings of the American Psychological Association, 1990.

Herek, Gregory M., and Eric K Glunt. "An Epidemic of Stigma: Public Reactions to AIDS." *American Psychologist* 43(11) (1988): 886–891.

––––––. "Identity and Community among Gay and Bisexual Men in the AIDS Era: Preliminary Findings from the Sacramento Men's Health Study." In *AIDS, Identity, and Community: The HIV Epidemic and Lesbians and Gay Men*, edited by Gregory M. Herek and Beverly Greene, 55–84. Thousand Oaks, CA: Sage Publications, 1995.

Hickey, Neil. "There She Is . . . : or, Through the Years with Bert Parks and Miss America." *TV Guide*, September 5, 1970, 11.

Hilbert, Jeffrey. "The Politics of Drag." In *Out in Culture: Gay, Lesbian, and Queer Essays on Popular Culture*, edited by Corey K. Creekmur and Alexander Doty, 463–469. Durham, NC: Duke University Press, 1995.

Hinojosa, Magda, and Jill Carle. "From Miss World to World Leader: Beauty Queens, Paths to Power, and Political Representations," *Journal of Women, Politics, and Policy* 37(1) (2016): 24.

Hoad, Neville. "World Piece: What the Miss World Pageant Can Teach about Globalization." *Cultural Critique* 58(1) (2004): 56–81.

hooks, bell. "Is Paris Burning?" In *Black Looks: Race and Representation*. Chicago: South End Press, 1992.

Hopkins, Steven J. "Let the Drag Race Begin": The Rewards of Becoming a Drag Queen." In *The Drag Queen Anthology: The Absolutely Fabulous but Flawlessly Customary World of Female Impersonators*, edited by Steven P. Schacht and Lisa Underwood, 135–150. New York: Harrington Park Press, 2004.

Horn, Katrin "The History and Theory of Camp." In *Women, Camp, and Popular Culture*, Chapter 2. Cham, Switzerland: Springer, 2017.

Horowitz, Katie Rebecca. "The Trouble with 'Queerness': Drag and the Making of Two Cultures." PhD diss., University of California, Berkeley, 2012.

Hymes, Dell. "Breakthrough into Performance." In *Folklore: Performance and Communication*, edited by Dan Ben Amos and Kenneth S. Goldstein, 13. The Hague: Mouton, 1975.

Ivannone, Jeffry J. ""Dancing on My Own": On Bodies, Belonging, and Gay Male Culture." *Medium*. December 31, 2018. https://medium.com/th-ink/dancing-on-my-own-on-bodies-belonging-and-gay-male-culture-223597e07640.

Janson, Donald. "Miss America Asked to Quit over Photos Showing Her Nude." *New York Times*, July 21, 1984.

Jensen, Erin. "Miss America Just Isn't the Same: Twitter Rips New Red-Carpet Competition." *USA Today*, September 10, 2018. https://www.usatoday.com/story/life/entertainthis/2018/09/10/twitter-miss-america-2019-critics-say/1253506002/.

Jewel, K. Sue. *From Mammy to Miss America and Beyond: Cultural Images and the Shaping of U.S. Social Policy*. London: Routledge, 1993.

John Milner Associates. *Atlantic City Schools: A Historic Overview, Context and Survey*. West Chester, PA, 2006.

Johnson, Mark. "Negotiating Style and Mediating Beauty: Transvestite (Gay/Bantut) Beauty Contests in the Southern Philippines." In *Beauty Queens on the World Stage: Gender, Contest, and Power*, edited by Colleen Ballerino Cohen, Richard Wilk, and Beverly Stoeltje. New York: Routledge, 1996.

Johnson, Nelson. "Atlantic City's Next Gamble." *New York Times*, September 5, 2014.

———. *Boardwalk Empire: The Birth, High Times and Corruption of Atlantic City*. Medford, NJ: Plexus Publishing, 2002.

———. *The Northside: African Americans and the Creation of Atlantic City*. Plexus Publishing, 2010.

Kaminski, Elizabeth, and Vera Taylor. "We're Not Just Lip-Synching up Here": Music and Collective Identity in Drag Performances." In *Identity Work in Social Movements*, edited by Jo Reger, Daniel J. Myers, and Rachel L. Einwohner. Minneapolis: University of Minnesota Press, 2008.

Kastor, Elizabeth. "Miss America Asked to Resign: Pageant Officials Act after Learning of Nude Photos." *Washington Post*, July 21, 1984.

———. "Miss America Resigns amid Controversy." *Washington Post*, July 24, 1984.

———. "Miss America Says Photos Were Private." *Washington Post*, July 23, 1984.

Kerr, Peter. (1984) "Penthouse Says Nude Photos Are Those of Miss America." *New York Times*, July 20, 1984.

Kessler, S. J., and W. McKenna. *Gender: An Ethnomethodological Approach*. New York: John Wiley and Sons, 1978.

King-O'Riain, Rebecca Chiyoko. "Making the Perfect Queen: The Cultural Production of Identities in Beauty Pageants." *Sociology Compass* 2(1) (January 2008): 74–83.

———. *Pure Beauty: Judging Race in Japanese American Beauty Pageants*. Minneapolis: University of Minnesota Press, 2006.

Klein, Jack. "When Premature Babies Were 'Stars' on Atlantic City Boardwalk." *Annals of Southern Jersey History*, October 7, 1979.

Kohler, Will. "The Very Gay and Interesting History of the Almost Lost Tradition of the Sunday Tea Dance." Back2Stonewall.com, May 26, 2019. http://www.back2stonewall.com/2019/05/gay-history-lost-tradition-sunday-tea-dance.html.

Kozol, Wendy. "Miss Indian America: Regulatory Gazes and the Politics of Affiliation." *Feminist Studies: FS* 31(1) (2005): 64.

Kuperinsky, Amy. "At Miss America Parade in Atlantic City, Tradition Trumps Controversy." NJ.com, September 8, 2018.

LaBruce, Bruce. "Notes on Camp/Anti-Camp." *Manifestos*, October 6, 2014. http://brucelabruce.com/2015/07/07/notes-on-camp-anti-camp/.

Lakoff, Robin T., and Raquel L. Scherr. *Face Value: The Politics of Beauty*. Boston: Routledge and Kegan Paul, 1984.

Lave, Jean, and Etienne Wenger. *Situated Learning: Legitimate Peripheral Participation*. Cambridge: Cambridge University Press, 1991.

Lavenda, Robert H. "'It's Not a Beauty Pageant!': Hybrid Ideology in Minnesota Community Pageants." In *Beauty Queens on the World Stage: Gender, Contest, and Power*, edited by Colleen Ballerino Cohen, Richard Wilk, and Beverly Stoeltje, 31–46. New York: Routledge, 1996.

Leach, Ben. "Atlantic County among Nation[']s Top 20 for Rate of AIDS, HIV." *Press of Atlantic City*, June 23, 2009. https://www.pressofatlanticcity.com/news/breaking /atlantic-county-among-nation-s-top-for-rate-of-hiv/article_c3744eb6-5f4c-11de -bc1e-001cc4c03286.html.

Leap, William L. *Word's Out: Gay Men's English*. Minneapolis: University of Minnesota Press, 1996.

Lee, Crystal. "My Bikini Moment in Miss America Wasn't Demeaning, It Was Empowering." Op-ed, *Los Angeles Times*, June 12, 2018.

Limata, Carole Lee. *Luna Babies: A Story of the Incubator Babies Exhibit at Luna Park, Coney Island, New York*. Amazon Digital Services, 2016.

Lipsitz, George. *Time Passages: Collective Memory and American Popular Culture*. Minneapolis: University of Minnesota Press, 1990.

Lopez, Barry. *About This Life: Journeys on the Threshold of Memory*. New York: Vintage Books, 1998. (interview) Poets and Writers, Vol. 22, Issue 2, March/April 1994.

———. *Arctic Dreams*. Open Road Media (online books), 2013.

———. Facebook post, October 30, 2011.

Lowder, Bryan J. "Can Camp Help Us Deal with a Tragedy on the Level of AIDS?" *Slate*, April, 9, 2013.

Lucksinger, Annette. "Ecopedagogy: Cultivating Environmental Consciousness through Sense of Place in Literature." In *Pedagogy* 14(2) (Spring 2014): 355–369.

Macedo, D., and S. R. Steinberg. *Media Literacy: A Reader*. New York: Peter Lang, 2007.

Malinowska, Anna. *The Aesthetics of Camp: Post-Queer Gender and Popular Culture*. I. B. Tauris, 2018. (unpublished work in progress)

Mann, Dorrie S. "There She Is: Miss Atlantic City Beauty Pageant." *Atlantic City Press*, November 4, 1979, 8–9.

Marching.com. "Miss America Show Us Your Shoes Parade, Atlantic City." Marching.com, 2018. http://www.marching.com/events/miss-america-show-us -your-shoes-parade/.

Margolis, Charles J. *Did I Really Say That? A Complete Pageant Interview Guide*. CreateSpace Independent Publishing Platform, 2012.

Martin, Nancie S. *Miss America through the Looking Glass: The Story behind the Scenes*. New York: Messner Books, 1985.

McCune, Jeffrey Q. "Transformance: Reading the Gospel in Drag," In *The Drag Queen Anthology: The Absolutely Fabulous but Flawlessly Customary World of Female Impersonators*, edited by Steven P. Schacht and Lisa Underwood, 151–168. New York: Harrington Park Press, 2004.

Merleau-Ponty, Maurice. "The Body in Its Sexual Being." In *The Phenomenology of Perception*, translated by Colin Smith. Boston: Routledge and Kegan Paul, 1962.

Meyer, M. "Reclaiming the Discourse of Camp." In *The Politics and Poetics of Camp*, edited by M. Meyer, 1–22. New York: Routledge, 1994.

Miller, Stephen. *Ancient Greek Athletics*. New Haven, CT: Yale University Press, 2006.

Miss America: American Experience. People and Events: The Miss America Organization. PBS. http://www.pbs.org/wgbh/amex/missamerica/peopleevents/p_mao.html (accessed October 15, 2012).

Mockridge, Norton. "Pageant Judges' Work Absorbing." *Atlantic City Press*, September 11, 1970.

Moncrieff, Michael, and Pierre Leinerd. "A Natural History of the Drag Queen Phenomenon." *Evolutionary Psychology* 15(2) (May 2017): 16.

Moore, Fiona. "One of the Gals Who's One of the Guys: Men, Masculinity and Drag Performance in North America." In *Changing Sex and Bending Gender*, edited by Alison Shaw and Shirley Ardener, 103–118. New York: Berghahn Books, 2005.

Moseley, Seth. "Miss America: Half a Century Later." *Asbury Park Press*, September 8, 1974, A23.

Muñoz, José Estaban. *Disidentifications: Queers of Color and the Performance of Politics*. Minneapolis: University of Minnesota Press, 1999.

Myers, Daniel J. "Ally Identity: The Politically Gay." In *Identity Work in Social Movements*, edited by Jo Reger, Daniel J. Myers, and Rachel L. Einwohner, 167–188. Minneapolis: University of Minnesota Press, 2008.

Napikoski, Linda. "What's Wrong with Beauty Pageants?," *ThoughtCo.*, January 29, 2020. http://thoughtco.com/whats-wrong-with-beauty-pageants-4072580.

Nelson, Tiffany Renee. "A Movement on the Verge: The Spark of Stonewall." Mad-Rush Undergraduate Conference, Paper no. 1. *Proceedings of 6th Annual Conference.* James Madison University, April 10, 2015. https://commons.lib.jmu.edu/madrush/2015/SocialMovements/1/

Newton, Esther. *Mother Camp: Female Impersonators in America*. 3rd ed. New York: Prentice-Hall, 1979.

———. "Role Models." In *Camp Grounds: Style and Homosexuality*, edited by David Bergman, 39–53. Amherst: University of Massachusetts Press, 1993.

Niles, Richard. "Wigs, Laughter, and Subversion: Charles Busch and Strategies of Drag Performance." In *The Drag Queen Anthology: The Absolutely Fabulous but Flawlessly Customary World of Female Impersonators*, edited by Steven P. Schacht and Lisa Underwood, 35–54. New York: Harrington Park Press, 2004.

Norkunas, Martha K. *The Politics of Public Memory: Tourism, History, and Ethnicity in Monterey, California*. Albany, NY: SUNY Series in Advances in Applied Anthropology. 1993.

Ochs, Elinor. "Linguistic Resources for Socializing Humanity." In *Rethinking Linguistic Relativity*, edited by John J. Gumperz and Steven C. Levinson (Cambridge: Cambridge University Press, 1996), 407–437.

O'Flaherty, Erin. "First Openly Gay Miss America Contestant Is More Than Just Her Sexual Identity." In *NJ.Com*, September 8, 2016. https://www.nj.com/entertainment/2016/09/miss_america_miss_missouri_erin_oflaherty_first_op.html

Oliver, M. Cynthia. *Queen of the Virgins: Pageantry and Black Womanhood in the Caribbean*. Jackson: University Press of Mississippi, 2009.

Omoto, Allen M., and A. Lauren Crain. "AIDS Volunteerism: Lesbian and Gay Community-Based Responses to HIV." In *AIDS, Identity, and Community: The HIV Epidemic and Lesbians and Gay Men*, edited by Gregory M. Herek and Beverly Greene, 187–289. Thousand Oaks, CA: Sage Publications, 1995.

Oppliger, Patrice. *Girls Gone Skank: The Sexualization of Girls in American Culture*. Jefferson, NC: McFarland and Co., 2008.

Osbourne, Angela. *Miss America: The Dream Lives On; A 75 Year Celebration*. Dallas: Taylor Publishing, 1995.

Parry, Wayne. "Atlantic City Welcomes Home Miss America Pageant." Associated Press, February 14, 2013.

Patterson, Eleanor. "The Golden Girls Live: Residual Television Texts, Participatory Culture, and the Queering of TV Heritage through Drag." *Feminist Media Studies*, 16 (5): 838–851. 2016. DOI:10.1080/14680777.2016.1149087.

Pendergast, Frank J. "City Reborn: Casinos, New Charter Win." *Press of Atlantic City*, November 2, 1976.

———. "Miss America to Appear in New Hall Ceremonies." *Atlantic City Press*, September 27, 1970.

Prentice, Claire. "How to Save the Miss America Pageant before It's Too Late!" *Press of Atlantic City*, November 2, 2018. https://www.pressofatlanticcity.com/opinion/editorials/how-to-save-the-miss-america-pageant-before-it-s/article_e43bb490-689c-5b5f-a93b-4eec35ef3f52.html.

———. "The Man Who Ran a Carnival Attraction That Saved Thousands of Premature Babies Wasn't a Doctor at All." Smithsonian.com, August 19, 2016. https://www.smithsonianmag.com/history/man-who-pretended-be-doctor-ran-worlds-fair-attraction-saved-lives-thousands-premature-babies-180960200/.

———. *Miracle at Coney Island: How a Sideshow Doctor Saved Thousands of Babies and Transformed American Medicine.* Amazon Digital Services, 2016.

Pugliese, Nicholas. "'It's Our Pageant:' As Miss America Leaves Atlantic City, Residents Get Territorial." WHYY, July 25, 2019. https://whyy.org/articles/its-our-pageant-as-miss-america-leaves-atlantic-city-residents-get-territorial/.

Raffel, Dawn. *The Strange Case of Dr. Couney: How a Mysterious European Showman Saved Thousands of American Babies.* New York: Blue Rider Press, 2018.

Raheem, Turiya S. A. *Growing Up in the Other Atlantic City.* Bloomington, IN: Xlibris, 2009.

Raspberry, William. "Missed America." *Washington Post,* July 23, 1984.

Raymond, Janice. "The Politics of Transgenderism." In *Blending Genders: Social Aspects of Cross-Dressing and Sex-Changing,* edited by Richard Ekins and Dave Kind, 215–223. New York: Routledge, 1996.

———. *The Transsexual Empire: The Making of the She-Male.* New York: Teachers College Press, 1994 [1979].

Reger, Jo, Daniel J. Myers, and Rachel L. Einwohner, eds. *Identity Work in Social Movements.* Minneapolis: University of Minnesota Press, 2008.

Remien, Robert H., and Judith G. Rabkin. "Long Term Survival with AIDS and the Role of Community." In *AIDS, Identity, and Community: The HIV Epidemic and Lesbians and Gay Men,* edited by Gregory M. Herek and Beverly Greene, 169–187. Thousand Oaks, CA: Sage Publications, 1995.

Reynolds, Daniel. "Trans *Drag Race* Alum Says 'Some Things Need to Be Changed.'" *Advocate,* April 2, 2014. http://www.advocate.com/politics/transgender/2014/04/02/trans-drag-race-alum-says-some-things-need-be-changed.

Reynolds, W. M. "Iron Man Democracy: Militainment and Democratic Possibilities." In *Educating for Democratic Consciousness: Counter-Hegemonic Possibilities,* edited by Ali A. Abdi and Paul. R. Carr. New York: Peter Lang, 2012.

Rhyne, Ragan. "Racializing White Drag." In *The Drag Queen Anthology: The Absolutely Fabulous but Flawlessly Customary World of Female Impersonators,* edited by Steven P. Schacht and Lisa Underwood, 181–194. New York: Harrington Park Press, 2004.

Rice, June. "Why Interview Miss America Contestants about Political Views?" *Kentucky Today,* September 15, 2017.

"Ripley's Believe It or Not!: "A Century of Strange." Ripley's Believe It or Not!, 2019. https://www.ripleys.com/a-century-of-strange/.

Riverol, Armando. *Live from Atlantic City: The History of the Miss America Pageant before, after, and in Spite of Television*. Bowling Green, OH: Bowling Green State University Popular Press, 1992.

————. "The Miss America Pageant: A Comparative Structural Analysis of the Pre- and Post-Television Event." PhD diss., New York University, 1989.

Rivers, Jason. "Me but Not Me: Drag Queens and the Discontinuity of Selves." Paper presented at American Anthropological Association Annual Meetings, San Jose, California, November 15, 2018.

Roberts, Blaine. "The Miss America Pageant Still Sends the Wrong Message." Op-ed, *New York Times*, September 13, 2013.

————, Blaine. *Pageants, Parlors, and Pretty Women: Race and Beauty in the Twentieth-Century South*. Raleigh: University of North Carolina Press, 2014.

Roberts, Kathleen. "Speech, Gender, and the Performance of Culture: Native American 'Princesses.'" *Text and Performance Quarterly* 22(4) (2002): 261–279.

Robertson, Pamela. *Guilty Pleasures: Feminist Camp from Mae West to Madonna*. Durham, NC: Duke University Press, 1993.

Ross, A. "Uses of Camp." In *Camp: Queer Aesthetics and the Performing Subject; A Reader*, edited by Fabio Cleto, 308–329. Ann Arbor: University of Michigan Press, 1999.

Rossiello, Robert. "Show Us Your Shoes Parade." *Casino Connection* 10(12) (September 12, 2013). http://casinoconnectionac.com/issue/vol-10-no-12-september-12-2013/article/show-us-your-shoes-parade.

Rousselle, Christine. "Miss America Contestants Were Asked Politically Charged Questions Last Night." Townhall Media (townhallmedia.com), September 11, 2017.

Rowe, Rochelle. "Glorifying the Jamaican Girl: The 'Ten Types—One People' Beauty Contest, Racialized Femininities, and Jamaican Nationalism." *Radical History Review* 103 (2009): 36–58.

RuPaul. *Letting It All Hang Out: An Autobiography*. New York: Hyperion, 1995.

————. "Tranny Chaser" (song). Champion. Prod. Lucian Piane. Los Angeles: RuCo Inc.

Rupp, L. J., V. Taylor, and E. I. Shapiro. "Drag Queens and Drag Kings: The Difference Gender Makes." *Sexualities* 13 (2010): 275–294.

Rupp, Leila, and Verta Taylor. *Drag Queens at the 801 Cabaret*. Chicago: University of Chicago Press, 2003.

Russell, John. "Miss'd America Contestants on the High Cost of Pageantry in the Age of *Drag Race*." *Queerty*, September 29, 2018. https://www.queerty.com/missd-america-contestants-high-cost-pageantry-age-drag-race-20180929.

Safire, William. "There She Goes . . ." *New York Times*, July 23, 1984.

Sawicki, Jana. *Disciplining Foucault: Feminism, Power and the Body.* New York: Routledge, 1991.

Sayles, Genie Polo. *How to Win Pageants.* Plano, TX: Wordware Publishing, 1990.

Schacht, S. P. "Four Renditions of Doing Female Drag: Feminine Appearing Conceptual Variations of a Masculine Theme." *Gendered Sexualities* 6 (2002): 157–180.

Schacht, Steven P., and Lisa Underwood, eds. *The Drag Queen Anthology: The Absolutely Fabulous but Flawlessly Customary World of Female Impersonators.* New York: Harrington Park Press, 2004.

Schackt, Jon. "Mayahood through Beauty: Indian Beauty Pageants in Guatemala." *Bulletin of Latin American Research* 24(3) (2005): 269–287.

Scharf, Lois. "There She Is, Miss America." Rev. in *American Beauty: A Social History through Two Centuries of the American Idea, Ideal, and Image of the Beautiful Woman,* by Lois Banner. *Reviews in American History* 12(1) (March 1984): 125–129.

Schechner, Richard. *Between Theater and Anthropology.* Philadelphia: University of Pennsylvania Press, 1985.

———. *Performance Theory.* New York: Routledge, 1988.

Schottmiller, Carl. "A Drag Primer: Situating *RuPaul's Drag Race* within Academic Drag Studies." Paper presented at PCA Conference, Indianapolis, Indiana, March 29, 2018.

Schröder, Ingo W. "Parades and Beauty Pageants: Encountering Authentic White Mountain Apache Culture in Unexpected Places." *Etnofoor* 17 (1/2) (2004): 116–132.

Sengupta, S., B. Banks, D. Jonas, M. S. Miles, and G. C. Smith. "HIV Interventions to Reduce HIV/AIDS Stigma: A Systematic Review." *AIDS and Behavior* 15(6) (2011): 1075–1087. doi:10.1007/s10461-010-9847-0.

Serpico, Erin. "Locals Keep Tradition and Gear Up Their Cars for Miss America Parade." *Press of Atlantic City,* August 26, 2018. https://www.pressofatlanticcity.com/missamerica/locals-keep-tradition-and-gear-up-their-cars-for-miss/article_483ed1c1-1da5-5c09-aa37-4b8e3c1fd395.html#6.

Shaw, Alison. "Changing Sex and Bending Gender: An Introduction." In *Changing Sex and Bending Gender,* edited by Alison Shaw and Shirley Ardener. New York: Berghahn Books, 2005.

Shaw, Alison, and Shirley Ardener, eds. *Changing Sex and Bending Gender.* New York: Berghahn Books, 2005.

Shenon, Philip. "Where Beauty Queens Preen: No Eyesores, Please." *New York Times,* August 21, 1991.

Shindle, Kate. *Being Miss America: Behind the Rhinestone Curtain.* Austin: University of Texas Press, 2014.

Shugart, Helene A., and Catherine Egley Waggoner. *Making Camp: Rhetorics of Transgression in U.S. Popular Culture.* Tuscaloosa: University of Alabama Press, 2008.

Simon, Bryant. *Boardwalk of Dreams: Atlantic City and the Fate of Urban America*. London: Oxford University Press, 2006.

———. "New York Avenue: The Life and Death of Gay Spaces in Atlantic City, New Jersey, 1920–1990." *Journal of Urban History* 28(3) (2002): 300. DOI: 10.1177/0096144202028003002.

Singleton, Don. "Miss (NY) America!" *New York Daily News*, September 16, 1983.

Sisson, Patrick. "How Gay Bars Have Been a Building Block of the LGBTQ Community." *Curbed*, June 17, 2016. https://www.curbed.com/2016/6/17/11963066/gay -bar-history-stonewall-pulse-lgbtq.

Smit, Peter J., et al. "HIV-Related Stigma within Communities of Gay Men: A Literature Review." In *AIDS Care*, 24 (3–4) (2012): 405–412. Published online November 25, 2011. doi:10.1080/09540121.2011.613910.

Sontag, Susan. "Notes on 'Camp.'" In *Against Interpretation*, 275–292. New York: Farrar, Straus and Giroux, 1966.

Spruill, Jennifer. "Ad/Dressing the Nation: Drag and Authenticity." In *The Drag Queen Anthology: The Absolutely Fabulous but Flawlessly Customary World of Female Impersonators*, edited by Steven P. Schacht and Lisa Underwood, 91–112. New York: Harrington Park Press, 2004.

Stegner, Wallace. *The Sense of Place*. New York: Random House, 1992.

Stoeltje, Beverly. "The Snake Charmer Queen: Ritual, Competition, and Signification in American Festival," In *Beauty Queens on the World Stage: Gender, Contest, and Power*, edited by Colleen Ballerino Cohen, Richard Wilk, and Beverly Stoelje, 11–30. New York: Routledge, 1996.

Strübel-Scheiner, J. "Gender Performativity and Self-Perception: Drag as Masquerade." *International Journal of Humanities and Social Science* 13 (2011): 12–19.

Swarr, Amanda Lock. "Moffies, Artists and Queens: Race and the Production of South African Gay Male Drag." In *The Drag Queen Anthology: The Absolutely Fabulous but Flawlessly Customary World of Female Impersonators*, edited by Steven P. Schacht and Lisa Underwood, 73–90. New York: Harrington Park Press, 2004.

Taylor, V., and L. J. Rupp. "Chicks with Dicks, Men in Dresses: What It Means to Be a Drag Queen." In *The Drag Queen Anthology: The Absolutely Fabulous but Flawlessly Customary World of Female Impersonators*, edited by Steven P. Schacht and Lisa Underwood, 113–134. New York: Harrington Park Press, 2004.

———. "Learning from Drag Queens." *Contexts* 5(3) (2006): 12–17.

———. "When the Girls Are Men: Negotiating Gender and Sexual Dynamics in a Study of Drag Queens." *Signs* 40.4 (2005): 2115–2139.

Taylor, V., L. J. Rupp, and J. Gamson. "Performing Protest: Drag Shows as Tactical Repertoire of the Gay and Lesbian Movement." *Research in Social Movements, Conflicts and Change* 25 (2005): 105–137.

Tewksbury, R. "Men Performing as Women: Explorations in the World of Female Impersonators." *Sociological Spectrum* 13 (1993): 465–486.

Tewksbury, R. "Gender Construction and the Female Impersonator: The Process of Transforming 'He' to 'She.'" *Deviant Behavior* 15 (1994): 27–43.

Thomas, June. "The Gay Bar." *Slate*, June 28, 2011. http://www.slate.com/articles /life/the_gay_bar/2011/06/the_gay_bar_4.html.

Thomson, Rosemary Garland. Extraordinary Bodies: Figuring Disability in American Culture and Literature. New York: Columbia University Press, 1997.

———, ed. *Freakery: Cultural Spectacles of the Extraordinary Body*. New York: New York University Press, 1996.

Thursby, Keith. "Jean Bartel Dies at 87; Miss America 1943 Pushed Pageant to Give Scholarships." *Los Angeles Times*, March 9, 2011. http://articles.latimes.com/2011 /mar/09/local/la-me-jean-bartel-20110309.

Tice, Karen W. *Queens of Academe: Beauty Pageantry, Student Bodies, and College Life*. Oxford: Oxford University Press, 2012.

Trescott, Jaqueline. "Miss America Winning Ways: Vanessa Williams Breaks One Racial Barrier." *Washington Post*, September 19, 1983.

Turner, Paige. "The 11 Most Common Styles of Drag." *Queerty*, June 3, 2014. https:// www.queerty.com/11-common-drag-queen-styles-20140603.

Turner, Victor. *Dramas, Fields, and Metaphors*. Ithaca, NY: Cornell University Press, 1974.

———. "Liminality and the Performative Genres." In *Rite Drama, Festival, Spectacle: Rehearsals toward a Theory of Cultural Performance*, edited by John J. MacAloon, 19–41. Philadelphia: Institute for the Study of Human Issues, 1984.

———. *From Ritual to Theater: The Human Seriousness of Play*. New York: PAJ Publications, 1982.

United Press International. "Beauty Queen Abdicates." United Press International, July 20, 1970.

Urla, Jaqueline, and Alan C. Swedlund. "The Anthropometry of Barbie." In *Deviant Bodies: Critical Perspectives on Difference in Science and Popular Culture*, edited by Jennifer Terry and Jacqueline Urla. Bloomington: Indiana University Press, 1995.

Valentine, David. *Imagining Transgender: An Ethnography of a Category*. Durham, NC: Duke University Press, 2007.

Van Derber, Marilyn. *Miss America by Day: Lessons Learned from Ultimate Betrayals and Unconditional Love*. Denver: Oak Hill Ridge Press, 2003.

Vinkin, Barbara. *Fashion Zeitgeist: Trends and Cycles in the Fashion System*. Oxford: Berg, 2005.

Visage, Michelle. "Michelle Visage Talks Miss'd America Pageant, Being Mistaken for a Drag Queen, and More." *Huffington Post*, September 18, 2013. https://

www.huffingtonpost.com/2013/09/18/michelle-visage-missd-america-drag
-queens_n_3936947.html.

Von B, Mr. "Drag Orphan." *Huffington Post*, February 2, 2016. https://www
.huffingtonpost.com/tom-bartolomei/drag-orphan_b_3725071.html.

Wardhaugh, Ronald, and Janet M. Fuller. "Language, Gender and Sexuality." In
An Introduction to Sociolinguistics, 7th ed. New York: John Wiley and Sons, 2015.

Warren, Stephan. "Suspicious Fire Guts $1.5 M Building in Atlantic City," *Press of
Atlantic City*, November 7, 1981.

Watson, Elwood, and Darcy Martin. *There She Is, Miss America: The Politics of Sex,
Beauty, and Race in America's Most Famous Pageant*. New York: Palgrave Macmil-
lan, 2004.

Weintraub, Daniel J., and Mickey Eisenberg. "The Shape of Things to Come: Miss
America versus the Golden Rectangle." *American Psychologist* 21(3) (1966): 246–247.

Wenger, Etienne. "Communities of Practice: Learning as a Social System." *Systems
Thinker*, Leverage Networks, 2018. https://thesystemsthinker.com/communities-of
-practice-learning-as-a-social-system/.

———. *Communities of Practice: Learning, Meaning, and Identity*. Cambridge:
Cambridge University Press, 1998.

Weston, Keith. *Families We Choose: Lesbians, Gays, and Kinship*. New York:
Columbia University Press, 1991.

Whitestone, Heather. "An Interview with Heather Whitestone Callum, Miss
America 1995, Cochlear Implant Candidate." Audiologyonline.com, 2002.

Wilcox, Ed. "Is It Miss . . . or Myth America?" *New York Sunday News*, September 6, 1970, C20–21.

Wilk, Richard. Introduction to *Beauty Queens on the Global Stage: Gender, Contests, and Power*, edited by Colleen Ballerino Cohen, Richard Wilk, and Beverly
Stoeltje. New York: Routledge, 1996.

———. "The Local and the Global in the Political Economy of Beauty: From Miss
Belize to Miss World." *Review of International Political Economy* 2(1) (1995): 117–134.

Williams, Caroline. "It's Not a Beauty Pageant: An Examination of Leadership Development through Alaska Native Pageants." PhD diss., University of Arizona, 2013.

Williams, Vanessa, and Helen Williams. *You Have No Idea*. New York: Gotham
Books, 2012.

Williamson, Judith. *Consuming Passions: The Dynamics of Popular Culture*. London: Marion Boyars, 1986.

Willis, Susan. *A Primer for Everyday Life*. New York: Routledge, 1991.

Winfrey, Lee. "Miss America Pageant to Ignore Casino Gambling." *Atlantic City
Press*, August 31, 1978.

Yahr, Emily. "Miss America 2019: The Best, Worst and Weirdest Moments from the Swimsuit-Free Competition." *Washington Post*, September 10, 2018. https://www.washingtonpost.com/news/arts-and-entertainment/wp/2018/09/10/miss-america-2019-the-best-worst-and-weirdest-moments-from-the-swimsuit-free-pageant/?utm_term=.5438b5c56f6e.

Yan, Holly. "Vanessa Williams Gets Miss America Apology 32 Years Later." CNN, September 14, 2015.

"Young's Pier—Infant Incubators." *Press of Atlantic City*, July 3, 1905.

Zoppo, Avalon. "Atlantic City's Dormant Drag Scene May Be Coming Alive." *Press of Atlantic City*, July 10, 2019. https://www.pressofatlanticcity.com/news/atlantic-city-s-dormant-drag-scene-may-be-coming-alive/article_a4afbob9-ofe8-518a-8010-6dcafa2871cd.html.

VIDEOS

"Behind the Tiara: Randy Rainbow and Alexia Love." YouTube video, 2013. Accessed, September 2016. https://www.youtube.com/watch?v=RotCvs1hNQI.

"Behind the Tiara: Randy Rainbow and Chantel Reshae." YouTube video, 2013. Accessed, September 2016. https://www.youtube.com/watch?v=WsKRJOS005U.

"Behind the Tiara: Randy Rainbow and Honey Davenport." YouTube video, 2013. Accessed September 2016. https://www.youtube.com/watch?v=hToDDlm5ta4.

"Behind the Tiara: Randy Rainbow and Ivy Profen." YouTube video, 2013. Accessed September 2016. https://www.youtube.com/watch?v=W-VPfBeFE30.

"Behind the Tiara: Randy Rainbow and Mirkala Crystal." YouTube video, 2013. Accessed September 2016. https://www.youtube.com/watch?v=BRdJ9kLU1xo.

"Behind the Tiara: Randy Rainbow and Victoria Porkchop Parker." YouTube video, 2013. Accessed September 2016. https://www.youtube.com/watch?v=Q30NM57IQso.

"Behind the Tiara: Randy Rainbow and Victoria Venom." YouTube video, 2013. Accessed September 2016. https://www.youtube.com/watch?v=jrDn3aA90RY.

"Ivy Profen Alexia LoveVideo: Behind the Tiara: Randy Rainbow and Victoria Venom (2013). Accessed, September 2016. https://www.youtube.com/watch?v=jrDn3aA90RY

"Meet Miss America 2017." *People>bodies*. Online video advertisement. Accessed August, 2016. https://people.com/bodies/miss-america-first-openly-gay-contestant-hopes-to-break-another-ceiling/

"Miss'd America Coming Home." YouTube video, 2010. Accessed September 2016. https://www.youtube.com/watch?v=16CjuQmMGgA.

"Miss'd America Past Winners, Pre-2010." YouTube video. Accessed September 2016. https://www.youtube.com/watch?v=pQoCSvBfoxY.

"Miss'd America 2003." YouTube video. Accessed September 2016. https://www
.youtube.com/watch?v=9bcsot3RceU.

"Miss'd America Coming Home 2010." Accessed September 2016. https://www
.youtube.com/watch?v=16CjuQmMGgA

"Miss'd America 2010 Highlight Reel, no. 1." February 2, 2010. Accessed September 2016. https://www.youtube.com/watch?v=6IERTi3usNQ.

"Miss'd America 2010 Highlight Reel, no. 2." February 2, 2010. Accessed September 2016. https://www.youtube.com/watch?v=0iOsBmmEmf8.

"Miss'd America 2013." YouTube video, September 24, 2013. Accessed September 2016. https://www.youtube.com/watch?v=FSu40G_9MHk.

"Miss'd America 2017 (Tina Burner)." YouTube video. Accessed October, 2017. https://www.youtube.com/watch?v=pHXsWKtBY_Y.

"Raw Video: There He Is! Miss'd America!" YouTube video, February 1, 2010. Accessed, September 2016. https://www.youtube.com/watch?v=IGSb_OtkPG0.

"Show Us Your Shoes Parade Preview: 2014 Miss America Competition." YouTube video. Accessed September 2016. https://www.youtube.com/watch?v=eOx839SXjTY.

Index

Note: Pages in *italic type* refer to illustrative matter.

About the Author

Laurie A. Greene is an associate professor of anthropology at Stockton University, where she has taught since 1986. She is the founder of the LGBTQ Youth Safe Space Initiative at Stockton University, and an advocate for the local LGBTQ community. She is the author of *A Grammar of Belizian Creole: Compilations from Two Existing United States Dialects* and of various articles on Creole language and culture, gender, and somatic ritual. She is the mother of three grown children and the "drag stepmom" to some fine young gay men.